PRAISE FOR THIS BOOK

"One might say that liturgical institutions are the forms and social structures of the Church *par excellence*. It is these which draw her boundaries, illuminate her definitions, direct her prayer, and provide an exact and profound theological link from which her doctors can bolster up and illustrate their theses. How indebted, then, must we find ourselves to Dom Guéranger for having cast light upon the manifold grace of Christ transmitted through the Church in the course of her history, through her rites and Sacraments."
 — from the Foreword by **DOM GÉRARD CALVET**, OSB†, Founder and first Abbot of Le Barroux

"For those who understand something of the depths that liturgical conversations and controversies have plumbed in the past six decades of Church history, this excellent translation of Dom Prosper Guéranger's masterpiece will be most welcome. Being both a 'courageous defender of the prerogatives of the Roman Pontiff' (Brief of Pope Pius IX, 1875) and a witness to the best liturgical tradition, Dom Guéranger can provide precious insight for the Church in our time. Open this new edition of an old volume and find out for yourself."
 — **RT. REV. PHILIP ANDERSON**, OSB, Abbot of Our Lady of Clear Creek

"All who love the sacred liturgy will be glad that the heart of this classic work is at last available in English. Dom Guéranger helps his readers to grow in a supernatural and intelligent appreciation for the gift that is the liturgy of the Latin church."
 — **FR. THOMAS CREAN**, OP, author of *The Mass and the Saints*

"One hundred and fifty years after the death of the first abbot of Solesmes, there could be no finer tribute to him, nor any work more useful, than this English edition of his famous and influential *Liturgical Institutions*. His denunciation of the 'anti-liturgical heresy' remains incredibly relevant. To rebuild the liturgical movement that went astray after him, to rediscover the sense of the sacred, the beauty of the liturgy, and the love of Christian worship, we must urgently return to the wisdom of Guéranger."
 — **FR. REGINALD M. RIVOIRE**, FSVF

"In his renowned *Liturgical Institutions*, the father of the Liturgical Movement, Dom Prosper Guéranger, unmasks the 'anti-liturgical heresy' — a spiritual disease that leads to the degradation of divine worship, the fracturing of ecclesial unity, and the collapse of faith itself. Though written in the nineteenth century, his analysis proves strikingly prophetic. With unmatched erudition and fervor, Guéranger shows that liturgy — not merely the *idea* of liturgy, but its *concrete traditional form* — is no matter of aesthetics or discipline alone, but the very heart of Catholic life. Essential reading for anyone seeking to grasp the roots of today's liturgical crisis—roots, alas, embedded deep in the Church's own history and mindset."

—**TOMASZ DEKERT**, Institute of Cultural Studies, Jesuit University Ignatianum, Krakow

"We are familiar with Dom Guéranger's *Liturgical Year*, a day-by-day commentary on the annual cycle, but we are often unaware of his masterpiece, the *Liturgical Institutions*, published between 1840 and 1851, which is of the utmost importance in the history of the Roman rite. This historical compendium, conceived as a weapon of war, is in fact the main work of the abbot of Solesmes, who re-established Benedictine life after the turmoil of the Revolution.

"The work is of great interest as a history of the Roman liturgy, due to its scope, its precision, and the number of ancient authors consulted, and it remains very useful even if historical science has progressed since its time. But one can say the *Institutions* is an essential book above all as an integral part of the very history of the liturgy it concerns. Among the leading Catholic counter-revolutionaries of the time—Bishops de Salinis, Gerbet, and Parisis, Cardinal Gousset, and many others—who advocated a rallying of Catholics around the Vicar of Christ in an age bereft of Christian princes, Guéranger became the tireless propagandist of the 'pure' Roman liturgy.

"In concrete terms, he called for the rejection of the missals and breviaries published in France at the end of the seventeenth and eighteenth centuries, which had reorganized the readings and fashioned antiphons, chants, hymns, and sequences of their own, supplanting a Roman liturgy that the dioceses of France had inherited from the Middle Ages and had developed in localized ritual and textual practices. Guéranger described these new books as 'neo-Gallican,' denouncing Gallican, Jansenist, and 'enlightened' influences, and speaking of 'anti-liturgical heresy.'

"The very harsh controversy, in keeping with the spirit of the times as well as the notable support of Pius IX, ensured that the *Institutions* received widespread publicity. It also proved irresistibly effective: from 1839 to 1875, all French dioceses adopted the Roman books in their entirety (together with some collateral damage: the disappearance of many proper customs and texts, including in the monastic liturgies). This was nothing less than a total victory for Dom Guéranger. We may thus say that the *Liturgical Institutions*, while not as important in the history of liturgy as the liturgical books of the Carolingian period, of Innocent III, and of Pius V, nevertheless marked the final step in the complete Romanization of the Latin liturgy."

—**FR. CLAUDE BARTHE**, author of *A Forest of Symbols: The Traditional Mass and Its Meaning*

LITURGICAL INSTITUTIONS

OS JUSTI STUDIES
in
LITURGICAL HISTORY AND REFORM

General Editor
MATTHEW HAZELL

DOM PROSPER GUÉRANGER

LITURGICAL INSTITUTIONS

An Abridged Edition

Foreword by
DOM GÉRARD CALVET†

Translated by
DAVID M. FOLEY
and
GERHARD EGER

OS JUSTI PRESS

Based on Dom Prosper Guéranger,
Institutions liturgiques, 1840–1851: Extraits,
Éditions de Chiré, 1977
Copyright © 2025 David M. Foley

Os Justi Press
P.O. Box 21814
Lincoln, NE 68542
www.osjustipress.com

Send inquiries to
info@osjustipress.com

ISBN 978-1-965303-48-1 (paperback)
ISBN 978-1-965303-49-8 (hardcover)
ISBN 978-1-965303-50-4 (ebook)

Book design by Michael Schrauzer
Cover: The Christmas Mass, from *Les Très Riches Heures du
duc de Berry*, Folio 158r, the Musée Condé, Chantilly.

CONTENTS

FOREWORD

T IS SUFFICIENT FOR US TO EXAMINE THE portrait of Dom Guéranger by Gaillard, to cast our eyes over the fire of his gaze, if we wish to understand that the founder of Solesmes was illuminated and inhabited by an idea that consumed his entire person.

His massive head seems to be directed towards an approaching assailant. We are in the presence of a man who is both a contemplative and a fighter — two characteristics that are only apparently in opposition, for the object of contemplation is always under attack here below. The contemplative should consent to this combat, in the way that a fighter should be animated by an inner vision.

The vision that Dom Guéranger bore within himself, that which he has transmitted to us, is the liturgical idea.

Amid the fumes of the religious sentiment of his age, this contemporary of Victor Hugo and Lammenais, a distinguished writer who was by no means insensible to the power of words to convey his idea, devoted his pen to the service of a monumental work whose purpose and result was the restoration of the Roman liturgy to every place where it had perished.

In the course of the eighteenth century, the joint influence of the encyclopedists and Jansenists had subjected the Catholic liturgy, both in the Canonical Hours and the Mass, to a twofold process of profanation and fragmentation.

The process of profanation came first. Under the pretext of rendering the liturgy more accessible to the faithful, certain men despoiled the forms of worship of their majesty and their mystery. The vernacular language was widely adopted, while the new offices clung to the pretense of offering instruction without being able to edify the faithful. It is thus that the ancient lure of naturalism periodically arises in the history of souls.

The process of fragmentation followed. By unduly expanding the power of bishops over the liturgy, to the end of vaunting diversity (and its riches) to the detriment of unity (and its alleged monotony), it came about that a Breviary was created for each diocese, or very nearly, while the Missal suffered from the same outrages.

Through the working of this twofold *leaven of malice*, namely humanization and particularization, the ancient and majestic liturgical edifice that dated, in its broader structure, to St. Gregory the Great, had been toppled.

The Church of France was secretly grieving for the magnificence of the Antiphonary and the Gregorian Responsorial, for the forms of worship were in a state of profound degradation.

The Abbot of Solesmes, who suffered more gravely over this state of affairs than any other, preferred to light a lamp in his home rather than to hurl curses at the darkness. Day after day, at the cost of an unrelenting labor that was enveloped in prayer, the Benedictine savant accomplished an immense work: the restoration of the Roman liturgy in France. His learned, impassioned, and unfailingly relevant argumentation is set forth in the four volumes of his *Liturgical Institutions*, selections of which are here published in this new edition.

Dom Guéranger found himself facing two problems in need of resolution: the one, of a canonical order, concerning a bishop's rights over the liturgy in his diocese; the other, of a liturgical order, touching upon the pre-eminence of the Roman books, which had not been altered in any essential way ever since Christian antiquity.

The canonical and liturgical arguments proposed by Dom Guéranger were so clear, so compelling, so full of ardor, that in only a few years they won the support of all the bishops of France. All ended up adopting the liturgical rites of the Church of Rome, their Mother and Teacher, overcome as they were by the fragrance of antiquity that exhaled from these rites, their sober elegance and perfection.

Nevertheless, two bishops put up a memorable resistance: those of Toulouse and Orléans. This resulted in a correspondence with the Abbot of Solesmes which serves as a model of intelligent, courageous, and indeed effective debate; in the end, the opponents were routed.

This victory for traditional liturgy, following a century and a half of innovation and degradation, is singularly encouraging for us, who find ourselves in a situation analogous to that of Dom Guéranger.

Indeed, a situation analogous but still worse. We also have returned to a process of profanation and fragmentation, but it has advanced to a citadel that the Jansenists and rationalists of the eighteenth century never dared to besiege: the Canon of the Mass. In the worst years of the French Revolution and the Empire, the clergy of the Constitution and the Concordat always respected the Canon. The priests continued to recite it in Latin (only rarely in French); undoubtedly, many pronounced it aloud to make it common and banal, but no one ever dared to alter the text; the stronghold was invaded, but the citadel always held.

It is in our times, when nothing remains intact among the monuments bequeathed to us by Christian antiquity, neither the Canon of the Mass, nor the Divine Office, nor the Sacraments, that we turn towards Dom Guéranger to draw the guiding idea for our own restoration. This idea is the strong, unbreakable bond between the faith of the Church and her liturgical tradition.

The entire work of Dom Guéranger is nothing other than an illustration of the famous axiom, so frequently and so justly invoked: *Legem credendi statuat lex supplicandi.* That is, the law of prayer (inscribed upon the monuments of the liturgical tradition) fixes, or establishes, the rule of faith.

The word *statuat* here is noteworthy. In it, we find the root for the word "institution." The verb *statuere* signifies to establish, to found, to build up. In the *Robert*, we find the following definition under the entry for "institution": "a set of forms or social structures as established by law or custom."

One might say that liturgical institutions are the forms and social structures of the Church *par excellence.* It is these which draw her boundaries, illuminate her definitions, direct her prayer, and provide an exact and profound theological framework from which her doctors can bolster up and illustrate their theses.

How indebted, then, must we find ourselves to Dom Guéranger for having cast light upon the manifold grace of Christ transmitted through the Church in the course of her history, through her rites and Sacraments; for having designated the Apostolic See, that Rome of the Apostles to which we are attached with all the fibers of our being, as the center and the foundation of liturgical unity.

And if we should regret today that this resonant voice is now silent, that there is so grave a lack of the faith, eloquence, and fighting spirit of him whom the Church might one day name her "Liturgical Doctor" (*Doctor liturgicus*), then let it suffice for us to devote our attention to this profound study of our patrimony, lest we prove unworthy of it.

Dom Gérard Calvet, O. S. B.
Priory of Sainte-Madeleine
11 November 1976
Feast of St. Martin

TRANSLATOR'S PREFACE

OM PROSPER GUÉRANGER (1805–1875) must be numbered among the most heroic figures of modern ecclesiastical history. From his earliest years, despite the expulsion of monasticism from France during the bloody ravages of the French Revolution, Guéranger sensed his vocation to the religious life. Entering the minor seminary at Tours as an adolescent, Guéranger was ordained to the priesthood in 1827, and was shortly after named a canon regular at the cathedral chapter of Tours.

At the age of thirty-two, Dom Guéranger received permission from Pope Gregory XVI, himself a Benedictine, to found the Abbey of Solesmes upon the ruins of a medieval priory, thereby restoring to France her venerable tradition of Benedictine monasticism. The Abbot of Solesmes devoted the remainder of his life, through his scholarly works and zealous observance of the monastic rule, to liturgical restoration, with a particular dedication to reclaiming for France the Roman liturgy from its corruptors and fostering a revival of Gregorian chant from its decadent stupor. Although he is principally famous today in the English-speaking world for his fifteen-volume commentary on the liturgy of the Roman Church, *The Liturgical Year*, Dom Guéranger produced another work of a grand scale that proved no less influential for liturgical theology and practice.

Originally published over the course of eleven years (1840–1851) in three ample volumes that span nearly two-thousand pages, Dom Guéranger's *Liturgical Institutions* sets forth an erudite and impassioned history of the Roman Rite and of the depredations it suffered at the hands of various "anti-liturgical heretics" over the centuries. Like the Roman Rite to which he devoted his life's work, Guéranger's French prose is at the same moment elegant and virile, replete with delicate imagery and forceful argumentation. Guéranger's *Institutions* possesses all of the liturgical piety and spiritual genius of a medieval mind, joined with the precise methodology of the practitioner of a modern science. This ambitious monument of liturgical scholarship, which equally serves as a startlingly prescient exposition of the liturgical revolution of the mid-twentieth century, has never been dignified by an English translation. The essential core of the French *Liturgical Institutions* was deftly extracted by Jean Vaquié in 1977; this serves as the basis for the present English edition. Although a complete translation would grant access to Guéranger's full weight of reasoning and full breadth of research, it must be admitted that the sheer magnitude of the original, replete with long flights of nineteenth-century rhetoric, makes that goal a more remote task and one that is less likely to be welcomed by modern readers eager to get to the meat of the argument.

While I have generally preserved the structure of the abridgment, and reproduced Vaquié's chapter headings and textual interventions (bracketed in italics), it seemed appropriate to introduce some editorial interventions of my own. First, following the original three-volume structure of the first edition of the *Institutions*, I have subdivided the text into three books, for which I have provided descriptive headings, and, moreover, numbered the chapters consecutively, as is customary in a book today, although Guéranger himself divided his three-volume work into two parts, each with separately numbered chapters. Frequently, in order to admit the reader into the wider context of the *Institutions*, I found it necessary to supply passages from the original text — whether short phrases or complete paragraphs — that were omitted by the compiler. Since very few source notes appear in the abridgement, I have ventured to add citations for all of Guéranger's direct quotations, generally with recourse to the first edition of the *Institutions*, although I do not always direct the reader to specific editions of Guéranger's sources. Wherever Dom Guéranger quotes Latin sources, I have translated from the original text unless otherwise specified. When it seemed necessary to supply a word or phrase to clarify the sense of the text, these insertions have been made in brackets and italicized, undifferentiated from Vaquié's interventions. Occasionally, I have also provided short explanatory footnotes to clarify a liturgical custom, historical event, or figure to which Guéranger attaches particular importance, or which may be especially unfamiliar to the twenty-first century reader.

In closing, I must express my special gratitude to Gerhard Eger, whose vast liturgical erudition has elevated this volume far above my unaided powers. In addition to painstakingly revising my translation against the original edition of Guéranger's *Institutions*, Gerhard was able to shed light on many arcane liturgical and historical details scattered throughout the text, and a number of his explanations have been distilled in the volume's notes. I would also like to acknowledge Kolya Sidloski and Zachary Thomas, who had no direct hand in this project but whose edifying friendship and liturgical piety always exert a distant causality. Particular thanks are due also to Canon Jason Apple, ICKSP, who placed a copy of the 1977 abridgment of the *Institutions* into my hands five years ago during a visit to Gricigliano, as well as to Mr. Chris Horan, a Benedictine oblate who has generously supported this project from the outset. Penultimately, I am indebted to Peter Kwasniewski, who warmly encouraged me to undertake this translation, bore gracefully with my delinquency in its completion, and finally saw it through to publication. *In finem, offero gratiarum actionem Tibique æterno Deo, vivo et vero.*

David M. Foley
Festo S. Benedicti MMXXV

METHOD OF COMPOSITION

[by the Compiler of the 1977 Abridged Edition]

HE FIRST EDITION OF THE *LITURGICAL Institutions* was produced in the lifetime of Dom Guéranger. It consisted of three volumes, the publication of which spanned from the years 1840 to 1851. Consequently, it dates from the final years of the reign of Louis Philippe and the period of the Second Republic.

After Guéranger's death, Dom Ildelphonse Guépin published a new edition of the work in 1878. To the content of the first edition, he added several supporting booklets that Dom Guéranger had written to defend his work against the attacks of the Archbishop of Toulouse and the Bishop of Orléans. The second edition, which is also the last one since no other was issued afterwards, thus consists of four volumes instead of three.

The selections that we are now publishing here have been drawn from the first three volumes of the second edition; therefore, they do not touch upon the supporting booklets, despite their intrinsic interest, because it was necessary to limit our selection, as a completely new edition was not possible at this time. Rather, we had to content ourselves with the choicest sections of the text, or indeed extracts, as will be seen below.

Our problem was this: to condense three large volumes into one while remaining faithful to the spirit of the text, which is to say without disfiguring its line of reasoning. The resolution at which we arrived is as follows.

Evidently, it was necessary to sift through a number of paragraphs distributed throughout the chapters, since indeed every book is made this way. We completely omitted paragraphs that constitute an overabundance, inasmuch as they contain only supplementary evidence; consequently, these paragraphs may be regarded as laps that cannot be run by the hurried men we are today. These omissions do not alter the text's argumentation, but they draw away from its richness.

On the other hand, we have preserved intact the essential paragraphs, namely those in which Guéranger's historical and liturgical reasoning unfolds with force and clarity.

Between the paragraphs that have been omitted and those that have been wholly preserved, there remains a number of very important "mixed" paragraphs that contribute to the argument (and thus they cannot be discarded), but which also contain an overabundance of material. Seeing that we cannot reproduce these paragraphs in their entirety, for fear of exceeding the limits imposed upon this selection, what should be done about them?

In cases of this kind, it would have been possible to produce our own paraphrase of the text. But then this book would have been, in great part, our own composition. And indeed, the purpose of this new edition was precisely to make known the very characteristic style of Dom Guéranger — a style that might be reproached for a certain grandiosity, but which unquestionably contains an admirable and informative enthusiasm for all things liturgical. Paraphrases inserted by a strange hand would have completely disfigured the tranquil and vibrant rhythm of the text. Thus, we were forced to reject that first solution.

Consequently, for the paragraphs that we have called "mixed," we have proceeded in the same way as with the rest of the work: that is, by omitting phrases and incidental comments that were not indispensable for an understanding of the argument, while preserving the essence of the text. Everything that the reader encounters within has issued from the pen of Dom Guéranger. But, of course, one will not read here all that he wrote, precisely for the reason that it was necessary to condense the text. This is most regrettable, since the sections omitted are nearly as rich as those which have been preserved.

Therefore, readers must continue to await a completely new edition of the four volumes of the second and final edition of the *Liturgical Institutions*, which was published by Dom Guépin in 1878.

Some other alterations of minor details were necessary to make the text more readable. Thus, it was convenient to shorten the chapter titles, which were overly long in the original, according to the convention of the time. We have also seen fit to divide bulky chapters into sections, whose subtitles have been drawn from the text itself.

To serve as a marker and to facilitate reading, italics are reserved for the compiler, since it was necessary for him to provide a number of explanatory notes for contemporary readers.

It should be noted here that we did not take advantage of this work of abridgement to deform the sense of the text or direct it to our own ends. Indeed, to avoid doing so, we have presented our selections in the same order as that in which they appeared in the original text. Moreover, we did not wish to group together those passages dealing with a single subject, since this would have constrained us to upset the order and succession of ideas established by the author, and therefore would have resulted in a mutilation of the text.

For the same reason, we have reproduced certain arguments that are no longer invoked by contemporary traditionalists, who no longer find them defensible in our times. Indeed, we would not wish to incur the reproach of having removed them for the sake of advancing a cause. These selections, then, do not constitute a commentary so much as a record.

Jean Vaquié
1977

SELECTIONS FROM THE BRIEF
OF HIS HOLINESS POPE PIUS IX[1]

in honor of the memory of the Most Reverend Father
DOM PROSPER GUÉRANGER
Abbot of Solesmes

MONG CHURCHMEN ARISEN IN OUR times who are most distinguished for their piety, their zeal, their learning, and their devotion to advancing the interests of the Catholic religion, it is indeed just that one should name our dear son Prosper Guéranger, Abbot of St. Peter of Solesmes and superior general of the Benedictines of the Congregation of France. Endowed with a prodigious intellect, an admirable erudition, and a profound mastery of canon law, he dedicated himself, over the course of his long life and by means of his most compelling writings, to a courageous defense of Catholic doctrine and the prerogatives of the Roman Pontiff, thus shattering the efforts and refuting the errors of the Church's adversaries . . .

The principal object of his thoughts and labors was the restoration of the Roman liturgy to its ancient rights in France. He undertook this mission so well that it was by virtue of his writings, and at the same time of his constancy and singular ability, more than by any other influence, that all of the dioceses of France embraced the rites of the Roman Church before he departed from this life . . .

Given in Rome, at St. Peter's,
under the Ring of the Fisherman,
19 March, 1875,
in the twenty-ninth year of Our Pontificate

---

[1] *Acta Sanctæ Sedis* 8 (1875), 375–77.

I

THE APOSTOLIC AGE TO THE COUNCIL OF TRENT

I
Preliminary Observations

DEFINITION OF THE LITURGY

ONSIDERED IN A GENERAL WAY, THE LIT-
urgy is the collection of symbols, chants, and actions by
means of which the Church expresses and manifests her
religion towards God. Consequently, liturgy is not simply
prayer, but rather prayer considered in its social dimension. An individual prayer, offered in the name of an individual, is by
no means liturgy.

PERSONAL PRAYER

Nevertheless, the formulas and signs of the liturgy can be legitimately
and appropriately employed by individuals with the intention of giving
greater force and efficacy to their own works of prayer, as when one recites
hallowed prayers, hymns, or responses to excite within oneself the virtue
of religion. Therefore, within the realm of vocal prayer, this is the best
kind of prayer, because it unites the merits and consecrated devotion of
the entire Church to the efforts of the individual.

THE THREE ELEMENTS OF THE LITURGY

Confession, Prayer, and Praise: these are the principal acts of religion, and
they are also the principal forms of the liturgy.

Confession, by which the Church pays homage to God for the truth
that she has received from Him, repeating a thousand times in His presence
the triumphant creed which, written though it is in the language of earth,
contains the truths of heaven. It is this creed that she repeats in brief many
times each day within the Canonical Hours, and in a more elaborate form
within the action of the Sacrifice on Sundays and high solemnities. Finally,
she makes this confession in the fullest sense within the whole of the
liturgical year, in the course of which the creed is represented, mystery by
mystery, with all the richness of her rites, all the splendor of her language,
all the depth of her adoration and fervor of faith.

This is why every age has placed such importance, particularly for the
understanding of dogma, upon the words and actions of the liturgy. The
axiom is well known: *Legem credendi statuat lex supplicandi* ("the law of
prayer establishes the law of belief"). It is in the liturgy that the same Spirit
who inspired the Sacred Scriptures speaks again. In this way, the liturgy is
tradition itself, in its highest degree of power and solemnity.

Prayer, by which the Church expresses her love, her desire to please God and to be united with Him, a desire that is at once humble and forceful, timid and bold, for the reason that she is loved, and the One who loves her is God. It is in prayer, which naturally arises from confession, just as hope does from faith, that the Church expresses her petitions, lays bare her needs, and relates her necessities, for she knows what God wants from her and how far she remains from accomplishing it, until the number of the elect has been fulfilled.

Praise, because the Church cannot contain in silent contemplation the transports of love and admiration which the sight of the divine mysteries stirs up within her. Like Mary, when she beheld the great things which He who is mighty had done unto her (Lk. 1:49), she delights in Him and glorifies Him. The Church therefore celebrates the victories of the Lord as well as her own triumphs. The commemoration of the wonders of ancient times thrills and exalts her; she thus begins to recall these events with grandeur, as if to rekindle the sentiments that they inspire within her.

THE POETRY OF THE RITES AND CHANTS

These three principal elements — Confession, Prayer, and Praise — become a threefold source of poetry within the liturgy: poetry inspired by the same Spirit that dictated the canticles of David, Isaiah, and Solomon; poetry that is as enthralling in its imagery as it is profound and inexhaustible in its feeling.

But since all of the great impressions of the soul — faith, love, the sense of wonder, the joy of triumph — cannot be adequately expressed except through song, it naturally follows that the Church must sing her praise, prayer, and confession, setting forth a chant that is as beautiful as the words, and words as lofty as the sentiment they express, while the sentiment itself is in harmony with Him who is its object and source.

Now the Church is a society, not of spirits but of men, that is, of creatures composed of body and soul who communicate every truth through signs and images. We must say, then, that in the Church, this heavenly union of Confession, Prayer, and Praise is expressed in a hallowed language, and one that is modulated by a supernatural rhythm; likewise, it is set forth through exterior signs, rites, and ceremonies, which constitute the body of the liturgy.

2

The Importance of
Studying the Liturgy

NE CAN READILY PERCEIVE THAT MATE-
rial for a veritable science must emerge out of this complex
of Confession, Prayer, and Praise that constitutes the liturgy:
a science of the divine offices, which is to say the part of
the liturgy that consists in the "sacrifice of the lips" (see
Heb. 13:15); a science of the Real Sacrifice with all its rites and mysteries; a
science of the Sacraments, the organs of man's sanctification; a science of
blessings and sacramentals by means of which every creature is purified and
reconciled by the power of the Cross; finally, a science of supplication and
other solemn rites that the Church employs on extraordinary occasions.

LIGHT FOR THE MIND AND WARMTH FOR THE HEART
Who can relate the graces of salvation which are communicated to the
Christian people as a direct effect of teaching which is based on the explanation and comprehension of these mysteries, of the words and rites of the
liturgy? If men of our times but knew and savored that which was known
and savored by the simple catechumens of the Church of Milan, of Hippo,
and of Jerusalem, who were initiated by Ambrose, Augustine, and Cyril!
And again, centuries later in our new Churches of the West: what light did
they draw from the liturgical teaching of Rabanus Maurus, Ivo of Chartres,
Honorius of Autun, Hildebert of Le Mans, or Durandus of Mende!

What influence did the likes of these exert over Catholic morals! What a disposition towards perceiving the things of the supernatural life did they inspire
among the people, instructed with such care about the secrets that Christ and
His Church had hidden under the vast and profound emblem of the liturgy!

THE LITURGY AS THE LOFTIEST SCHOOL OF DOGMA
And indeed, what other means could there be for human minds to pen-
etrate into the understanding of dogma than that which the Author and
Redeemer of our nature has chosen as the place where His invisible grace
would descend to sanctify us? "The words that I have spoken to you are
spirit and life" (Jn. 6:64), says the Savior: they provide a light to the mind
while simultaneously giving the heart charity, which is life.

The liturgy has therefore always been considered as the higher learning
of dogma, while it is at the same moment the most universally accessible.

3

Liturgy in the Time of the Apostles

HE LITURGY IS SO SUBLIME A THING that its origin must be traced back to God; for God, in the contemplation of His infinite perfections, glorifies and praises Himself unceasingly, just as He loves Himself with an everlasting love. Nevertheless, these diverse acts, which are accomplished in the Divine Essence, found a visible and truly liturgical expression only at the moment that one of the Three Persons, by taking on a human nature, was Himself able to render the duties of religion to the glorious Trinity.

THE CELESTIAL LITURGY

"God so loved the world that He gave His only begotten Son" (Jn. 3:16), and He did this in order to give instruction by the accomplishment of a liturgical work. Having been prefigured and announced over the course of forty centuries, a divine prayer was offered and a divine sacrifice fulfilled. And so, from now until eternity, the Lamb that was slain from the foundation of the world offers Himself upon the sublime altar of heaven and in an infinite manner renders up to the ineffable Trinity all of the duties of religion, in the name of the members of which He is the Head.

Infinitely beneath the Lamb, and yet incomparably above every creature, stands Mary, the Mother of God, assisting in body and soul, in order that nothing should be lacking in the fulness of the liturgical expression; thus, she offers up to God the purest and most complete prayer, apart from that of her Son, before whom she brings the wishes of creation.

The choirs and angelic spirits likewise celebrate God's praises. They never cease to cry out one to another: "Holy, holy, holy!" They fulfill all the duties of religion on their own behalf as well as on behalf of the rest of creation, and particularly men, to whom God has entrusted the honor of His service, even as He did to them.[1]

Those chosen and glorified men, the saints, united in a perfect harmony full of grace and glory, also chant the divine praise, continuing as it were their songs from earth. And in the fulness of time, so that nothing should be missing from their liturgy, they will one day resume their bodies, in order to give a visible form to their worship.

---

[1] See the Collect for the Dedication and Apparition of St. Michael, which begins: *Deus qui miro ordine angelorum ministeria hominumque dispensas* ("O God, who dispose in marvelous order ministries both of angels and men . . . ").

THE TERRESTRIAL LITURGY

Lastly, the Church Militant praises God together with the Lamb who is her Spouse; with Mary who is her merciful Queen; with the angels who govern her under the watchful eye of the Almighty; with the saints who love her everlastingly with filial tenderness. In this mortal dwelling where the divine ordinances hold her, the Church admirably fulfills all of the conditions of the liturgy, as we will observe in depth throughout the *Institutions*.

But first, let us examine the principles and developments of the liturgy in its general forms. To begin with, let us acknowledge that the world has never been without it; since the Church dates back to the beginning of the world, according to the teaching of St. Augustine, the liturgy has this same beginning.[2] Indeed, since man was at no time without the knowledge of God, at no time did he fail to adore Him, to entreat Him, to celebrate His grandeur and His blessings, and these sentiments have never existed in man without producing certain words and acts.

God deigned to reveal these liturgical forms just as He gave to man speech and understanding, and as He manifested Himself to him as the Author of nature, of grace, and of glory. Therefore, from the very beginning, we observe the liturgy offered by the first men according to the chiefest and most august of these acts: sacrifice.

SACRIFICE BEFORE THE FLOOD

Despite the difference of their offerings, and even because of this difference, the diverse offerings of Cain and Abel bear witness to a pre-established order, a common ritual, although the sacrifice of the second brother was bloody and that of the first was not.

Before long, within this same epoch before the Flood, which was so rich in divine communication, we read that Enos, who was a righteous man and a servant of God, began to call upon the name of the Lord (Gen. 4:26). This is to say, according to the understanding of the Church Fathers, he began to enrich with more abundant developments this first form of sacrifice that originated on the very day of man's creation. Sacrifice was preserved throughout this entire period, for Noah, as he emerged from the Ark at the same moment that the Lord's rainbow was emblazoned on the horizon, in an act of thanksgiving immolated many clean animals, which God had ordered to be preserved in great number for this very action.

SACRIFICE BEFORE THE TIME OF MOSES

In this way, the liturgical principle had been saved from the utter cataclysm which forever consumed the greatest part of this early world's monuments; the liturgy survived with the language and sacred tradition of the Patriarchs.

---

[2] St. Augustine, *Retractationes*, bk. 1, ch. 13, n. 3.

We find frequent testimony to this in the brief pages of the pre-Mosaic narrative. Abraham, Isaac, and Jacob offered the sacrifice of animals;[3] they dedicated to the Lord places where they sensed His presence;[4] and they raised up stones for altars.[5] Like today, these stones had to be anointed with oil to become worthy to receive the majesty of God.[6] Yet it was not only the altar that emerged; the sacrifice which was to come could be seen from afar. For suddenly, bearing bread and wine in his hands, a King-Priest offered up a sacrifice of peace.[7]

Throughout this entire primitive epoch, liturgical traditions were in no way formless and arbitrary, but rather precise and determinate; they were always performed in the same manner. One clearly sees that these rites are not of man's invention, but of God's own imposition. And indeed, the Lord praises Abraham for having preserved, not only His laws and precepts, but also His ceremonies.[8]

THE SACRIFICE OF MOSES

The Mosaic Law was subsequently promulgated in order to give a still more precise and solemn form to the liturgy, to create a body of priests presided over by a High Priest, and to fix by means of written regulations the traditions that had been preserved inviolate until that time, but whose integrity was threatened by the general defection of the people.

Nevertheless, before Moses ascended Mount Sinai, where he was to receive the Law, the paschal lamb had already been immolated in the midst of the most mysterious rites, and already the leader of the Hebrews had chanted the hymn of passage through the Red Sea.

It is thus that God speaks and reveals this group of rites in which one can discern, in an admirable order, the diverse kinds of sacrifice: expiations, the offering of the firstfruits, the sacred fire, the use of incense, priestly vestments, and so on ...

The liturgy then grew out of its infancy and entered into its intermediary age, during which it was no longer to be practiced under a simply domestic form, but under a more social form, by means of a consecrated tribe; but even so, the symbols of this liturgy, rich as they were, could not contain the realities that they signified.

THE SACRIFICE OF THE GENTILES

Furthermore, we must not fail to mention a remarkable phenomenon that has always astonished the student of ancient religions; namely, the striking

---

[3] Gen. 15:19, 22:13.
[4] Gen. 12:7, 8; 26:25; 28:16; 32:30.
[5] Gen. 28:18, 22; 33:20.
[6] Gen. 28:18; 31:13; 35:14.
[7] Gen. 14:18.
[8] Gen. 26:5.

resemblance between the religious forms employed by the greater part of the Gentile nations and the liturgical rites of the people of Israel. This is an incontestable fact, and, as it was observed long ago, it has contributed powerfully to preparing the way for the Christian religion, whether it is explained, as it was by the greater part of the ancient Fathers, by a series of communications between these peoples and the Jews, or whether it is regarded as a vestige of patriarchal traditions of which the Mosaic cult was only one vast development.

THE PERFECT SACRIFICE

Be that as it may, when the fulness of time had come, "the Word was made flesh and dwelt among us" (Jn. 1:14): He gave Himself to be seen, heard, and touched by men; He descended from heaven to fashion adorers in spirit and in truth; He came, not to abolish, but to fulfill and perfect the liturgical traditions.[9]

After His birth, Christ was circumcised, offered in the Temple, and redeemed.[10] At the age of twelve, He made His visit to the Temple, and later on He went there frequently to offer His prayers. He carried out a fast of forty days; He kept the sabbath holy; He sanctified, by His example, night prayer. At the Last Supper, when Christ celebrated the great liturgical act and made preparations for its coming fulfillment, He first undertook the washing of feet (which the Church Fathers have called "a mystery") and concluded with a solemn hymn before departing for the Mount of Olives.

A few hours later, His mortal life, which was itself nothing other than a sublime liturgical act, was ended with the outpouring of blood upon the altar of the Cross. The veil of the Old Temple was rent, being opened like a passage into new mysteries, thus proclaiming a new tabernacle and an eternal Ark of the Covenant. From this time forth, the liturgy entered its period of perfection insofar as worship in this life allows.

Jesus Christ therefore left His apostles upon the earth, being invested with His power and sent forth as He Himself had been sent. It is thus that they presented themselves, not only as messengers of the word of God, but also as ministers and dispensers of the mysteries (1 Cor. 4:1).

THE APOSTOLIC LITURGY

The apostles were therefore bound to establish and promulgate a collection of rites, superior to those of the Mosaic liturgy in every respect.

Such was the nature of the new religion, as it is with all religions; for, as St. Augustine says: "Men can never be united under the name of any religion, whether it be true or false, unless they are bound by an association of signs or visible sacraments."[11]

---

[9] Cf. 1 Jn. 1:1; Jn. 4:24; Mt. 5:17.
[10] "Redeemed," i.e., by the payment of two turtle doves (Lk. 2:24).
[11] St. Augustine, *Contra Faustum*, bk. 19, ch. 9.

This is why the holy Council of Trent, which treated of the august ceremonies of the Holy Sacrifice of the Mass in its twenty-second session, declares, with the full authority of knowledge and religious teaching, that we must trace back to apostolic origin all of the

> mystical blessings, lighted candles, incense, sacred vestments, and generally all such details calculated to emphasize the majesty of the great sacrifice and to elevate the minds of the faithful to the contemplation of the sublime truths which are concealed in this profound mystery by means of these visible signs of religion and piety.[12]

Now this holy Council did not come to make this assertion by a doubtful conjecture deduced from vague premises. Rather, it invoked the primitive, which is to say the apostolic, tradition, just as Tertullian so eloquently invoked it in the third century to account for so many of the rites which did not seem to be founded upon the letter of the holy Gospels, such as the renunciation of the devil before baptism and threefold immersion; the fixed reception of Eucharistic communion in the morning, before any other nourishment; offerings for the dead; the prohibition against fasting on Sunday and during Paschal time; the very special care taken for the consecrated species; and the continual use of the sign of the Cross.[13]

St. Basil likewise indicates the apostolic tradition as the source of these same observances, to which he adds the following examples: prayer towards the east, consecration of the Eucharist according to a formula of invocation that is found neither in St. Paul nor in the Gospels, the blessing of baptismal water and the oil of anointing, and so on.[14]

And not only St. Basil and Tertullian, but all of antiquity without exception clearly expressed this great rule articulated by St. Augustine, which has become almost banal by force of repetition: *Quod universa tenet ecclesia, nec consiliis institutum, sed semper retentum est, non nisi auctoritate apostolica traditum rectissime creditur* ("What is held by the universal Church, and not ordained by any council, but has always been retained, is most rightly believed to have come down from no other source than apostolic authority").[15]

The great Cardinal Bona admirably summarized this entire question with the following words:

> In every liturgy, there are certain things in which all of the Churches agree. These are the things without which the essence of the Sacrifice would no longer exist: for instance, the preparation of the bread and wine, the oblation, the consecration, the

---

[12] Council of Trent, Session 22, ch. 5.
[13] Tertullian, *De corona militis*, ch. 3.
[14] St. Basil, *De Spiritu Sancto*, ch. 27.
[15] St. Augustine, *De Baptismo contra Donatistas*, bk. 4, ch. 24.

consumption, and finally the distribution of the Sacrament to those who wish to communicate. Furthermore, there are other important parts which, although they do not pertain to the integrity of the Sacrifice, are nevertheless found in all the liturgies: for instance, the chanting of the psalms, the reading of Holy Scripture, the presence of ministers, the use of incense, the exclusion of catechumens and profane things, the breaking of the host, the giving of peace, the multiplication of prayers, thanksgiving, and other things of this kind.[16]

But if the apostles should without any doubt be regarded as the creators of all the universal liturgical forms, one is equally justified in attributing to them a large number of those liturgical forms of a more limited extension whose origin is no less lost in the mists of time. Indeed, the apostles must have condescended more than once to adapt these sorts of forms, in their accidental aspects, to the customs of different places and the genius of different peoples to facilitate the diffusion of the Gospel.

Let us conclude, then, that this is no reason to deny the apostolic origin of both general and particular liturgies: namely, the fact that the liturgies bearing the names of Sts. Peter, Paul, James, Mark, and so on, do not accord amongst themselves or other Western liturgies in things of secondary importance, such as the order and content of the formulas of supplication.

THE BREAKING OF THE BREAD: ITS LITURGICAL SIGNIFICANCE

But in order to clarify further the true state of affairs on this subject and to support our observations with some positive facts, we will venture to set out some characteristics of the primitive liturgy as a whole. We will draw our evidence from the Acts of the Apostles and the Epistles, as well as from the testimony of tradition in the first centuries, when these usages were regarded as dating back to the very origin of Christianity, while at the same time offering an idea of these general rites which, by their very generality, must be deemed apostolic, following the rule of St. Augustine that we cited above, and which this great doctor expresses elsewhere in a manner no less precise: "There are many things universally accepted in the Church and, for this very reason, they are rightly held to have been enjoined by the apostles."[17]

Let us begin with the Eucharistic Sacrifice. There can be no doubt that everything surrounding it is at the forefront of liturgical prescriptions. The Breaking of the Bread appears from the first page of the Acts of the Apostles (Acts 2:46). Likewise, in his first Epistle to the Corinthians, St. Paul teaches what the liturgical significance of this act is (1 Cor. 10:16).

---

[16] Giovanni Bona, *Rerum liturgicarum*, bk. 1, ch. 1, n. 1.
[17] St. Augustine, *De baptismo*, bk. 5, ch. 23.

From the first, this celebration took place in a dignified and adorned room, to the extent that this was possible, for the Savior Himself had established this practice at the Last Supper: "Then he will show you a large dining room, furnished. And there prepare" (Lk. 22:12).

Sometimes, too, numerous lamps were provided there to provide illumination in place of daylight: "And there were a great number of lamps in the upper chamber where we were assembled" (Acts 20:8). One must also understand that the "Breaking of the Bread" of heaven, in the house of Gamaliel in Jerusalem or the senator Pudens in Rome, was accomplished with greater pomp than when it took place in the house of Simon the tanner.

THE ANCIENT ORIGIN OF THE ALTAR

The place for the celebration was conspicuous by the presence of an altar. This was no longer a table. Indeed, St. Paul emphatically declares: *Altare habemus* (Heb. 13:10). We have an altar, and the ministers of the tabernacle — which is to say, the priests of the Temple of Jerusalem — have no power to assist there.

THE ANCIENT ORIGIN OF THE MAJOR DIVISIONS OF THE LITURGY

When the faithful were thus gathered together in the place of Sacrifice, what did the priest do in the apostolic age? Just as today, he presided first over the reading of the Epistles of the apostles, then the recitation of certain passages from the Gospel, which constitutes the origin of "the Mass of the Catechumens." We need not search farther than the apostles themselves to determine the source of this observance ...

From the time of the Old Law, the people were greeted with the words: "The Lord be with you." Thus, Christ says to His Church: *Ecce ego vobiscum sum* (Mt. 28:20: "Behold, I am with you"). The Church also preserves this custom from the apostles, as evidenced by the uniformity of this practice in the ancient Churches of the East and the West alike.

The Collect, a form of prayer that contains the intentions of the assembly uttered before the offering of the Sacrifice, likewise has a primitive origin. Such is the teaching of St. Augustine: the concordance of all the liturgies equally demonstrates this fact. The conclusion of this and all other prayers by the words "forever and ever" is universal, from the earliest days of the Church.

During the preparation of the matter of the Sacrifice, the commingling of the water and wine that are to be offered takes place. St. Cyprian teaches us to trace this observance, one of such profound symbolism, back to the tradition of Our Lord Himself: "Be assured, then, that in the offering of the chalice, we are instructed to preserve the tradition handed down to us by the Lord, and to do nothing that Our Lord has not first done before us: so that the chalice which is offered in remembrance of Him should be offered mixed with wine." He goes on: "In which portion we find that the chalice which the Lord offered was mixed."[18]

Upon this follows the Trisagion (*Sanctus, sanctus, sanctus*). It was Isaiah, under the Old Law, who heard this chanted at the foot of the throne of Jehovah. Under the New Law, the prophet of Patmos repeats this, having heard it resound before the Altar of the Lamb (Apoc. 4:8). All liturgies are familiar with it, and one can be assured that the Eucharistic Sacrifice is never offered without these words being uttered.

The Canon then begins, and what man would dare to deny its apostolic origin? Could the founders of the Church have left this principal part of the sacred liturgy vague and arbitrary? If they had adjudicated on so many secondary matters, what care would they have taken to determine the words and rites of the most venerable and foundational of all the Christian mysteries? "It is from the apostolic tradition," writes Pope Vigilius in his letter to Profuturus of Braga, "that we have received the text of the Canonical prayer."[19]

It is this same "Canonical prayer" that St. Paul had in mind when he distinguished, in his discussion of the solemn prayers to be addressed to God, between supplication, petition, intercession, and thanksgiving: *Obsecro igitur primo omnium fieri obsecrationes, orationes, postulationes, gratiarum actiones pro omnibus hominibus*—"I desire therefore, first of all, that supplications, petitions, intercessions and thanksgivings be made for all men" (1 Tim. 2:1).

One should here read St. Augustine's commentary on this passage:

> In these words, I choose to understand that which all or nearly all of the Church repeatedly does, so that by supplications (*precationes*) we understand the prayers that we say in the celebration of the Sacraments, before that which is upon the Lord's Table begins to be blessed; by petitions (*orationes*), those which are said when it is blessed, consecrated, and broken for distribution, which nearly the entire Church concludes with the recitation of the Lord's Prayer ... By interpellations (*interpellationes*), or petitions (*postulationes*) as some of our versions read, those which are said when the people are blessed, because at this time bishops, in the role of advocates, offer their clients up before the most merciful Judge. When all of these are accomplished, and the most sublime Sacrament partaken of, thanksgiving (*gratiarum actio*) concludes all things.[20]

---

[18] St. Cyprian, *Epistles* 63.2.1 and 9.11.
[19] Vigilius, *Letter to Profuturus* (*Patrologia Latina* 84:829–32).
[20] St. Augustine, *Epistle* 149 (to Paulinus), n. 16.

A LITURGY MORE TRADITIONAL THAN SCRIPTURE

Let it suffice to conclude this chapter with some foundational observations.

1. The liturgy as it was established by the apostles must necessarily have contained everything that was essential for the celebration of the Christian Sacrifice and the administration of the Sacraments, both in terms of the essential forms and of the rites required by the dignity of the mysteries.

2. Apart from a small number of allusions in the Acts of the Apostles and the Epistles, the apostolic liturgy stands completely outside of Scripture and belongs to the pure domain of tradition. These allusions, even the most unambiguous of them — for example, that of St. James to extreme unction (Jas. 5:14–15) — although they attest that rites and formulas existed, teach us nothing about the nature of the rites nor the content of the formulas. It requires little study or long reflection to conclude that the liturgy was practiced by the apostles, and by those whom they had consecrated bishops, for a long time before the complete redaction of the New Testament.

4

The Liturgy in the
First Three Centuries

T IS POSSIBLE TO SUGGEST THAT, during the first three centuries, the liturgical life enjoyed its fullest force and extension, since at this time Confession, Praise, and Prayer encompassed the entire existence of Christians. We may also observe that the Apostle, speaking to the faithful of his time, exhorts them not only to prayer but also to chant, as if for an unending feast: "Be ye filled with the Holy Spirit, speaking to yourselves in psalms and hymns and spiritual canticles, singing and making melody in your hearts to the Lord" (Eph. 5:18–19). And again: " . . . in all wisdom, teaching and admonishing one another in psalms, hymns and spiritual canticles, singing in grace in your hearts to God" (Col. 3:16).

In the writings of the Fathers of this primitive epoch, as well as in the Acts of the Martyrs, we learn that Christians devoted themselves to psalmody and the celebration of the divine praises practically without ceasing. And they did so not according to vague and arbitrary forms, but rather exact and determinate ones; not at a moment of caprice, but at precise and mysterious hours that had been determined by apostolic institution. Such is the character of the liturgy, properly so called.

THE ANCIENT ORIGIN OF THE CANONICAL HOURS

If we examine the *Apostolic Constitutions*, an important liturgical collection which scholars do not hesitate to place at the end of the second century or in the course of the third at the latest, we read these words:

> Offer up your prayers in the morning, at the hour of Terce (*tertia*), of Sext (*sexta*), of None (*nona*), in the evening (*vespere*), and at the crowing of the cock. In the morning, returning thanks that the Lord has sent you light, that He has brought you past the night and brought on the day; at the hour of Terce, because at that hour the Lord received the sentence of condemnation from Pilate; at Sext, because at that hour He was crucified; at None, because all of nature was in horror at the crucifixion of the Lord, trembling at the audacity of the Jews and not bearing the outrage offered to its crucified Lord; in the evening, giving thanks that He has given you the night to rest from the daily labors; at the

crowing of the cock, because that hour brings glad tidings of the coming day, in which we must perform the works of light.[1]

Yet this is not only a discipline of the Eastern Church, to which the *Apostolic Constitutions* seem primarily to bear witness; indeed, the Latin Fathers of the same period give the same testimony for the West. Tertullian writes:

> In the Acts of the Apostles, we learn that it was at the hour of Terce that the apostles, being first infused with the Holy Spirit, entered into prayer and were regarded by the Jews as drunk; that it was at the hour of Sext that Peter ascended to the higher parts of the house; that it was at the hour of None that he entered the Temple with John. Do we not observe from this account that these three hours, so conspicuous in the course of human affairs and so constantly recalled to divide the day in the midst of its labors, must also have occupied a more solemn status in the divine prayers?[2]

Further on, Tertullian uses the word *officium* to designate the ecclesiastical prayers made at these hours.

Accordingly, in order to celebrate the praises of God, Christians would gather at the hours that we have noted, but principally at the time that preceded sunrise. They kept vigil with psalmody and, turning towards the East, they stood ready to salute with their chants "the Sun of Justice," for which the visible sun had always been the symbol in the monuments of the universal liturgy.

From the year 104, Pliny the Younger, writing to Trajan to consult him on the treatment that should be given to Christians, attests that the religious gatherings of this new sect took place before dawn and that they sang hymns to Christ at this time as to a god.[3]

Nevertheless, the same observances were also made at the other hours, for St. Cyprian attests that the Eucharistic offering was made in the afternoon as well as the morning, although he judges that it is better done in the morning.[4]

THE PRIMITIVE FEASTDAYS

The feastdays observed during the first three centuries [of the Church] were as follows. Apart from the Commemoration of the Passion, Resurrection, and Ascension of Jesus Christ, and the Descent of the Holy Spirit, there were the Nativity of the Savior on the twenty-fifth day of the ninth month, and His Epiphany on the sixth day of the tenth month.[5] To these, one must add the anniversary of the glorious death of the martyrs.

---

[1] *Apostolic Constitutions*, bk. 8, ch. 34.
[2] Tertullian, *De Ieiunio*, ch. 10.
[3] Pliny the Younger, *Letters*, bk. 10, letter 96.
[4] St. Cyprian, *Epistle* 63.
[5] See *Apostolic Constitutions*, bk. 5, ch. 13. Guéranger's account is here following the *Apostolic Constitutions*, which names the months of the feastdays according to the Hebrew reckoning.

THE SHAPE OF THE SANCTUARY

It would be impossible in our times to determine, in a precise manner, the configuration of primitive sanctuaries. With the exception of certain rooms in the catacombs, adorned with paintings and mosaics, many of which date back to the second or third centuries, nothing remains of these holy places. Even so, one can reasonably conjecture that the first temples erected at the time of the Peace of the Church, of which such a magnificent description has come down to us,[6] must have been built according to the model of the temples which preceded them. The conversion of the emperors to Christianity could not have suddenly given rise to new liturgical habits, and the shape that seemed best for such edifices under Diocletian (in the time of persecutions and the catacombs) must have certainly remained acceptable twenty years later under the reign of Constantine.

Through the munificence of the emperors, churches of the fourth century were sumptuously enriched and decorated. Nevertheless, those of the preceding centuries were by no means neglected by the faithful. We learn not only that the churches were endowed with fixed revenues, but we can also observe from indisputably authentic documents that the objects used for worship bore witness to a veritable opulence.

THE ANCIENT ORIGIN OF THE BISHOP'S CHAIR

St. Cyprian, the holy Bishop of Carthage, spoke vigorously about the chair of the bishop, the inalienable seat established in each church at the centre of the apse, and upon which the elect of the Holy Spirit alone could sit.[7] Some of these chairs have been found in the very heart of the catacombs; until our own times, the chair upon which Pope St. Stephen was martyred has been carefully preserved, and it still bears traces of his blood. The Basilica of St. Peter still preserves to this day the chair of the Prince of the Apostles.

Christians of this period took part in the prayers of the Church by facing towards the east and extending their hands in the form of a cross, a gesture which the Latin Church has retained for the priest during the most solemn moment of the Sacrifice.

THE SECRET OF THE RITES

But how many other details, how many precious liturgical formulas might have reached us today, if the Secret that enshrouded the Christian mysteries in this epoch had not forbidden their manifestation in public writing! This consideration must always be present for anyone who wishes to write or describe something about the liturgy, not only of the first three centuries, but

---

[6] Guéranger appears to be referring to Eusebius' *Ecclesiastical History*, although he provides no citation in the first edition, nor does the original context clarify his reference.
[7] St. Cyprian, *Epistle* 72 (to Jubaianus, concerning the Baptism of Heretics).

one might even say of the three or four centuries that followed them. This is not the place to give evidence for the existence of the august Secret that so faithfully guarded the Christian traditions and kept them pure of any contact with the profane. The testimonies to this fact are most abundant in the writings of the Fathers, both before and after the Peace of the Church, and no one today, to our knowledge, would dispute such a palpable material fact.[8]

THE DETERMINATION OF THE DATE OF EASTER

Providence permitted that one of the most characteristic acts of pontifical authority, during these first three centuries, was at the same time a sovereign exercise of Roman power over liturgical matters.

In the second century, the Churches of Asia followed a different practice from that of Rome in the celebration of Easter. Instead of holding the feast on Sunday, which is the day of the creation of light, of the Resurrection of Christ, and the Descent of the Holy Spirit, they followed the Jewish observance of commemorating it on the fourteenth lunar day of March.

This divergence in the custom of celebrating the principal event of Christianity gravely undermined the unity of worship, which is the first consequence of the unity of faith. The persistence of the customs of the Synagogue in the heart of Christian society posed a dangerous threat to the integrity of the Christian rites. Lastly, prudence obliged the Church to use every means of isolating herself from the Jewish sect.

All of these weighty considerations led Pope St. Victor to make an energetic effort to restore Christian unity on a point of such importance. He therefore ordered that provincial councils be held through the entire Church on this question. Having thus determined that the Roman practice of celebrating Easter on Sunday was almost universally admitted, he believed that it was necessary to deal severely with the Churches of the province of Asia, which seemed likely to persist in the opposing custom.

The Pope went as far as to cut them off from communion with the Church—a severe penalty, and indeed so severe that it was later revoked. But the bishops, and notably St. Irenaeus, who considered it their duty to voice their objections to the Pope on this subject, did not reproach him for having exceeded the limits of his apostolic authority; rather, they simply entreated him not to permit so many Churches which otherwise adhered to the soundest traditions to remain separated. The forbearance of the Apostolic See soon brought about the restoration of peace, but this important act remains as a manifestation of the uncontested power of the Roman Church over liturgical matters, and as a prelude to the efforts that Rome would have to make, over the course of time, to reunite all of the Churches in a communion of the same rites and prayers.

---

[8] Guéranger's understanding of the discipline of secrecy in the early Church with respect to ancient liturgical documents is more fully expressed below, in chapter 26.

THE LITURGICAL ACTIVITY OF THE HERETICS

Just as the liturgy revealed itself as one of the principal forces of Christendom, heresy, which always seeks to counterfeit orthodoxy and to turn to the advantage of its pernicious designs all of the same means that are used to maintain tradition, was already laying its hands on this sacred weapon.

The precursor of Arius, Paul of Samosata, abolished the chants with which his church had hitherto resounded in honor of Christ, replacing them with other hymns for which he received the sacrilegious flattery of his followers.[9]

The schismatics who, going by the name of Donatists, had belabored the Church of Africa from the end of the third century until the fifth, also invented chants of their own, according to the witness of St. Augustine, in the form of psalms which were calculated to spread the venom of their errors among the multitude gathered for prayer.[10]

A long time before these, the infamous Valentinus had also composed psalms, which he did with great impudence according to Tertullian.[11] Likewise, St. Epiphanius teaches us that a certain sectarian, Hieracas, also imitated Valentinus with the same purpose of corrupting the faith through misleading prayers.[12] In later epochs, we will see new applications of this same faithless system, which is common to nearly all the separated bodies.

In concluding this chapter, we observe that the Roman Church was from this time the heart of the liturgy, in the same way that she was the heart of the faith, to such an extent that, even from the perspective of our times, we may apply to her the solemn words of St. Irenaeus: *Ad hanc quippe Ecclesiam, propter potentiorem principalitatem, necesse est omnem convenire Ecclesiam, id est qui sunt undique fideles* ("For it is to this [Roman] Church, on account of the primacy of her power, that the entire Church, that is, those who are faithful everywhere, must necessarily turn").[13]

---

[9] See Eusebius, *Historia ecclesiastica*, bk. 7, ch. 30.
[10] St. Augustine, *Epistle* 34.
[11] Tertullian, *De carne Christi*, bk. 4, ch. 17.
[12] St. Epiphanius, *Adversus hæreses*, bk. 2, ch. 77.
[13] St. Irenaeus, *Adversus hæreses*, bk. 3, ch. 3.

5

The Liturgy in the Fourth Century

T LAST, THE CHURCH EMERGED FOREVER from the crypts which too often had concealed in their shadows the majesty of her mysteries. She brought her rites out into the open, and by their glory and sanctity she would complete the victory over paganism that the august truth of her dogmas and the beauty of her morals had already secured.

The character of this epoch is one of triumph: it is at this time that the Savior's words were accomplished: "That which you hear in the ear, preach ye upon the housetops" (Mt. 10:27). The pomp and richness of worship, however splendid under the largesse of the patrician disciples of Christ, surpassed every measure at the moment that the emperors crossed the threshold of the Church.

"And so," writes Eusebius of Caesarea, "if the temple in one city situated in Palestine was worthy of wonder, how much more for their multitude and magnitude and beauty are the churches of God that have been erected throughout every region!"[1]

THE FIRST DEDICATIONS

Everywhere, therefore, churches demolished during the persecution were restored, and new ones raised up through the entire Empire. The dedication of these temples was marked by ever greater splendor, with bishops gathering in large numbers.

The first dedication of a church that we encounter after the Peace of Constantine is that of the Basilica of Tyre, around the year 375. This city, under Bishop Paulinus, had seen its church perish during the persecution of Diocletian, with the pagans there even attempting to deface the church by heaping up all kinds of filth on the site. A different location could easily have been found to build a new church when peace had been restored to Christianity, but Bishop Paulinus preferred to have the first place cleansed and to have the foundations of the second basilica laid there, in order to make the victory of the Church all the more palpable. Moreover, this second temple surpassed the first in grandeur. Eusebius of Caesarea was charged with delivering the homily for the dedication, in the midst of a vast multitude gathered there to take part in the feast:

---

[1] Eusebius of Caesarea, *Commentary on Isaiah*, trans. Jonathan J. Armstrong (IVP Academic, 2013), 266.

Then [Paulinus], building in righteousness, divided the whole people according to their strength. With some he fortified only the outer enclosure, walling it up with unfeigned faith; such were the great mass of the people who were incapable of bearing a greater structure. Others he permitted to enter the building, commanding them to stand at the door and act as guides for those who should come in; these may be not unfitly compared to the vestibules of the temple . . . Still others he joined together about the royal edifice on both sides; these are the catechumens who are still advancing and progressing, and are not far separated from the inmost view of divine things granted to the faithful. Taking from among these the pure souls that have been cleansed like gold by divine washing, he then supports them by pillars, much better than those without, made from the inner and mystic teachings of the Scripture, and illumines them by windows. Adorning the whole temple with a simple and imposing vestibule, to signify the adorable majesty of the only God . . . But the great and august and unique altar, what else could this be than the pure holy of holies of the soul of the common priest of all?[2]

In the West, the traditions of the Roman Church teach us that Pope St. Sylvester, in the fourth century, instituted and regulated in detail the rites that we practice to this day in the dedication of churches and altars.[3] This Pontiff had the most magnificent occasions to observe these rites in the dedication of basilicas founded in Rome through Constantine's munificence.

But an event that particularly stirred Christians in the same century, and which furnished an occasion for the most sumptuous acts of the liturgy, was St. Helena's restoration of the holy places of Palestine, which had served as testimonies to the life, miracles, and sufferings of the God-Man.

Zealously supporting the pious intentions of his mother, Constantine put the treasures of the Empire at the disposal of St. Macarius, the Bishop of Jerusalem, to ensure that the church which was to be built over the Holy Sepulcher would surpass in magnificence all of the edifices found in any of the cities of the world.[4]

THE BIRTH OF PSALMODY

These vast and opulent basilicas resounded day and night with the chants of the clergy and the faithful. As the majesty of these rites grew, the chant became more melodious. Day by day, the sacred formulas took on a greater grandeur and eloquence. Distinguished bishops devoted their attention

---

[2] Eusebius, *Historia ecclesiastica*, bk. 10, ch. 4.

[3] Cf. *Breviarium Romanum*, 9 November, ad Matutinum, lectio 4: "Ritus quos in consecrandis ecclesiis et altaribus Romana servat Ecclesia, Beatus Silvester Papa primus instituit." ("The blessed Pope Silvester I instituted the rites that the Roman Church preserves for the consecration of churches and altars.")

[4] See the letter from Constantine to St. Macarius, in *Eusebius, Vita Constantini*, bk. 3, chs. 30–32.

to perfecting the rites and prayers and enriching the hallowed traditions of antiquity with new inspirations. And yet, as all things conspire to accomplish God's designs for His Church within the plans of Providence, the Arian heresy, disastrous as it was in its ravages, served as an occasion for new developments in liturgical forms.

The city of Antioch having been seized by the Arians through the perfidy of its bishop Leontius, two illustrious members of this great Church, Diodorus and Flavian, stood in opposition to this torrent of iniquity with a generosity of spirit and untiring vigilance. Desiring to fortify the people against the seduction of the heretics and to confirm them in the solidity of the faith through the most solemn observances of the liturgy, these men had decided that the time had come to give a new beauty to psalmody. Until this time, cantors alone had sung the psalms in church, and the faithful listened to their voices with reverence. Diodorus and Flavian divided the entire holy assembly into two choirs and instructed the faithful to sing the Psalms of David in alternation. After relating this story, Theodoret reports that this form of alternating chant, which had begun in Antioch, spread from this city to the extremities of the earth.[5]

Likewise provoked, so to speak, by the insolence of the Arians, the Church of Constantinople followed the example of Antioch a few years later. These heretics, like every sect, sought out every means of attracting the multitudes; thus, they presumed to appropriate the alternating chant that the orthodox had recently inaugurated in Antioch. Since, under the reign of Theodosius, the heretics had lost the churches they previously had in Constantinople, they were forced to hold their assemblies under the public porticoes. There, they divided themselves into choirs and sang the psalms in alternation, inserting into the sacred chants certain sentences that expressed their impious dogmas.

St. John Chrysostom, fearing with good reason that some of his flock, being seduced by these new liturgical forms, might run the risk of being corrupted, exhorted the faithful to imitate this alternating chant. After a short time, they had little trouble surpassing the heretics, both by the melody with which they executed the chants and by the splendor with which the entire Church of Constantinople, processing with crosses of silver and torches, inaugurated this new mode of psalmody.[6]

In the West, the alternating chant of the psalms had its beginning in the Church of Milan, around the same time that it had been established in Antioch, and with the same end of repelling Arianism by introducing a new liturgical form. St. Augustine, who witnessed this felicitous innovation, has left us an account. Let us see how he expresses himself in the ninth book of his *Confessions*:

---

[5] Theodoret, *Historia ecclesiastica*, bk. 2, ch. 24.

[6] See Sozomen, *Historia ecclesiastica*, bk. 8, ch. 8.

How greatly did I weep in Your hymns and canticles, deeply moved by the voices of Your sweet-speaking Church! Not long had the Church of Milan begun to employ this kind of consolation and exhortation, the brethren singing together with great earnestness of voice and heart. For it was about a year, or not much more, since Justina, the mother of the boy-Emperor Valentinian, persecuted Your servant Ambrose in the interest of her heresy, to which she had been seduced by the Arians. The pious people kept guard in the church, prepared to die with their bishop, Your servant... We, still unmelted by the heat of Your Spirit, were yet moved by the astonished and disturbed city. At this time it was instituted that, after the manner of the Eastern Church, hymns and psalms should be sung, lest the people should pine away in the tediousness of sorrow; which custom, retained from then till now, is imitated by many, yea, by almost all of Your congregations throughout the rest of the world.[7]

THE FIRST HERETICAL LITURGIES

Furthermore, while the Church employed forms of the liturgy against heresy, it must be said that heresy itself, from the fourth century, sought to deflect the blow by propagating sacrilegious errors on the subject of the sacred rites.

Throughout this entire history, we will see heretics adhere faithfully to this diabolical scheme: 1) either they adapt popular forms of worship to their own ends; or 2) they denounce these same forms as dangerous, superstitious, or of human invention.

Above all, the heretics will repeat this sophism: that anything in the liturgy that is not supported by Sacred Scripture must be removed as contrary to the purity of the divine service, thus willfully disregarding the great principle established above, that the entire liturgy pertains especially to tradition.

Now, in the fourth century, a Gaul named Vigilantius was raised up by Hell to be the first anti-liturgical heretic, whose succession we will recall in short order. He too believed and maintained that worship became increasingly filled with novel practices, which threatened to alter its purity.

The magnificence of exterior worship, the influx of people to the tombs of the martyrs, the cult rendered to fragments of their bones, the candles and torches lighted in full daylight to mark the joy of the Church, the profusion of feastdays: all of these things incited within the soul of Vigilantius an unparalleled fury.

St. Jerome, with his incisive eloquence, took it upon himself to confound this new Pharisee, and the arguments that the saint used to eradicate Vigilantius's sophistries almost seem to have been directed against modern

---

[7] St. Augustine, *Confessions* (trans. Philip Schaff), bk. 9, chs. 6–7.

sectarians, just as the errors of the latter are nothing but a pale imitation of the proclamations of our Gallic heresiarch.[8]

THE BIRTH OF THE MONASTIC LITURGY

It remains for us here to set forth another liturgical development that we will continue to trace through the course of this history. This development has its place within the churches of monks and the forms of worship observed within them. Now indeed, under the regime of peace which the Church now enjoyed, monasteries could not exist for long if those inhabiting them did not have the means to fulfill all the duties of the Christian faith. Therefore, from this time, monastic institutions had to include a church, an altar for the Sacrifice, and ministers for the Sacraments.

Furthermore, since the Divine Office was the principal occupation of monks, the manner of its celebration had to become the object of particular liturgical rules which, while remaining closely connected to the general usages of the Church, had to represent the principles and customs of the cloister in a special manner.

In each monastery, the celebration of the Sacred Mysteries required the presence of one or more priests or deacons, whether monks of the community or clergy of a neighboring church. Nevertheless, the first Fathers of monasticism, such as St. Pachomius, were not very inclined to ordain subjects who had already made their profession to the monastic life. Rather, they preferred to employ, for the ministry of the altar, priests who were already honored with the priesthood by the time they had embraced the perfect life of the desert.

The Church did not delay to manifest her intentions on this subject, and letters from the supreme pontiffs, as well as decrees from the councils, established rules for the ordination of monks, whose very state of life they regarded as a veritable preparation for the priesthood.

We will here limit ourselves to citing a fourth-century authority, the famous decretal of Pope St. Siricius: "We desire and wish that monks who are commendable for the gravity of their morals, as well as by a holy life and irreproachable faith, be elevated to the offices of the clergy."[9]

---

[8] St. Jerome, *Contra Vigilantium.*
[9] St. Siricus, *Epistle* (to Himerius of Tarragona), ch. 13.

6

The Liturgy During the Fifth and Sixth Centuries:

THE FIRST ATTEMPTS TO ESTABLISH UNITY

HE PERIOD OF PEACE UNDER WHICH the Church now lived and her liberation from all outward attacks gave her the leisure to regulate all of the secondary forms of her government and institutions. Yet nothing was more urgent for her than to apply more fully the great principle of unity that she received from Christ as her fundamental law, under the aegis of which she was able to traverse three centuries of bloody persecutions and the no less terrible tempests of Arianism. The perfection of liturgical forms by means of unity therefore became indispensable.

UNITY IN THE ESSENTIAL AND THE ACCIDENTAL

It should be clearly noted that we are not here dealing with unity as regards the essential things of divine worship, such as the form and matter of the Sacrifice and other Sacraments, or the general rites that accompany them. Indeed, we have already proven that, from the origin of the Church, there had been perfect unity in all of these matters.

Here, we are treating of a new degree of unity in the formulas that are not essential for the validity of the Sacraments or the completeness of the Sacrifice: in Confession, Prayer, and Praise, in the ceremonies with which worship was developed and enriched; in short, unity in the ensemble of rites that express either the mysteries of Christian initiation or the service offered to the Author of the Faith by the redeemed City of God.

The first apostles of the different Churches, the union of which formed such a magnificent empire for Christ from the time of Constantine, had brought with them the liturgical usages of the Mother Churches that sent them. Yet they interpreted and completed whatever needed to be perfected. Following them, their successors in every place, always while guarding the inviolable foundation of unity, had added new parts to the primitive liturgy, with more or less happy results, to meet new needs. But this divergence, which was less perceptible during the course of the persecutions and violent upheavals of Arianism, posed a serious inconvenience at the moment when the Church had to address the specific institutions suited for the age of peace that was opening before her.

The admirable words of Pope St. Siricius, pronounced at the end of the fourth century, reveal the full gravity of the consequences of unity in the liturgy, whether observed or violated: "The apostolic rule teaches us that the confession of all Catholic bishops must be one. If, therefore, there is only one faith, there can only be one tradition. If there is only one tradition, there should be only one discipline observed in the Churches."[1] This is a fundamental axiom of Catholicism: one faith, and one form of the faith.

This being the case, the liturgy, if it is also one within the Church of God, must be an authentic expression of this Church's faith and a lasting resolution of the controversies that might arise on the points of dogma professed in the sacred formulas of the liturgy.

It is a Pope of the fifth century who will furnish us with this natural conclusion. Let us read what St. Celestine wrote to the bishops of Gaul in his celebrated letter against the error of the Pelagians:

> Besides the inviolable decrees of the Apostolic See which have taught us the true doctrine, let us consider the mysteries contained in the formulas of priestly prayers, which, having been handed down by the apostles, are repeated in a uniform manner throughout the entire world and in every Catholic Church, such that the rule of prayer may establish the rule of belief (*ut legem credendi lex statuat supplicandi*).[2]

PUTTING AN END TO INNOVATIONS

The interests of the faith, no less than the order of discipline, thus demanded that measures be taken at an early stage to arrest innovations that tended to separate the Churches rather than unite them. One of the first documents of this principle is a canon from the second Council of Milevis, which sixty-one bishops from the Province of Numidia attended in the year 416, during the ravages of Pelagianism. Here is what the canon contains:

> It has also pleased the bishops that the prayers, orations, and Masses which have been approved in a council, as well as the prefaces, commemorations, and imposition of hands, should be observed by all. Only the prayers that have been composed by men of authority and approved by a council should be recited in the Church, lest anything be found in them that is contrary to the faith or that has been written in ignorance or lack of diligence.[3]

---

[1] Pope Siricius, *Epistle* 10 (*Patrologia Latina* 13:1181–96).
[2] St. Celestine, *Epistle* 21.
[3] Second Council of Milevis (416), can. 12.

In this way, limits were placed upon the effects of an unenlightened zeal, as well as on the love of novelty which so often works upon men, even without their realizing it.

Betaking ourselves now to Gaul, we will see that liturgical unity was proclaimed by the bishops of the Council of Vannes in 461:

> It seems good to us that, in our province, there be only one custom for the sacred ceremonies and psalmody, in order that, just as we have only one faith by our confession of the Trinity, we might also have only one rule for the [Divine] Offices, lest a variety of observances in certain things may give place to the belief that there are also differences in our devotion.[4]

Assuredly, nothing could be stated with greater precision, and in the centuries that followed, the doctrine of liturgical unity was never expressed with more directness than it was by the Breton bishops of this council.

Let us now turn, again with the same purpose, to the second canon of the Council of Toledo in 633:

> After having provided for the confession of the true faith which must be proclaimed in the Holy Church of God, it pleased us that all of us priests, who are joined by the unity of the Catholic faith, should no longer suffer any variety or dissonance in the ecclesial Sacraments, lest the slightest discrepancy might seem, in the eyes of the ignorant or carnally-minded, to give rise to some kind of schismatical error and lest variety among the Churches cause scandal for many. Therefore, throughout all of Spain and Narbonne, there shall be preserved only one order of prayer and psalmody, one usage in the solemnity of the Mass, and one rite in the Offices of the evening and morning.[5]

A NUANCED APPROACH

The Roman Pontiffs, who were attentive to all of the needs surrounding the inheritance of the Lord committed to their care, did not unduly hasten the consummation of this happy unification. Instead, they prepared for it at great length, by taking advantage of every occasion to settle liturgical controversies submitted to their tribunal.

Thus, Pope St. Innocent wrote to the Bishop of Gubbio in a decretal from the year 416:

> If the priests of the Lord wished to safeguard ecclesiastical institutions such as they were handed down by the Holy Apostles, there would be no discord in the [Divine] Office and consecrations. But when each priest supposes that he can observe, not that which derives from tradition, but that which seems good

---

[4] Council of Vannes (461), can. 15.
[5] Fourth Council of Toledo (633), can. 2.

to him, there comes about the diversity of celebration that we
see according to the diversity of places and Churches. This gen-
erates a scandal for the people who, not understanding that the
ancient traditions have been altered by human presumption,
begin to think either that the Churches are not in accord with
one another, or that the Apostles or apostolic men established
these contradictory practices.[6]

Following these remarks, Pope Innocent concludes in these terms:

It is thus, dearest brother, that we have taken upon ourselves the
duty, in accordance with our power, to respond to that which
your charity demands of us, so that your Church may be able
to observe and safeguard the customs of the Roman Church,
from which she derives her origin. As for the rest, which it is
not permitted to put into writing, we will be able to satisfy your
requests when you are present with us.[7]

Here, Innocent is treating of questions surrounding the words of the
Canon or the form of the Sacraments, elements which were still shrouded
in the greatest mystery.

The East, on the other hand, did not enjoy the advantages of complete
unity. Too many obstacles prevented the zeal of the Popes from thinking
that, even for an instant, they could establish an absolute devotion to the
Roman liturgy among the patriarchates of Alexandria, Antioch, Constantinople, and Jerusalem. They contented themselves with guarding the more
general unity, which consisted in the integrity of the rites of the Sacrifice,
the valid and proper administration of the Sacraments, the observance
of the Hours of the Divine Office and psalmody, and, later on, in the
veneration of sacred images.

It is thus, according to different times and places, that the Holy See was
able to exercise, in different degrees, the fulness of power which resides
within it, such that the Roman Pontiffs have never forgotten the doctrine
of the first of them: "Feed the flock of God which is among you, taking
care of it, not by constraint but willingly, according to God: not for filthy
lucre's sake but voluntarily: Neither as lording it over the clergy but being
made a pattern of the flock from the heart" (1 Pet. 5:2–3).

TRADITION: WRITTEN OR ORAL?

This is a fitting place to examine the tantalizing question of when the
mysterious formulas of the Christian Sacrifice and those which attended
the rites of initiation were first entrusted to writing. The learned Pierre
Le Brun, in the third volume of his excellent work *Explication de la Messe*,
has asserted that, before the fifth century, none of the ancient liturgies,

---

[6] Pope Innocent I to the Bishop of Gubbio, decretal 416.
[7] Ibid.

whether Greek or Latin, had been preserved in writing, but were simply transmitted by oral tradition.

It is our opinion, along with Ludovico Antonio Muratori, that this assertion is exaggerated, and that a more cogent interpretation can be given to the passages from antiquity cited by the learned Oratorian.

Indeed, how could such a degree of uniformity have been conserved in the general formulas and rites—a uniformity which, as we have shown above, was maintained in its entirety throughout the first centuries of the Church—if a written text was not present in each church to correct innovations and to prevent the effects of carelessness and neglect?

Granted, perhaps such a formulary was not placed on the altar, but rather guarded in some secret place, far away from profane eyes. Even so, in time of need, a celebrant could appeal to its authority to reinforce a faulty memory and to rectify anything that might have been introduced that was not consistent with antiquity. With these precautions, the secret of the sacred mysteries would have been no less safe.

The holy doctors upon whom Fr. Le Brun relies were speaking of tradition as opposed to Sacred Scripture, and did not mean to say that the liturgies were never written. Here, we may refer, among other testimonies, to that of St. Basil:

> We do not limit ourselves to the account given by the Apostle or in the Gospel [on the subject of the Eucharist]; rather, there are other things that we recite both before and after [the consecration], which have a great importance in the mystery and which we have received from an unwritten tradition.[8]

It is evident that the holy bishop here refers to a source distinct from the Holy Scriptures, and that he asserts that the formulas of the Canon of the Mass emanated from this source by way of tradition. We readily agree with him and do not say otherwise; nevertheless, it does not follow from this account that these traditions were not committed to writing by some human hand and preserved in the archives of the Church.

TWO LITURGICAL POPES: ST. CELESTINE AND ST. GELASIUS
Without a doubt, it is a point of the greatest importance to establish, in the study of antiquity, that universal secrecy concealed our sacred mysteries for so many centuries. However, it is also important to show that the principal forms of Christian worship reach back to an origin that precedes the external peace of the Church.

Accordingly, when the Popes of the fifth century concentrated their efforts on improvements to be introduced into the liturgy of the Church of Rome, there can be no doubt that this Church already possessed a

---

[8] St. Basil, *De Spiritu Sancto*, ch. 27.

corpus of liturgical formulas suited to the contemporary necessities of divine worship.

The first Pope of this period whom the *Liber Pontificalis* notes established rules for the Divine Office is St. Celestine, who reigned from the year 422. The chronicle reads:

> He ordained that the 150 Psalms of David should be chanted antiphonally before the Mass, with an antiphon . . . He also established that before the Mass, following the office, the Gradual should be chanted, which is to say the responsory which is said upon the steps (*gradus*).[9]

The Psalm with its antiphon chanted before Mass is what we call today the Introit. The Gradual, which has kept the same name the chronicle gives to it, is considered a responsory because it is chanted, like all responsories in former times, with the repetitions that are still in use today for the short responsories of the Office. In this way, the Mass was enriched with a solemn introduction and no longer began with readings from the Epistles and the Gospel, as it had in the time of St. Justin Martyr.

St. Gelasius reigned towards the end of the fifth century. About him, the *Liber Pontificalis* relates: "He composed Prefaces for the mysteries, and orations in a refined style."[10] This precious reference alludes to the publication of the so-called Gelasian Sacramentary that this Pontiff compiled, partly from formulas composed by his predecessors and partly from those which he himself added in a truly liturgical style.

---

[9] *Liber Pontificalis*, ch. 45: Celestine I (Paris, 1886), vol. 1, p. 230.
[10] Ibid., ch. 51: Gelasius I, 1:255.

7

The Work of Saint Gregory the Great

OWARDS THE END OF THE SIXTH CENTURY a man ascended to the Apostolic See whose pontificate of thirteen years and six months ended in the year 604. St. Gregory the Great left for the centuries that followed a glorious renown that might perhaps have been equaled but was never surpassed.

THE PRINCIPLE OF ENRICHMENT

In the preceding chapter, we related the work of St. Celestine and St. Gelasius during the fifth century, which was a brilliant moment for the liturgy throughout the entire Church, for the greatest bishops of the time devoted all of their attention to its perfection.

Towards the end of the sixth century, it became necessary to complete and improve the works of the preceding centuries; for indeed, the liturgy, as the symbol of the Church and the repository of her discipline, ought to be enriched over the course of the centuries, although it cannot be changed in a fundamental manner. True progress, as directed by a competent authority, satisfies new needs while never jeopardizing the integrity of the ecclesiastical rites, nor leading to offensive alterations in the holy formulas that the centuries have consecrated.

And thus, from the first years of his pontificate, St. Gregory undertook the reform of the Roman liturgy.

Walafrid Strabo, one of the historians of St. Gregory's pontificate, writes the following in his treatise *De rebus Ecclesiasticis*:

> Gelasius, the fifty-first Pope, organized the prayers composed both by himself and by those who came before him. The Churches of the Gauls made use of his prayers, and they still enjoy a wide application to this day. Nevertheless, since many of these formulas seemed to have an uncertain authorship, or were not clear and complete in meaning, the blessed Gregory took pains to collect everything that was consistent with the original purity of the text, and having omitted anything that was excessively long or composed in bad taste, he compiled a book which is called *Sacramentorum* ("On the Sacraments").[1]

This was the origin of the Gregorian Sacramentary, which, together with the Antiphonary mentioned above, forms even to this day, with some

---

[1] Walafrid Strabo, *De rebus Ecclesiasticis*, ch. 22.

slight alterations, the Roman Missal, which is used by the entire Western Church, save for *de facto* or *de jure* exceptions.

This Pontiff likewise re-established customs that had fallen into disuse, and instituted others which seemed useful to him; he selected, from the various rites of the Churches subject to Rome, customs which seemed appropriate to adopt; he asserted the sovereign right he had received, even over the See of Constantinople, to suppress abuses; and finally, he declared his willingness, so wisely and so frequently put into practice by the Holy See, to imitate whatever is found to be best in the uses of the various Churches. Throughout all of the centuries, we will constantly see the Popes following these lines, which he so forcefully traced.

THE CODIFICATION OF THE CHURCH'S CHANT

St. Gregory the Great also undertook the correction of ecclesiastical chant, whose majestic melody was to add a new splendor to divine worship.

We need not concern ourselves here with the characteristics of ecclesiastical chant, but only remind the reader in passing that every learned man who has discussed the origins of music recognized in ecclesiastical or Gregorian chant the rare and precious vestiges of ancient Greek music, of which so many marvels are told. Indeed, this music, so grandiose yet at the same time simple and popular, was naturalized in Rome at an early stage. The Christian Church appropriated without great difficulty this inexhaustible source of solemn and religious melodies . . .

Evidently, the Pontiffs preferred to instruct the faithful through the doctrine contained in the sacred text rather than to beguile their ears through the richness of extravagant harmony. Nevertheless, the necessities of worship had given rise to a great many pieces of chant in the Church of Rome, whose lyrics were all in prose. The motifs of most of these chants were inspired by reminiscences of certain familiar melodies that were simple to execute, which a trained ear still recognizes in the Gregorian repository and which would be easy to restore to their original color.

This collection of chants also called for a correction, and God, who had given to St. Gregory the noble and cadenced diction that enabled him to revise the Sacramentary of St. Gelasius, likewise gave him a sensibility for the ecclesiastical music to which his name would be rightfully attached. The historian John the Deacon writes: "Gregory, being like a new Solomon in the house of the Lord for the compunction and sweetness of his music, compiled an Antiphonary according to the style of the *cento*, which was of the greatest utility for cantors."[2] The expression *compilavit centonem* shows that St. Gregory cannot be considered as the author, properly speaking, of the chants which constitute his Antiphonary. So it is with ecclesiastical chant, as with every great institution of the Catholic Church: the first

---

[2] John the Deacon, *Vita Sancti Gregorii Magni*, bk. 2, ch. 6.

time that it is encountered in the monuments of tradition, it appears as an already existing fact, its origin lost in an impenetrable antiquity.

Nevertheless, it is certainly permissible to believe that St. Gregory did not content himself simply with collecting melodies: he must not only have corrected but also have composed many of the chants contained in his Antiphonary, in a method of working analogous to that by which he completed the Sacramentary.

The Antiphonary of St. Gregory was divided into two parts. The first contained the chants used in the Mass, and has for a long time been known as the *Gradual*. The second part, called the *Responsorial* in antiquity, contained the responsories and antiphons for the Office; this part has retained the name *Antiphonary*.

To ensure the perfect execution of the chants that he had collected and revised with such care, St. Gregory established a *Schola cantorum* (school of singers). The holy Pope richly endowed this Schola and assigned it two houses in Rome, one under the steps of the Basilica of St. Peter and the other in the vicinity of the patriarchal Lateran Palace. John the Deacon writes: "Still preserved in this latter house is the bed upon which he took repose while repeating the modulations of chant, the whip with which he threatened the children, and the authentic exemplar of the Antiphonary."[3]

The *Schola cantorum* established by St. Gregory endured through the centuries, and, after having undergone various alterations and obtained important privileges from the Apostolic See, it still exists in Rome. The Schola alone performs its chant service in the papal chapel and basilicas when the Supreme Pontiff celebrates the sacred mysteries there.

THE ROMAN LITURGY IN ENGLAND AND GERMANY

The provincial council of England held in 747 contains these words:

> The holy and sacrosanct solemnities of our redemption shall be celebrated according to the rule that we have in writing from the Roman Church, in all of the rites pertaining to them, whether for the office of baptism, the celebration of the Mass, or the style of chant. In like manner, through the entire course of the year, the feasts of the saints shall be venerated on fixed days according to the Martyrology of the same Roman Church, and with the appropriate psalmody and chant.[4]

The same thing must have perforce happened in all of the Churches founded by Rome in the West, from that of England founded by St. Augustine to those of the various Germanic and Slavic regions founded by St. Boniface, St. Adalbert, and so many others. These apostles, who were all Benedictine monks sent by the Apostolic See, could not have brought with them any books other than those of the Roman Church, from which they received their mission.

---

[3] Ibid.   [4] Council of Cloveshoe (747), can. 13.

8

The Ambrosian, Gallican, and Mozarabic Liturgies

HE NECESSITIES OF THE HISTORY THAT we are now writing obliges us to suspend our narrative in order to make some observations about the various liturgies that have already been mentioned on several occasions, and some of which survive to this day. We will devote this chapter to the liturgies of the West, and the next to those of the East.

THE AMBROSIAN LITURGY OF MILAN

The oldest liturgy in the West, after that of Rome, is the liturgy of Milan, known as the Ambrosian rite. According to Giuseppe Visconti (in his *De Ritibus Missæ*), St. Barnabas, whom the Milanese have venerated as their apostle for many centuries, established the order of the Mass; St. Mirocles, Bishop of the same Church, set down the rule for their psalmody; and finally, St. Ambrose completed and perfected this ensemble. Regrettably, there is no evidence to support these claims, and it is much simpler to agree that the origin of the forms of divine worship in the Church of Milan are intertwined with the very origin of Christianity there.

Nevertheless, the name "Ambrosian," which has always been attached to the liturgy of Milan, certainly proves that as great a doctor as St. Ambrose, along with all of the illustrious bishops of antiquity, took pains to correct the liturgy of his Church. One can therefore attribute to St. Ambrose a work analogous to that of St. Gelasius or St. Gregory on the Roman Sacramentary. Moreover, apart from the institution of alternating chant in the West, we can attribute to St. Ambrose a great number of hymns which were enthusiastically adopted by many Churches.

It is here worth remarking upon the frequent conformity of the Ambrosian liturgy with the Roman. Not only is the Canon almost entirely the same, but a great number of the Introits, Collects, Epistles, and Gospels are identical in the Missals of these two Churches. The Breviary likewise presents many similarities of the same kind. It even seems that the Roman books were intentionally imitated in Milan, for in the Ambrosian Missal, one finds the commemoration of St. Anastasia in the second Mass of Christmas, a commemoration proper only to the station held in Rome at the church of this saint. Furthermore, one finds in the Ambrosian Canon the addition of St. Gregory: "Diesque nostros in tua pace disponas."

Should this conformity be attributed to a demand of the Apostolic See that the Church of Milan, which was under its primacy like all of the Churches of Italy, should have in its liturgical usages at least something in common with the Church of Rome, especially the Canon? Or should we explain the common features of these rites and prayers by voluntary, and perhaps reciprocal, borrowings?

Indeed, the Roman Church had always been in the habit of adopting that which seemed to her praiseworthy in the other Churches, and one finds in the Sacramentary of St. Gregory many prayers which bear the name of St. Ambrose in their title. It is probable, then, that both of these hypotheses contain some truth.

The Church of Milan had always been very jealous of the integrity of her usages. Charlemagne, having conceived the idea of establishing the Roman Rite in all of the Western Churches, wished to extend this rigorous measure even to the Church of Milan. However, he was forced to abandon this enterprise in the face of the profound veneration that this Church attached to a liturgy attributed to St. Ambrose.

Many centuries later, in 1440, Cardinal Branda da Castiglione, who was sent as a legate to Lombardy by Pope Eugene IV, conceived a plan of his own to abolish the Ambrosian rite. Daring to seize an ancient Sacramentary that was believed to have come from St. Ambrose himself, the cardinal had Mass chanted in the Roman Rite on Christmas day, in the very Church of that holy doctor. In a fury, the people immediately besieged the legate's residence, threatening to set it aflame if he did not return the Sacramentary that he had removed. Frightened by the riot, the cardinal threw the book out of the window and fled the city the next day.

When St. Pius V, through the Bulls that we will discuss in due course, exempted all the Churches whose Breviaries [and Missals] dated back more than two centuries from the obligation to adopt the Roman books, he thereby indirectly but clearly recognized the legitimacy of the Ambrosian rite in Milan and its territories.

THE GALLICAN LITURGY

The liturgy of the Gallican Church differs too much from that of the Roman to believe that the one arose from the other. On the contrary, there is every reason to deem it of Eastern origin. First, the Gallican liturgy in itself bears many similarities to the rites of the Eastern Churches, and, considering the places that the first apostles of the Gauls came from, this conformity is easily explained. St. Trophimus, the founder of the Church of Arles, was a disciple of St. Paul; St. Crescens, a disciple of the same apostle, preached among the Gauls; Sts. Pothinus and Irenaeus, the apostles of Lyon, came from Asia, as did St. Saturninus, the apostle of Toulouse.

The Gallican liturgy, then, along with the Ambrosian, is one of the most precious monuments of the early Church. We will soon have to recount its destruction through the combined efforts of the Apostolic See and the Carolingian princes. Therefore, we can now postpone what remains to be said about this important liturgy, all the splendor of which the illustrious Mabillon detailed in his specialized treatise *De liturgia Gallicana*, by transcribing the mutilated vestiges of its books.

THE MOZARABIC LITURGY IN SPAIN: ST. LEANDER

The first question to be addressed is what liturgy was originally practiced in Spain after the establishment of Christianity there. Many authors, among whom we should first mention the learned Fr. Le Brun, maintain that the usages of the Roman Church were initially observed in Spain. They base this conclusion on the fact that this Church was founded by seven bishops sent by St. Peter, as well as on certain canons from the ancient councils of Spain, which demonstrate that many practices in force were identical to those of Rome.

To this, one can add that the affinity of the liturgical uses of Rome and Spain could not be more energetically attested than by the dispatch of the ordinary of the Roman Mass by Pope Vigilius to the Bishop of Braga in 538. Assuredly, no Pope had ever made a dispatch of this kind to the Patriarch of Constantinople or of Alexandria. It necessarily follows, then, that the bishops of Spain had recourse to the Apostolic See as the source of their liturgical traditions. This conjecture becomes all the more certain when we consider that a council in Spain, thirty years later, decrees that all priests should celebrate the holy mysteries in the form given by the Apostolic See to the Bishop of Braga.

However, if we consider the liturgy of the Churches of Spain in the state in which the efforts of St. Leander and St. Isidore fixed it fifty years later, we cannot help being struck by its total dissimilarity from the customs of the Roman Church. What, then, took place in this interval?

The name "Gothic," which the liturgy of Spain still retains, attests to an entirely different origin. Fathers Le Brun and Pinius have solidly established that Eastern rites were introduced into Spain by the Goths (or Visigoths) who became the rulers of this land at the beginning of the fifth century and founded such a firm and imposing kingdom there.[1] In the course of their campaigns throughout Asia Minor, these barbarians had embraced Christianity. Their famous bishop Ulfilas, who translated the Holy Gospels into the language of the Goths, went to Constantinople. Regrettably, he was there infected with the errors of Arianism, which then reigned in that capital city, but during his stay must have acquired a great familiarity

---

[1] Cf. Pierre Le Brun, *Explication de la Messe*, vol. 1, diss. 5, art. 1; Pinius, *De Liturgia antiqua Hispanica*, ch. 1.

with the Greek liturgy, the only liturgy known to the Goths, since their conversion to Christianity had taken place in the East.

When the Goths had established themselves in Spain, we observe that certain previously unknown relations were established between the Church of the peninsula and that of Constantinople. St. Leander had lived in Constantinople for many years, and it was in this great city that he formed a close friendship with St. Gregory the Great, who was living there in the capacity of *apocrisiarius* of the Apostolic See. Now, the Goths were the conquerors of Spain, and having brought with them their own special liturgical usages, the Roman liturgy as it was practiced in this country before the conquest could not survive for long in an unmixed form, and everything indicated that it would eventually succumb.

A major event determined the absolute triumph of the Gothic liturgy over the old one: the complete conversion of the nation of the Goths to orthodoxy at the third Council of Toledo in 589. St. Leander, who was, so to speak, the author of this great achievement, was also the main author of the Gothic liturgy, which became the sole liturgy of Spain from this period onwards.

In summary, Spain enjoyed a completely Roman liturgy from its origins. The Visigoths, who were Arians, introduced into this country a liturgy that was at the same time Eastern (even though it was in the Latin language) and Arian. Nevertheless, their return to orthodoxy under St. Leander allowed for the extirpation of Arianism from the Spanish liturgy, which would later be called "Mozarabic," from the term designating the Christians living under the Moorish occupation. It was the sole liturgy of the land, but it was national.

It is evident, in the first place, that there were several different liturgies in the West more or less different from the Roman liturgy and that some still survive, dating back to antiquity; secondly, that these particular liturgies always tended to become more or less mixed with the Roman; thirdly, that, because they were particular liturgies, they were often exposed to the dangers of alteration and corruption.

9

A Digression on the Eastern Liturgies

UR HISTORY HAS ALREADY REACHED THE ninth century, and the development of the liturgy in the Latin Church, far from coming to a halt, promises only to expand in the following centuries. In the Eastern Church, on the contrary, from the ninth century, everything is about to come an end for both liturgical development and unity. Nevertheless, the point of departure for the liturgy in the East was formidable. First come the apostolic liturgies.

THE APOSTOLIC LITURGIES OF THE EAST

The liturgy attributed to St. James is the principal and most authentic, at least in its general content. For a long time, this liturgy was practiced in the Church of Jerusalem to the exclusion of every other. Subsequently, the Patriarch of Constantinople forbade its use even in Jerusalem, outside of 23 October, the day on which this Church celebrates the feast of St. James. On every other day of the year, the liturgies used in Constantinople were to be observed. Like Jerusalem, the Melchite Patriarch of Antioch and all the clergy under his jurisdiction have been constrained to follow the liturgy of Constantinople, at least since the twelfth century.

Let us here recount the origin of the term "Melchite." A violent schism arose between the Catholics of Antioch and the disciples of Eutyches,[1] which continues to this day. The Monophysites gave Catholics the name "Melchite," which means "partisans of the prince" (from *melek*, the Arabic word for king), since they complied with the edict of the emperor Marcian for the publication and reception of the Council of Chalcedon. For a long time, the name "Melchite" was synonymous with orthodox, but since the time of the Greek schism, it designates only the Greeks who are united with the Patriarch of Constantinople.[2]

In antiquity, the Church of Alexandria, founded by St. Mark, followed a liturgy named after this evangelist. Since the twelfth century, the use of this liturgy has been completely abolished in the Churches subject to the Melchite Patriarch of Alexandria. This patriarch and all his clergy are bound to use the liturgy of Constantinople.

THE TWO LITURGIES OF CONSTANTINOPLE

The principal see of the Greek Melchite Church, Constantinople, which

---

[1] That is, the heresiarch of Monophysitism.
[2] A schism among the Melchites in 1724 led to the creation of the Melchite Greek Catholic Church united to Rome.

subjects all the Churches that have remained faithful to it under the yoke of its liturgy, uses only two liturgies to celebrate the divine service throughout the entire year. The first, called the liturgy of St. John Chrysostom, is used at all times except on the days mentioned below. It is this liturgy alone that contains the Order of the Mass (*ordo missæ*) and the rubrics.

The second, called the liturgy of St. Basil, is used only on the Vigils of Christmas and Epiphany, on Sundays in Lent, on Maundy Thursday and Holy Saturday, and finally on the feast of St. Basil. Although this liturgy is longer than the first, it does not contain the Order of the Mass and the rubrics.

The use of the liturgy of Constantinople expanded under the new form given to it by Sts. Cyril and Methodius in the ninth century. These two valiant missionaries, brothers by blood as well as in zeal and monastic profession, began their apostolate to the Slavs on the banks of the Danube. To facilitate their conquests, the saints considered it useful to adopt the Slavonic language in divine worship. All the liturgical books of Constantinople were translated into this tongue, and it is in this form that they are still used in Bulgaria, Serbia, Albania, Dalmatia, and Hungary.

Dom Guéranger goes on to devote many pages to the Coptic, Maronite, Armenian, and Chaldean liturgies, pages that the complexity of the subject makes somewhat confusing. We will here refrain from reproducing or even summarizing them, since they are rather extraneous to the subject of the Liturgical Institutions, *which deals principally with the Latin Church. We only retain the conclusion, which reads as follows:*

✺❀✺

Let us therefore conclude, based on all the facts stated in this chapter, that:

  ◉ The unity and immutability of the liturgy are such a great good that the separated sects of the East owe to it absolutely everything that they have preserved of Christianity.

  ◉ This unity can bear good fruits only to the extent that it stems from the conformity of the liturgical uses of the various Churches with those of a principal Mother Church.

  ◉ When this conformity is destroyed, a Church which has thus isolated itself courts the greatest risks, since it is uncontrolled and can preserve only a *de facto* orthodoxy.

  ◉ The liturgy falls under the power of secular princes in proportion to how much it has separated itself from the highest ecclesiastical authority.

  ◉ A liturgy, even that of a great Church, when distinct from that promulgated by the Mother Church, thereby becomes estranged from the improvements that take place in it.

  ◉ The liturgy, which ought to seal the faith of the people, since it is the highest and holiest expression of faith, sometimes becomes an accursed instrument that uproots this faith and prevents its restoration.

Abolition of the Gallican Liturgy

E HAVE LEFT OUR NARRATIVE AT THE moment when the Roman liturgy, after it had left the hands of Gregory the Great, was beginning its future conquests by its peaceful introduction into the new churches that the sons of St. Benedict were founding day by day in Great Britain, Germany, and the kingdoms of Northern Europe.

At this time, a new phenomenon comes before our eyes. One of the great Churches, namely the Gallican Church, which had always remained orthodox from its origin, endowed with its own national liturgy composed by the holiest doctors and free from every error, renounced its use of this liturgy to embrace that of Rome, in order to further strengthen the bonds uniting her to the Mother and Teacher of all Churches, and to secure its own inviolable orthodoxy in perpetuity.

THE TEMPORAL SOVEREIGNTY OF THE POPES AND THE FRENCH LITURGY

It was to her great rulers Pepin and Charlemagne that France was indebted for this blessing. In justice, however, we must add that the clergy sincerely and zealously supported the pious intentions of their sovereigns. Alas that we must recount hereafter the efforts of this same clergy in a subsequent epoch to destroy this liturgical unity, so dear to our forefathers for so many centuries ...

The Carolingian dynasty had been destined by Providence to render the greatest service to Christian society by establishing the temporal independence of the Roman Pontiffs, and by lending the support of public authority to the reformation of the clergy by means of the immortal Capitularies promulgated by the first princes of this dynasty. Breathless Europe was in need of rest within the unity of a strong and protective government. Charlemagne would soon come on stage, but Pepin was to herald this unity to the world and to the Church.

The violence of the Lombards, which the emperors of the East could no longer restrain, now compelled the Popes to throw themselves into the arms of the French, whom they had always found faithful to the Apostolic See, and who seemed to be on the verge of receiving and carrying out, in concert with the Church, the lofty mission of organizing a new Roman Empire.

It came to pass that Pepin the Short was equal to this mission. He received with filial affection the plea for help made to him by Pope Stephen II in

754, who was then being oppressed by the King of the Lombards. When this Pontiff had expressed his desire to come and seek temporary asylum in France, Pepin sent the Bishop of Metz to meet him.

Pope Stephen thus entered France and was received by Pepin with every honor. The Pope discussed with this prince not only the liberty and defense of the Church of Rome against the Lombards, but also the current needs of the Church of France. The Pope asked the king, as a sign of faith that united France to the Apostolic See, to support his efforts to introduce the Offices of the Roman Church into this kingdom, to the exclusion of the Gallican liturgy. The king endorsed this pious design, which conformed so well to the frank orthodoxy of his own heart, and so the clergy in Pope Stephen's retinue instructed the French cantors in the manner of celebrating the Roman Offices.

The capitulary drawn up at Aachen formally expresses the sovereign act by which Pepin suppressed the Gallican office: "For the sake of a greater union with the Roman Church, and in order to establish a peaceful harmony in the Church of God."[1]

After having achieved this signal victory in favor of liturgical unity, Stephen crossed the Alps once again, and a few months later the Abbot of Monte Cassino deposited in the *Confessio* of St. Peter the keys for twenty-two cities that Pepin had just wrested from the Lombards. Thus, the temporal power of the Roman Pontiffs began at the same time as the reign of the Roman liturgy in the Churches of the Most Christian Kingdom.

A monk of St. Gall informs us in his chronicle that Pope Stephen sent Pepin, at his request, twelve cantors who, like the twelve apostles, were to establish the sound traditions of Gregorian chant in France.[2]

CHARLEMAGNE AND THE LITURGY

At last, Charlemagne makes his appearance. It is not here our subject to describe the grandeur and genius of this prince, or the sublime and holy employment that he knew to make of these qualities. Instead, we will only present certain facts of his life which fall in line with the events that we are now recounting.

The filial love that Charlemagne bore towards Pope St. Adrian, who ascended to the Holy See in 772, is well known. This holy Pontiff had barely taken his seat upon the Chair of St. Peter when he addressed to King Charles the liveliest entreaties to imitate the example of Pepin in promoting the Roman liturgy. The following address is preserved in the *Libri Carolini*:

> We, having been granted by God the Kingdom of Italy, have sought to exalt in turn the grandeur of the Holy Roman Church,

---

[1] Council of Aachen (816), ch. 90.
[2] *Chronicon San-Gallense*, bk. 1, ch. 10.

endeavoring to obey the salutary exhortations of the Most Reverend Pope Adrian. This is why we have brought it about that several Churches in this country, which had previously refused to receive the tradition of the Apostolic See in their psalmody, now embrace it with all diligence, and adhere in the celebration of ecclesiastical chant to this Church, to which they had previously adhered by the virtue of faith. This is now the practice, as everyone knows, not only of all the provinces of the Gauls, Germany, and Italy, but even of the Saxons and the other nations of the northern shores, which we converted, through the divine assistance, to the rudiments of the Faith.[3]

"SAVAGE, DRINK-RAVAGED THROATS"

Yet there was one point over which the French spirit, in spite of itself, resisted the pious intentions of Charlemagne and Pepin. The latter had indeed managed to introduce the chant of the Roman Church into the Churches of France, but it was not within his power to have it executed with the perfection of the Roman cantors, nor to defend it everywhere from the supposed improvements with which the skill of French clerics presumed to "enrich" it. Thus it happened that in only a few years the pure sources of Gregorian melody contained in the antiphonaries sent by Stephen II and Paul I had already been corrupted.

John the Deacon, in his life of Gregory the Great, states, with the candor of an artist, the reasons why Gregorian chant had not been preserved in our Churches without alteration. Let us read his words, full as they are full of naivety and not without a shade of invective:

> Among the various nations of Europe, the Germans and the French were the most capable of learning and re-learning the sweetness of the modulation of chant. Nevertheless, they could not preserve it without corruption, owing both to the fickleness of their nature, which made them contaminate the purity of the Gregorian melodies by mixing them with their own, and to their inherent barbarity. Their Alpine bodies and thundering voices cannot exactly reproduce the harmony of the chants taught to them. Because of the toughness of their savage, drink-ravaged throats, the moment that they apply themselves to produce a melodious expression of chant with their own inflections and repercussions, a tumult of brutal sounds confusedly resounds, like the wheels of a cart down steps.[4]

Charlemagne, who had a profound appreciation of the fine arts, could not long endure this dissonance, which tended to nothing less than the destruction of all the noble fruits that he had cultivated. In 787, while

---

[3] *Contra synodum Græcorum de imaginibus*, bk. 1.
[4] John the Deacon, *Vita Sancti Gregorii Magni*, bk. 2, ch. 7.

in Rome for Easter, he was witness to a dispute between the Roman and French cantors. The latter alleged that their chant was superior, and, confident of their king's protection, they harshly criticized the Romans. The Roman cantors, on the other hand, assured of the authority of St. Gregory and the traditions that had always been attached to his Antiphonary in Rome, ridiculed the ignorance and barbarity of the French cantors. Charlemagne was anxious to put an end to this dispute, and he said to his cantors: "Which is purer: the living source or the streams that flow from it?" They admitted that it was the source. The king then rejoined: "Return then to the source of St. Gregory, for it is clear that you have corrupted ecclesiastical chant."[5]

THE SCHOOL OF METZ

Wishing to remedy this problem as soon as possible, Charlemagne asked the Pope to provide skilled cantors who could guide the French back to the proper traditions. St. Adrian sent him Theodore and Benedict, who had been students in the school of chant founded by St. Gregory, and he also presented the king with the Antiphonaries of St. Gregory, scored by Adrian himself in the Roman notation.

On his return to France, Charlemagne installed one of the two cantors in Metz and the other in Soissons, and ordered all the chant-masters from the other towns in France to submit their antiphonaries to these cantors for correction, and to learn the true rules of chant from them. In this way, the antiphonaries of France, which had been corrupted through individual whims with additions or subtractions without rule or authority, were amended. Moreover, all the French cantors were taught "Roman notation" (*nota romana*), which has since then been called "French notation" ... It was at Metz that Gregorian chant was raised to a higher degree of perfection. The chronicler of Angoulême adds that the Roman cantors instructed the French in the art of playing the organ.[6]

This superiority that the School of Metz still retained in the twelfth century over the *scholæ cantorum* of the other cathedrals in France is unquestionably due to the discipline that St. Chrodegang had established among his canons. Traditions of this kind were naturally preserved more purely in this church, whose clergy so rigorously guarded the observances of the canonical life. It has long been observed that the traditions of ecclesiastical chant are better preserved among religious orders than the secular clergy.

Let us say another word about Charlemagne, that great liturgical figure. It has been noted that he was the author of the hymn *Veni Creator Spiritus*. Additionally, he assisted faithfully at the Offices, both day and night, in the palace chapel. He did not presume to raise his voice, as befits priests

---

[5] Adémar de Chabannes, *Chronicon* 2.8.
[6] Ibid.

alone, but he chanted only softly, and even then only at moments when laymen were permitted to join the choir.

When we say that the Gallican liturgy was irreversibly destroyed in France, we do not mean to imply that there did not remain some vestiges of it that were mingled with the Roman usages. The Churches of Lyon and Paris were undoubtedly those which preserved the greatest number of ancient Gallican customs, but all the other Churches preserved some parts to varying degrees. We can still find traces of it in the non-Roman customs found in the majority of the Office books formerly used in France.

THE INTRODUCTION OF TROPES AND SEQUENCES

"Tropes" were like the first draft of the sequences which would succeed them. These tropes were a kind of prologue in preparation for the Introit. We may cite, for example, the one that was chanted on the first Sunday of Advent in honor of St. Gregory.

Later on, tropes were interspersed within pieces of chant: in the body of the Introit itself, between the words *Kyrie* and *eleison*, in certain passages of the *Gloria in excelsis*, *Sanctus*, and *Agnus Dei*. Tropes were also placed after the Alleluia verse, set to the melody of the *jubilus*, which always follows this verse. This final type of trope was called a sequence, from the name given at that time to the succession of notes on the same final syllable.[7]

The consequences of instituting these kinds of poetic and rhythmically ornamented chants were important for the development of the liturgy.

First of all, with respect to the composition of holy texts, these tropes increasingly sanctioned the principle that sacred chants are not exclusively composed of the words of Sacred Scripture. Undoubtedly, the Antiphonary and Roman Responsorial already contained a certain number of pieces in an ecclesiastical style,[8] but the ever-growing number of tropes and sequences increasingly clarified this principle. Rome, which had not adopted hymns at first, seems later, in the eleventh century at the latest, to have imitated the Ambrosian, Gallican, and Gothic Churches; she had been naturally prepared for this practice by the use of tropes and sequences.

Another consequence of the institution of tropes was a revolution in the development of ecclesiastical chant. Initially, it did not lead chant to become truly measured, but the cadenced and nearly always rhymed composition of these pieces demanded a different manner of constructing the Gregorian phrase in order for these features to be perceived.

However, the pieces of the Gregorian repertoire were quite faithfully preserved, but they now stood in contrast with the style of the new compositions added to celebrate new feasts, those of patrons, and other local solemnities. We can group the ecclesiastical chants composed between the

---

[7] See Cardinal Bona, *Rerum liturgicarum*, bk. 2, chs. 3 and 6.

[8] The recurrent term "ecclesiastical style" refers to liturgical texts not taken from Scripture.

eighth and eleventh century in two main categories: one, consisting of pieces composed, wholly or in part, in the classic Gregorian style, and the other marked by a new character, at once rough and heavily melodious.

In the midst of this turmoil, the true traditions were neglected, and it can be asserted that, if the Roman books had not already been introduced into France by the irresistible wills of Pepin and Charlemagne, and the whole structure of the feasts of the Christian year had not already been based on this admirable repertoire, today we would know the ancient modes of music only in theory, and we would be ignorant of the past two-thousand years of this art.

Let us conclude this chapter with the following observations:

◉ In the eighth century, the Apostolic See began to establish as a principle the necessity for the ancient Churches of the West to embrace the Roman liturgy in its fulness.

◉ The Gallican Church saw its ancient usages give way to those of Rome, and abjured its own traditions, which were doubtlessly venerable, but it did this in order to embrace even more sacred ones.

◉ The intention of the Popes and French princes in this great enterprise was to strengthen the bond of unity by eliminating a liturgical divergence that they thought could have dangerous consequences.

◉ The French spirit willingly adopted this new liturgical structure, but wasted no time in manifesting its own fickleness by altering several aspects of the deposit of the Roman liturgy while claiming to perfect it.

◉ Nevertheless, these variations did not alter the substance of the liturgy, and the eighth century saw the beginning of a period of nearly a thousand years, during which the Church of France took pride in sharing one and the same prayer with the Church of Rome.

II

The Abolition of the Mozarabic Rite:

THE FORMATION OF
THE FRENCH-ROMAN RITE

 GREAT LITURGICAL EVENT MARKS THE era that we will take up in this chapter. The Gothic or Mozarabic liturgy in Spain succumbed under the efforts of St. Gregory VII, just as the Gallican liturgy had succumbed in France under the assault of Charlemagne.

Indeed, it was time that Christian Spain figured into the great unity of Europe. Its form of the Holy Sacrifice, although fundamentally the same as that observed elsewhere, differed in the ways that struck the eyes of the people. The chants were entirely different. Furthermore, heresy had long waited for the moment to latch onto the words of a liturgy that had no guarantee of purity, since it emanated from an authority that could not count on infallibility.

THE ROMANIZATION OF CATALONIA[1]

The influence of Rome in the suppression of the Gothic liturgy is clearly discernible in the case of Catalonia. The city of Barcelona and its territory, which was reconquered from the Moors by Charlemagne in 801, subsequently adopted the Roman liturgy, which is why it was called "Gallican" in Spain throughout the Middle Ages. Yet this vast province was not entirely under French control, and its original Gothic liturgy still persisted in many places. The year 1068 saw it abolished forever through the efforts of Cardinal Hugh of Remiremont, called Candidus ("the White"), the Legate of Pope Alexander II. In a council held in Barcelona, this great measure was accomplished. The Church owed this boon to the singular zeal of Princess Almodis, the wife of Ramon Berenguer, count of Barcelona. She was French, and all of the chronicles of the time agree that she was a princess of great character. Her authority, combined with that of the Legate, were decisive in the triumph of the Roman liturgy in Catalonia.[2]

THE ROMANIZATION OF ARAGON

Before this, in 1063, a synod had already been held at Jaca, in Aragon, which issued a decree prescribing that the liturgy would no longer be celebrated

---

[1] In the following sections, Guéranger confuses Catalonia and Aragon, an error that was repeated by the editor of the 1977 edition who supplied the following subtitles.

[2] See Pinius, *De Liturgia antiqua Hispanica*, ch. 6.

according to the Gothic Rite, but according to the Roman. History does not expressly record the direct reasons for this measure, but there can be little doubt that the influence of Rome played a significant part.

The illustrious successor of Pope Alexander II, St. Gregory VII, ascended the chair of St. Peter shortly after this, and he resolved to complete the victory of the Roman Church over the Gothic liturgy. In a letter that he addressed to the King of Aragon in 1074, the Pope commends this prince for his zeal for Roman usages in the following terms, so expressive of his intentions regarding the important subject at hand:

> By sharing with us your zeal and the orders that you have given to establish the Office according to the Roman Order in the lands under your dominion, you show yourself to be a son of the Roman Church. You demonstrate that you have with us the same concord and friendship that the kings of Spain once had with the Roman Pontiffs. Be constant, then, and have firm hope of completing what you have begun.[3]

THE ROMANIZATION OF CASTILE, LEON, AND NAVARRE

In the same year, 1074, Pope Gregory VII wrote to the King of Castile and Leon, as well as to the King of Navarre:

> Gregory, bishop, servant of the servants of God, to Alphonse and Sancho, Kings of Spain, and to the bishops of their states. The blessed Apostle Paul declared that he had visited Spain, and Your Zeal is not ignorant of the fact that the apostles Peter and Paul later sent seven bishops from Rome to instruct the peoples of Spain, and that these bishops, having exterminated idolatry in your land, there established Christianity, planted the true Religion, taught the order of the Office to be observed in divine worship, and dedicated the churches with their own blood. How much concord Spain enjoyed with the city of Rome in religion and the order of the divine Offices is manifest.
>
> But when, following the incursion of the Goths, and later the invasion of the Saracens, the Kingdom of Spain was for a long time corrupted by the perfidy of the Arians and separated from the Roman Rite; not only was the true Religion diminished, but the temporal powers of the State were greatly weakened.
>
> This is why, as our dearly cherished sons, we exhort and admonish you, after so long a separation, to recognize the Roman Church as your mother, in which you will find us your brethren; to receive the order of the Office of this holy Church, and not that of Toledo or any other Church ... For from the very source whence you do not doubt that you received the beginning of

---

[3] Pope Gregory VII, *Letter to the King of Aragon.* See H. E. J. Cowdrey, *The Register of Pope Gregory VII, 1073–1085: An English Translation* (Oxford, 2002), 67.

Religion, it follows that you should also receive the divine Office in the ecclesiastical order.[4]

To press for his wishes more effectively, St. Gregory VII dispatched a legate to the Churches of Spain, namely Richard, the Abbot of Saint-Victor of Marseille, who twice made the journey to Spain for this important mission. In a council held in Burgos in 1085, the legate, supported by the authority of Alphonse VI, promulgated with even greater solemnity the abolition of the Gothic liturgy (also called Mozarabic) in the kingdoms under the rule of this great prince.

TOLEDO ALSO SUBMITS

On 25 May 1085, Alphonse VI made his triumphal entry into Toledo. He immediately took all necessary measures to restore the Church of this illustrious city to its former glory. Yet the prince encountered great difficulties in his attempt to abolish the Mozarabic Rite in Toledo:

> The clergy and the people of Spain were agitated, because the Legate Richard and King Alphonse wanted to compel them to adopt the Roman Office. On the appointed day, when the king, the primate, the legate, and a great multitude of clergy and people were assembled, a long quarrel ensued, owing to the courageous resistance of the clergy, the knights, and the people, who opposed this change to the Office. For his part, the king, advised by the queen, thundered forth terrible threats. At last, the resistance of the soldiery was so great it was decided that the dispute would be settled by single combat. Two knights were chosen, and the king's knight was vanquished. But the king, at the urging of Queen Constance, refused to abandon his intentions, saying that "a duel is no law."[5]

The king eventually prevailed, and Rodrigo concludes his narration thus:

> All the people grieved and wept over such an unfortunate outcome, which gave rise to the proverb: *Quod volunt reges, vadunt leges* ("when kings desire, the laws retire"). And before long, the Roman Office, which had never before been received there, either in its Psalter or its Rite, came to be observed in Spain.[6]

THE RESTORATION OF THE MOZARABIC RITE IN TOLEDO

Nevertheless, Providence did not will that the Church of Spain should lose forever the glorious memory of her ancient Gothic Rites. When the danger had passed and Spain, wholly freed from the Saracen yoke and firmly integrated into European society, had merited in so many ways the

---

[4] Ibid., 68–69.
[5] Roderic of Toledo, *De Rebus Hispaniæ*, bk. 6, ch. 26.
[6] Ibid.

title of "the Catholic Kingdom," something befell her that had happened to no other nation. The past was exhumed from the dust, and Toledo thrilled to see the august mysteries of Isidore and Leander celebrated in broad daylight once more.

One of those men who do not belong only to the single nation that produced them but to all mankind is the great Cardinal Francisco Ximenes de Cisneros, Archbishop of Toledo, who lovingly gathered together the remnants of the Mozarabs who, under the tolerance of the kings of Castile, had continued to observe the rites of their forefathers in a few humble sanctuaries of Toledo. He had their books printed and assigned them a chapel in the cathedral and six churches in the city for the celebration of the Gothic liturgy. But in order to legitimize this restoration, Cisneros sought the approval of the Roman Pontiff, and Pope Julius II issued two Bulls at the cardinal's request, canonically establishing the Gothic Rite in the churches assigned to it.

UNITY PREVAILS OVER DIVERSITY

Superficial minds, who might imagine Julius II thereby contradicted Gregory VII, would fail to appreciate the various reasons prompting the actions of the two Popes. Unity, and all that it entails, is the highest good of the Church. Her social development, her felicitous influence on the good of mankind, her conservation of the deposit of faith, all depend on this unity. Consequently, in certain cases, even goods of a secondary order must be sacrificed for it. Now indeed, the antiquity and beauty of certain prayers are a good, but not goods that can claim equality with the general necessities of the Church. This is the principle that influenced St. Gregory VII.

On the other hand, when unity has been secured together with all the goods that flow from it, there is nothing to prevent granting some, or even a good deal, of leeway to legitimate desires that do not threaten what that unity established at such pains and for such great profit. In the six or seven churches of Toledo where it is confined, the Gothic Rite no longer poses an obstacle to the fusion of the Kingdom of Spain with the Catholic customs of the West. In Toledo itself, the Roman liturgy, far from being overshadowed, is rather enhanced by it.

Rome has never been afraid of antiquity. Rather, antiquity is the firmest foundation of her rights and those of the whole Church, of which Rome is the cornerstone. She delights to see these Ambrosian and Gothic Rites preserved, like two ancient monuments from the primitive age of Christianity.

THE COMPOSITION OF THE BREVIARY

St. Gregory VII does not appear in history only as a zealous propagator of the Roman liturgy. His efforts also had for their object the reduction of the Divine Office.

The momentous affairs that besieged a Pope in the eleventh century, along with the interminable details of administration to which he was bound to attend, made it impossible to reconcile these duties of such immense gravity with exact assistance at the long Offices according to the use of the preceding centuries. St. Gregory VII thus abridged the order of prayers and simplified the liturgy for the usage of the Roman Curia. Since that time, it has remained more or less as it was at the end of the eleventh century. St. Gregory VII's Breviary [or *"abridgement"*] was in line with that of the present day.

The reduction of the Divine Office carried out by Gregory VII was initially intended only for the Pope's chapel, but it quickly spread to the several churches of Rome. The Lateran Basilica was the only one that did not adopt it. Churches in the rest of the West remained more or less unaffected by this innovation. It came to pass, then, that many of the Churches in France and the other provinces of Christendom found themselves observing a liturgy [*i.e., the Canonical Hours*] that had more in common with that of Gregory the Great than with the new one instituted in Rome by Gregory VII. However, everything contained in the latter is found in the former, of which it was an abridgement.

THE INFLUENCE OF THE ROYAL CHAPEL OF PARIS

Among the various Churches of Europe, that of France stood out because of the fertility of her liturgical genius and the beauty of her chants. At the heart of our fatherland, the Church of Paris, at the time under discussion, worthily enjoyed an incontestable superiority.

One of the reasons that maintained the Romano-Parisian liturgy in such a flourishing state was the influence of the royal court under our kings of this period, whose chapel was served with marvelous pomp and devotion. Charlemagne, Louis the Pious, and Charles the Bald found worthy successors to their zeal for the Divine Offices among the kings of the Capetian dynasty, foremost among which we must place Robert the Pious and St. Louis.

Robert the Pious, who assiduously attended the Offices with even more zeal than Charlemagne, used to join the cantors vested in a cope and holding his scepter in hand. The eleventh century, so illustrious for the rebuilding of numerous cathedrals and abbatial churches, opened under the auspices of this pious king, who himself founded fourteen monasteries and seven churches. A great lover of ecclesiastical chant, he devoted himself to the composition of several pieces of sweet and mystical melodies. To propagate the chants of which he was particularly fond, Robert the Pious first had them performed in his palace chapel or the Abbey of Saint-Denis, and then in the cathedral of Paris; from there, they spread to the other cathedrals.

THE INFLUENCE OF THE BENEDICTINE ORDER

To make the influence of the Benedictines manifest, suffice it to say that, from the eighth to the twelfth century, monks filled all of the principal posts in the Church, while at the same being virtually the sole custodians of knowledge and tradition. They furnished the Church with Popes like St. Gregory the Great, St. Boniface IV, St. Agatho, St. Leo III, St. Paschal I, St. Leo IV, St. Leo IX, Alexander II, St. Gregory VII, Urban II, Paschal II, Callistus II, and Innocent IV. They also provided her with teachers of the liturgy and all kinds of doctrine.

It was thus that many Benedictine usages took root in the Western liturgy, such as, for example, the antiphons *Salve Regina* and *Alma Redemptoris Mater*; the use of hymns and sequences; the aspersion and procession before Mass on Sundays. All of these usages, and many others besides, have a monastic origin. It is also well known that the "Commemoration of All the Faithful Departed" on the second day of November was transmitted from the Abbey of Cluny, where it was instituted by St. Odilo, to the entire Western Church, as was the custom of chanting the hymn *Veni Creator* at Terce during the octave of Pentecost.

ST. BERNARD'S PRINCIPLES OF LITURGICAL COMPOSITION

"In the august solemnities, it is not fitting to hear new or frivolous things but rather authentic and ancient ones, which edify the Church and savor of ecclesiastical gravity.

"If one should desire to hear something new, and the occasion demands it, I deem that it should be accepted only if the dignity of its words and their author should render it both agreeable and profitable to the hearts of the listeners. Furthermore, its phrases should radiate with undoubted truth, they should resound with justice, urge humility, and teach righteousness. Likewise, they should engender the light of truth in the minds of men, shape their morals, crucify their vices, enflame their devotion, and discipline their senses.

"If there should be a new chant, it should be full of solemnity, resounding neither with levity nor vulgarity. Let it be sweet but not insipid, delighting the ear in order to stir the heart. It should lighten sadness and mitigate anger, neither should it empty the sense of the letter, but enrich it. For it is no slight loss of spiritual grace to be distracted from the profit of the sense of the words by the frivolity of the chant, and to focus more on producing virtuosic sounds than on understanding the meaning of the text itself."[7]

---

7 St. Bernard of Clairvaux, *Epistle* 398 (*Patrologia Latina* 182:610-11).

12

The Liturgical Pinnacle of the Thirteenth Century

N HIS REFORM OF THE ROMAN OFFICE [*i.e., the Canonical Hours*], St. Gregory VII had had the papal chapel principally in mind. Over time, most of the churches of Rome adopted this reduced form of the Office as well. However, neither this great Pontiff nor his successors had ordered that the diverse Churches of the West subject to the Roman liturgy should reform their books according to this latter revision. Consequently, a kind of confusion resulted which would some time later necessitate a solemn correction. This confusion was further exacerbated on account of the offices of saints which were everywhere added to the ancient calendar. This, together with the remnants of earlier liturgical practices that had been preserved, albeit in small number, increasingly threatened liturgical unity in the patriarchate of the West, at least concerning the offices of the Hours—for, as we do not tire of recalling, the Gregorian Sacramentary, which would soon change its name to the "Roman Missal," had remained generally intact.

FRANCISCANS PROPAGATE THE BREVIARY OF GREGORY VII
Pending the rigorous measures which would not be imposed until the sixteenth century, it was therefore greatly to be desired that the Breviary of the papal chapel, which had already conquered all the churches of Rome apart from the Lateran Basilica by the twelfth century, should be extended to the rest of the Western Church, whether *de facto* or *de jure*.

It was St. Francis of Assisi who would prepare the ground. This great patriarch, destining his numerous sons for apostolic preaching, expressly commanded them to preserve steadfast fidelity to the Roman Church. In order to reinforce this fundamental law with an external bond, he commanded that they observe, in its entirety, the same order of the Office followed by the Mother and Teacher of all the Churches.

Since St. Francis had given this law to his sons in 1210, it was natural that, when they asked Rome what Office they should follow, she assigned the one observed in the papal chapel and the various churches of this capital of Christendom. It was, therefore, the abridged Office [*the Breviary of St. Gregory VII*] that the Friars Minor followed. They entitled their Breviaries *secundum consuetudinem Romanæ Curiæ* ("according to the custom of the Roman Curia"). Furthermore, this Office, being shorter than the more ancient one, could be transcribed at a more modest expense, while its size was less cumbersome on journeys. As a result, the Franciscans were bound to prefer this Office to the ancient one still in use in the Lateran Basilica.

A great number of Churches in Italy had already adopted the abridged Office. The marvelous spread of the Order of the Friars Minor throughout Europe and beyond soon made this new form of the liturgy known everywhere. Whether one should attribute this to the influence of the Franciscans or to the natural preference for the more concise Office over time, the fact is that the Breviaries of all, or nearly all, of the Churches of Europe written or printed in the fourteenth and fifteenth centuries, and even in the first half of the sixteenth century — and thus before the Bull of St. Pius V — were generally arranged according to the form of the abridged Office, rather than the one in use prior to St. Gregory VII.

INSTITUTION OF THE DOMINICAN LITURGY

The Friars Preachers that God gave to His Church through the ministry of St. Dominic some years before the Friars Minor merit a distinguished place in the annals of the liturgy. After their foundation, they were soon established in Paris by St. Louis in the illustrious convent in the Rue Saint-Jacques (from which they drew the name "Jacobins"). The liturgical usages to which the Friars have remained faithful make known to us those of the Churches of France, and particularly the Church of Paris, in the thirteenth century.

With respect to the Mass, they have preserved many rites and prayers found in French Missals of the thirteenth to fifteenth centuries. The text of the Missal is otherwise purely Roman, save for some minor differences.

As for the Breviary, it was compiled in the convent of the Rue Saint-Jacques in 1253 by Humbert of Romans, who later became the Master General of the Order. With the exception of particular feasts of the Order and a few rites, everything in this Breviary that seems to be added to the Roman is found in the old Parisian Breviary. The Offices of Dominican saints in this Breviary are all composed in measured and rhymed prose, like those of the Friars Minor. However, the triumphant tone and exultant language, which are their foremost qualities, contrast characteristically with the naive simplicity of the Franciscan Offices.

It must also be said, to the praise of the Dominican Order, that it successfully defended its Breviary against the attempted innovations, and that it is the only Order in these latter days that has preserved liturgical inspiration in the composition of Offices for the feasts of its new saints. Those of St. Pius V, St. Rose of Lima, St. Louis Bertrand, and St. Catherine de' Ricci, are as perfectly in the style of the thirteenth century as the older Offices of the Dominican repertoire. The Office of the Holy Rosary, composed quite recently, serves to demonstrate that this illustrious Order has never lost hold of its traditions.

OFFICE OF CORPUS CHRISTI

The thirteenth century was the stage for a liturgical event of such great consequence that nothing similar has yet come to pass. We are referring to the institution of the feast of Corpus Christi, for all the universal feasts since established by the Apostolic See are not of such high rank, having neither their own octaves nor entailing the obligation to cease from servile labor. Consequently, it can be said that it was during the period described in this chapter that the Christian year reached its completion, at least with respect to the major outlines of the calendar. This solemnity, so dear to all the Catholic world, was established as a solemn testimony to the Church's faith in the august mystery of the Eucharist.

The heresy of Berengar had already in the eleventh century made necessary a solemn liturgical protestation in favor of the ancient belief. Hence, the rite of the elevation of the host and the chalice to be adored by the people immediately after the consecration was promptly instituted and spread everywhere.

In the thirteenth century, new attacks were being plotted against this central dogma of a religion founded upon the mystery of the Word that became incarnate to be united to human nature. Already, the precursors of the Sacramentarians had appeared.[1] The Waldensians and Albigensians prepared the way for Wycliff and John Hus, themselves precursors of Luther and Calvin.

It was time for the Church to make her great voice resound, and so the Feast of Corpus Christi was established by Pope Urban IV in 1264. Not only was a solemnity of the first order added to the ancient feasts instituted by the apostles, but soon a splendid procession, in which the Body of the Lord was to be borne, was joined to the ancient processions of Palm Sunday and the Rogation Days. To celebrate so great a mystery, it was necessary to compose a new Office that echoed the Church's enthusiasm and was equal to the grandeur of its subject. The liturgy did not disappoint the expectations of the Christian people on this occasion.

DIVINE INSPIRATION OF CERTAIN GREGORIAN CHANTS

What is most striking in this Office, as it issued from the hands of St. Thomas Aquinas, is its magnificently scholastic form. Each of the Matins responsories is composed of two sentences, one from the Old Testament and the other from the New, which thus together bear united witness to the great mystery that forms the theme of this solemnity. This ambitious idea was unknown to St. Gregory and the other authors of the ancient liturgy, and it must be acknowledged to be elegant and forceful, if it is applied in due measure on greater occasions.

---

[1] A name given in the sixteenth century to those of the Reformers who saw only a symbol without a reality in the Sacrament of the Eucharist.

The same methodological genius of the thirteenth century appears in the sequence *Lauda Sion*, an astonishing piece which is incontestably the work of St. Thomas. In it, we glimpse the immense potential of a Schoolman—not truncated and disembodied like today, but a whole man as in the Middle Ages—who could effortlessly apply the rhythm and allurements of the Latin language to the faithful and precise exposition of a dogma as intricate for the theologian as it is sweet and nourishing for the heart of the faithful. What majesty is there in the opening verses of this sublime poem! What delicate precision in the exposition of the faith of the Church! With what natural grace does it call to mind, in the conclusion, the figures of the Old Law that announced the true Bread of Angels, the Paschal Lamb, and the Manna! Thus do we have a confirmation of what was said above, that every rightly ordered sentiment resolves necessarily into harmony. St. Thomas, the most perfect of the thirteenth-century scholastics, is by virtue of the same fact also found to be the most sublime poet.

We have yet another work from the same period that deserves the same admiration: the sequence *Dies iræ*. There is no agreement on the name of the inspired poet who gifted Christendom this tender yet somber chant, which will no doubt accompany the Church on that last day whose terrors it so poignantly expresses. But what majesty, what unction, what rhythm worthy of such a fearful subject! One cannot help believing that the Holy Spirit granted a special assistance to the authors of the *Dies iræ* and the *Lauda Sion*, revealing to them heavenly tones perfectly suited to the solemnity of their themes.

13

Alterations to the Liturgy in the Fourteenth and Fifteenth Centuries

OLLOWING THE FRANCISCAN REFORMS, it was difficult for the liturgy to remain in a state of total purity. The Apostolic See had never obliged the Churches to accept these reformed liturgical books, and those places that had adopted them did so voluntarily. Moreover, the Churches that did accept them also retained many ancient usages, aggravating the confusion. At the same time, an ardent devotion continued to overburden the calendar with new saints, whose offices were of varying quality.

ALTERATION OF TEXTS

Although the ancient core of the Roman liturgy had remained intact, as one can confirm by leafing through the books that have come down to us today, it is easy to imagine what an anarchy of minor differences existed in the usages of the various dioceses. In the absence of the printing press to produce multiple uniform copies, it was necessary, however perilous, to rely on handwritten copies, which were rife with errors. These copies were corrupted not only by the ignorance or negligence of scribes, but also by the accumulation of a host of crude and even superstitious additions, as is evident from numerous decrees of councils in the fourteenth and fifteenth centuries that frequently complained about such abuses.

These additions consisted principally in apocryphal histories, unknown or even rejected by earlier centuries, that had been introduced into the lessons, hymns, or antiphons; in the barbarous formulas inserted to please the people; in votive Masses that replaced ordinary Masses and introduced superstitious elements into the rite; and in blessings, unknown in antiquity, furtively placed in the ecclesiastical books by private individuals. In short, instead of being the living rule, the teaching, and the supreme law of the Christian people, the liturgy had been reduced to serving the popular passions, and certain fictions that properly belonged in the plays of the Basoche had too often invaded the books of the altar and those of the choir.[1]

To grasp the full extent of the abuses of which we speak, one need only recall the indifference with which the clergy allowed cathedrals to be used

---

[1] The Basoche was the guild of law clerks in the Ancien Régime, known for their theatrical productions.

for the strange farces of the "Feast of the Ass" or the "Feast of Fools." It is easy to imagine how this impudent familiarity with the most sacred aspects of divine worship compromised the liturgy's purity.

In the last century [*i.e., the eighteenth century*], it was fashionable to vilify the Middle Ages as a time of barbarism. Today, fortunately, the trend seems to be to exalt the centuries called "the Catholic ages." This shift certainly represents a marked improvement. However, deeper study reveals that the twelfth and thirteenth centuries, although undoubtedly far superior to those that followed until the present day, also had their miseries, as we readily acknowledge. When, therefore, we point out serious problems of ignorance and superstition in those centuries, we echo the sentiments of the councils and doctors of those heroic times. Yet, by the very nature of the reproaches we level at them, we elevate them far above the centuries degraded by rationalism and materialism . . .

Furthermore, in its decline in the fourteenth and fifteenth centuries, the liturgy, as usual, mirrored the fate of the Church herself. The diminished authority of the papacy after Boniface VIII, the exile of the Popes in Avignon, and the Great Western Schism sufficiently explain the disorders that served as a pretext for the undertakings of the so-called Reformation.

ALTERATION OF CHANT

Ecclesiastical chant was not only transformed in this period, but almost perished forever.

Until this time, the Gregorian repertoire remained untouched, while pieces of a consistently religious character — drawn from the ancient modes, or at least compensating for departures from the consecrated rules with original and sometimes sublime beauties — were added to celebrate local solemnities more fully or to heighten the majesty of certain universal feasts.

The fourteenth and fifteenth centuries witnessed the rise of Descant (a chant based partly on a Gregorian theme) which absorbed and completely obliterated, with its bizarre and capricious inflections, all the unction of the ancient pieces. The venerable phrases of chant succumbed to the efforts of a hundred profane musicians whose only aim was to introduce novelty and to make a display of their talent for harmonies and variations.

But it was not in vain that the Holy Spirit had chosen St. Gregory the Great as the organ of Catholic melodies. His work, a sublime and inspired echo of ancient music, was destined to accompany the Church to the end of time. It therefore became necessary for the great voice of the Apostolic See to be heard, and for a solemn rebuke to be issued against the innovators attempting to give a human and mundane expression to the heavenly sighs of Christ's Church.

DEFINITION OF ECCLESIASTICAL CHANT

Now let us look to the words of Pope John XXII in his famous Bull *Docta Sanctorum*, issued in 1322:

> The learned authority of the holy Fathers decreed that during the Offices, in which man renders to God the tribute of praise and of service due to Him, the souls of all the faithful should be alert, so that their words should not falter and the modest gravity of those singing the psalms should render the chant with peaceful modulation. For it is written: *In ore eorum dulcis resonabat sonus* ("The sound resonated sweetly from their lips").[2] Indeed, a sweet sound resounds from the lips of those singing the psalms when they receive God in their hearts while they are speaking about Him with words and enkindling devotion to Him with their chants. Indeed, the chanting of psalms is prescribed in the Churches of God in order to arouse the piety of the faithful. It is for this reason that clergy and laity diligently sing the nocturnal and diurnal Offices and the Sacrifice of the Mass with perfect melody and distinct tonality, that its variety might be agreeable and its richness give delight.
>
> But certain followers of the new school, applying all of their attention to measuring time, attempt to invent their own melodies with new notes, at the expense of the ancient chants. Ecclesiastical chants are now sung with semibreves and minims, and are disturbed by these little notes. Such men sunder the melodies with hockets, deprave them with descants, and sometimes garble them with three-part polyphonies and secular songs. All this occurs to such an extent that they spurn the foundations of the Antiphonary and Gradual, ignoring that upon which they presume to build, forgetting the modes, confusing instead of discerning them...
>
> *A lascivious mind takes pleasure in the more lascivious modes, or is often softened or stirred up when it hears them.*[3] It is this, therefore, that stands in need of correction, as We and Our Brethren have for some time observed; it is this that We make haste to reject, nay, to cast out entirely and effectively banish from the Church of God. Wherefore, We expressly prescribe that no one should presume to undertake innovations of this kind, above all in the Canonical Hours or in the Mass.[4]

MISGUIDED EFFORTS OF THE HUMANIST POPES

We will later examine the series of efforts made by the Roman Pontiffs for the improvement of music at the time of the great Counter-Reformation. This reform was preceded, as is well known, by many unsuccessful attempts, which attest to the unrest that was felt in all parts of the Church.

---

[2] Resp. 1 ad Mat. in Communi Dedicationis Ecclesiæ.

[3] Boethius, *De musica*, bk. 1, ch. 1.

[4] John XXII, Bull *Docta sanctorum* (in *Extravagantes communes*, bk. 3, title 1). While Guéranger dates the Bull to 1322, scholars today generally agree that it was issued in 1324.

It was an inopportune moment to decide upon the best form of the liturgy, as Rome was then under the influences of profane literature born of an unduly exclusive study of the Greek and Latin classics.

The first impulse to correct the liturgy occurred to Pope Leo X, at a moment when the Roman Curia was teeming with poets and prose stylists whose taste could not tolerate the "barbarism of ecclesiastical Latin." Some of these poets referred to God as *Numen*,[5] others recited their Hours in Greek or Hebrew, and one even stopped reading the Epistles of St. Paul for fear that it would mar the purity of his taste.

They deemed, then, that the main flaw of the liturgy was its infelicity of style. As a result, without any concern for the rights antiquity had bestowed upon the sacred formulas, and failing to realize that respect for this venerable antiquity simply required the pruning of inexpedient additions and interpolations, they concluded, in this poetic age, that what was most in need of reform was the Hymnary.

And how did they go about it?

The genius of Catholicism, in every age, has been to refine, to complete, and to reform. The violent destruction of centuries-old usages, and the sudden substitution of entirely new forms for ancient ones, is without precedent in its history.

Nevertheless, this is what would have happened if Providence had allowed the project of Leo X to succeed. This Pontiff ordered Zacharias Ferreri, the Bishop of Guardia, to compose a collection of hymns for all the feasts of the year, employing a style that was worthy of sixteenth-century literature. The bishop devoted all his efforts to this work, but Leo X, taken by death, did not personally witness the fruition of Ferreri's labors. This work only saw the light of day under Leo X's successor, Pope Clement VII, who, like him, was a great enthusiast of pagan antiquity. In 1525, the long-awaited collection appeared in Rome.

The hymns it contains are precisely what one might expect of the author and his age. Everything is novel. The mysteries of the Savior's Nativity, Passion, and Resurrection, of Pentecost and the Blessed Sacrament, are all pompously celebrated in odes that have nothing in common with the ancient hymns of St. Ambrose, Prudentius, and the other poets of the Catholic Church. Instead, one finds, with astounding thoughtlessness, all of the images and allusions to pagan beliefs and customs that one might encounter in Horace. To cite only one example, when recounting St. Gregory's election to the papacy, Ferreri heedlessly writes that the *Flamines* chose him as the Supreme Pontiff.[6]

---

[5] A term for "divinity" used by the pagan poets of Latin antiquity, never applied by ancient Christian writers to the true God.

[6] The *Flamines* were priests of ancient Rome, devoted to the service of a pagan divinity for whom they performed sacrifices.

In a Brief dated 11 December 1525, Clement VII approved Ferreri's hymns: "We grant and order, by apostolic authority, through these presents, that anyone, even a priest, may use these hymns, even in the Divine Offices." By this unprecedented measure, the Pope had permitted every clergyman to use individually a liturgical text that was not universal. Each one could choose, at least to a degree, what prayers to recite.

The title of Ferreri's hymnary contained the announcement of a new Breviary that he himself had elaborated, commended for being "shorter and simpler [i.e., than the ancient one], and purged of every error."[7]

A DISASTROUS REFORM: THE BREVIARY OF QUIÑONES

Since Ferreri had died before being able to complete his "abridged" Breviary, Clement VII entrusted the task to Cardinal Francisco de Quiñones, known as the "Cardinal of the Holy Cross" because his titular church was the Basilica of the Holy Cross in Jerusalem. This prelate, who was a Franciscan and one-time Minister General of his order, actively devoted himself to fulfilling this commission. Finally, in 1535, he presented his work to Paul III, Clement VII's successor. The Pope gave his approval, and the "Breviary of Quiñones" was published in Rome.

Quiñones' intention, and the aim of Leo X, Clement VII, and Paul III, was to reform the Office of Hours by abridging it, and, to avoid attacking the older usages of the liturgy, to introduce a distinction between the Office as celebrated in choir and the Office recited privately. They hoped to revive the spirit of prayer among the clergy by means of a degree of variety in the prayers and readings, by avoiding repetitions, and by removing everything that was directed towards the assembly of the faithful, as if it were unnecessary in private recitation. However, they failed to see that this came at the expense of tradition; that the ancient deposit of liturgical prayers, once altered, would soon perish; that this form of the Office, unknown to all Christian ages, would before long insinuate itself into the Churches, greatly scandalizing the people; and, in a word, that this was a disastrous reform that sacrificed the liturgy's whole past.

The nature of the Apostolic See's influence over the publication of the Quiñones' Breviary stands in contrast to everything seen before or since. Rome appeared to encourage the adoption of this form of the Office while hesitating to impose it as law. One might understand this as a transitional period which would endure until St. Pius V — designated by God as the successor to Leo the Great, Gelasius, and Gregory the Great in liturgical matters — came forth worthily to reform divine worship, as the Church declares in the Collect of his feast day.[8]

---

[7] "Breviarium Ecclesiasticum ab eodem Zacharia *longe brevius et facilius redditum et ab omni errore purgatum* prope diem exibit."

[8] Cf. Collect for the feast of St. Pius V: "Deus, qui ad conterendos ecclesiæ tuæ hostes, et

In 1535, the same year that it appeared in Rome, Quiñones' Breviary entered France and faced a vigorous and ruthless attack from the doctors of the University of Paris. The matter had been deferred to the Faculty by the Parlement of Paris. Here are some excerpts from this censure, which begins as follows:

> First of all, it is necessary to note that the said Breviary stands in contradiction with all the other Breviaries of any diocese whatsoever, and particularly of the Roman Church, for all these other Breviaries contain many holy and salutary things ordered to foster the piety and devotion of the faithful. None of these things are found in the said Breviary...
>
> These salutary institutions have been preserved in the ecclesiastical Offices from the origin of the Church until our times, and so one cannot but be astonished to find that the writer of this new Breviary rejects all these things, claiming they are to be rejected because, he says, they are conducive neither to piety nor to the knowledge of Holy Scripture...
>
> This alteration of the Breviary seems to be a dangerous thing, for it is to be feared that if it is accepted, the Missal and the Office of the Mass might be altered in the same way...
>
> Moreover, it would pose an immediate and considerable danger if, at the urging of a private individual, we were to abandon the common usage hitherto observed in the Church. If cathedral, collegiate, and parochial churches were to accept this new Breviary, the Church would find herself in possession of an Office guaranteed solely by the signature of one man.[9]

This forceful critique, motivated by such grave circumstances, struck both against Quiñones and against the authority that appeared to endorse him [*i.e., the Pope*]. If the reign of this strange liturgy had been long, the ancient form of the Roman Offices would have been overthrown everywhere, and the link between antiquity and the modern age severed.

PUBLICATION OF THE RUBRICS

We shall now mention a significant event in the liturgy marking the end of the fifteenth century and the beginning of the sixteenth. It is the definitive publication of the body of rituals and sacred observances known under the name of "Rubrics": an admirable collection of laws at once mysterious and rational, dismissed only by those who have lost their faith or their taste for serious matters. These laws, whose origin is lost in the mists of time,

---

ad divinum cultum reparandum beatum Pium pontificem maximum eligere dignatus es" ("O God, who to the destruction of the enemies of Thy Church, and to the restoration of Thy holy worship, didst vouchsafe to elect blessed Pius to be Thy high priest ... ").

[9] "Rationes et motiva propter quæ videtur Universitati Parisiensi non recipiendum Breviarium, nuper editum et promulgatum," in Charles du Plessis d'Argentré, *Collectio Judiciorum de Novis Erroribus*, vol. 2, pp. 12–126.

appeared in increasingly detailed form in the series of "Roman Orders," intended for use in the papal chapel.

However, there was not yet a collection containing these rubrics described for the use of all priests, including details absent from the "Roman Orders," which had until this time been confined to oral tradition. This work was taken up and accomplished by Johann Burchard of Strasbourg, who held the important office of Master of Pontifical Ceremonies.

Let superficial spirits blaspheme what they do not understand and ridicule this admirable digest of all liturgical traditions ...

After Burchard, we must mention his successor in the office of Master of Papal Ceremonies, Paris de Grassis. He was found worthy to receive and transmit to others the liturgical traditions that Burchard had himself received from his predecessors.

Without these two illustrious men — one of whom closed the pomps of the papal chapel in the fifteenth century, and the other who reopened them in the sixteenth — the entire liturgical heritage of Rome might have perished. This was the time when the thirst for novelties prevailed everywhere, and when Quiñones, representing Clement VII and Paul III, regarded knowledge of the rules of divine worship as a source of unnecessary burdens, and the recitation of the Office merely as a private reading of the Bible.

As we close this chapter, we find a great number of considerations to gather for the articulation of the true teaching on the liturgy.

1. A liturgical form hastily created to satisfy supposed literary necessities cannot be enduring.

2. For liturgical reform to last, it cannot be carried out by learned hands, but by pious ones.

3. In reforming the liturgy, avoid the spirit of novelty, restoring any defects that might have slipped into the old forms, rather than abolishing them.

4. To shorten the liturgy is not to reform it; its length is not a defect in the eyes of those who are meant to live by prayer.

5. To read a great deal of Holy Scripture in the Office is not to fulfill the obligation of priestly prayer, for to read is not the same as to pray.

6. There is no basis for a distinction between public and private Office, for no two prayers are at the same time the official prayer of the Church. The cleric who is legitimately absent from the choir must remain united with his brothers, just as if he were present, reciting with them what they chant in union with him. The readings he might select from a learned Breviary isolate him from this common prayer.

7. It is not a bad thing that the rules of divine service are numerous and complicated, for the cleric thereby learns with what diligence he must

accomplish the Lord's work. Any derision of the Rubrics exposes a superficial man, and the Church has responded to these novel theories by promulgating more forcefully than ever the whole of her laws, so beautiful in their harmony and unity.

8. Finally, there can be no comparison, in good conscience, between St. Pius V, the Supreme Pontiff who solemnly re-established the ancient Office, and the Cardinal of the Holy Cross, Quiñones, the man responsible for the edition of a new Office unknown to all centuries. [10]

---

[10] The Breviary of Quiñones is also called "the Breviary of the Holy Cross."

14

The Anti-Liturgical Heresy and the Protestant Revolt[1]

HE ANTI-LITURGICAL HERESY, THAT which opposes the forms of divine worship, can only ferment in the heart of the true Church herself. Only where there is anything worth destroying will the spirit of destruction attempt to insinuate this pernicious poison.

PRECURSORS: VIGILANTIUS, BERENGAR, PETER WALDO

The known starting point of this heresy is Vigilantius, the Gaul immortalized by St. Jerome's eloquent sarcasms. This former declaimed against the pomp of ceremonies, grossly insulted their symbolism, blasphemed the relics of the saints, and attacked both the celibacy of the sacred ministers and the continence of virgins — all in the name of safeguarding the purity of Christianity. As one can see, this kind of thinking was not a little "ahead of its time" for a fourth-century Gaul.

After Vigilantius, the West enjoyed a period of rest for many centuries, but when the barbarian races, whom the Church initiated into civilization, started to become somewhat familiar with intellectual endeavors, men, and then sects, began to arise that denied what they did not understand. The heresy of the Sacramentarians began in twelfth-century France with the blasphemies of the archdeacon Berengar. The entire Church rose up against these monstrous teachings, but it was foreseeable that rationalism, once unleashed against the most august act of Christian worship, would not stop there. The mystery of the Real Presence of the divine Word under the Eucharistic symbols would become the focal point for every attack. God had to be distanced from man, and, in order to attack this central dogma more forcefully, it was essential to close off all avenues within the liturgy which, so to speak, lead to the Eucharistic mystery.

Berengar had only given the signal. His campaign would be reinforced in his own century and in those that followed, resulting in the most prolonged and appalling attack that Catholicism had ever suffered.

A new branch of the anti-liturgical sect sprouted up in Lyon from the

---

[1] In Dom Guéranger's terminology, the expression "anti-liturgical heresy" designates the hostility found in all true heresies towards the traditional Catholic liturgy. This term does not define a particular heresy, but a constant tendency that inevitably drives every heterodox school, from age to age, to transform and then to destroy the liturgy of the true Church.

trunk of Manichaeism. In 1160, the merchant Peter Waldo formed a sect of turbulent fanatics known as "the Poor of Lyon," but most commonly as "Waldensians," after their founder. It soon became evident that the spirit of this sect aligned with the anti-liturgical stance Berengar first propagated in France. Soon shedding their Manichaean opinions, unpopular in France, the Waldensians shifted focus to advocating for Church reform, and to achieve this, they boldly undermined the entire structure of her worship.

First of all, for them, there is no longer any priesthood; every layman is a priest. A priest in mortal sin cannot consecrate, thus making the Eucharist uncertain. Clerics cannot possess worldly goods. Churches, holy chrism, the cult of the Blessed Virgin and the saints, and prayer for the dead are abhorrent. Everything must be based on Sacred Scripture.

PROTESTANTISM'S ANTI-LITURGICAL COMPONENT

At last, Luther makes his appearance. He said nothing that his predecessors did not say before him, but claimed to liberate man both from the slavery of thought to teaching authority and from the slavery of body to liturgical authority.

It is necessary now to outline the course of the so-called reformers of Christianity over the past three centuries, and to present an overview of their deeds and teachings concerning the purification of divine worship.

1. The first characteristic of the anti-liturgical heresy is contempt for the tradition regarding the texts of divine worship. Any sectarian wishing to introduce a novel doctrine unfailingly clashes with the liturgy, which is tradition at its most powerful, and he cannot rest until he has silenced this voice and torn up the pages that contain the faith of ages past. Indeed, how did Lutheranism, Calvinism, and Anglicanism establish and maintain their influence over the masses? All it took was the substitution of new books and new texts for the old ones, and their whole work was accomplished. Nothing now stood in the way of these new teachers; they could preach to their heart's content: the faith of the people was now defenseless.

2. The second principle of the anti-liturgical sect is to replace texts in ecclesiastical style with readings from Sacred Scripture. This principle offers the sect two advantages: first, it silences the voice of tradition, which it always fears; secondly, it allows this heresy to propagate and support its dogmas through selective omission or emphasis. By omission, they adroitly bypass the texts that express doctrine opposed to the errors they wish to propagate. By emphasis, they highlight truncated passages that present only one side of the truth, concealing the other from the eyes of common folk.

It has been known for centuries that all heretics prefer Sacred Scripture over ecclesiastical definitions on account of the ease with which they can manipulate the Word of God to say whatever they want, by putting it on display or concealing it as it suits them.

3. Having expelled ecclesiastical texts and proclaimed the absolute necessity of using only the words of Scripture in the divine services, heretics discover that Scripture does not always bend to their every will. Hence the third principle: to fabricate and introduce various deceptive texts to ensnare the people more tightly in error, thereby consolidating the whole edifice of their godless reform for centuries to come.

4. We should not be surprised that heresy contradicts itself in its works, for its fourth principle, or rather the fourth necessity imposed on the sectarians by the very nature of their state of revolt, is habitual contradiction with their own principles.

Thus, all sectarians without exception begin by invoking the rights of antiquity. They want to free Christianity from everything that error and the passions of men have mixed into it that is false and unworthy of God. They want only what is primitive, and claim to return the original foundations of Christianity. To this end, they prune, erase, and cut away; nothing is spared their lash. But when one expects to see divine worship restored to its original purity, one finds oneself encumbered with new texts that date only from yesterday and are unquestionably man-made.

Every sect reaches this inevitable conclusion. We have seen it with the Monophysites, with the Nestorians, and we find the same thing in all the Protestant branches.

Let us note another characteristic of the liturgical changes effected by these heretics. In their furor for innovation, they do not content themselves with pruning away the texts of ecclesiastical style that they disparage as merely human words. Rather, they extend their condemnation even to the readings and prayers the Church has drawn from Scripture. All these they change and substitute, fearing even the slightest shred of the orthodoxy that guided the selection of these passages.

5. Since sectarians undertook the reform of the liturgy with the same aim as the reform of dogma of which it was the consequence, it follows that, just as Protestants have separated themselves from unity in order to believe less, they were led to remove from worship all of the ceremonies and formulas that express mysteries. They branded as superstition or idolatry anything that did not seem purely rational, thus restricting the expressions of faith, obstructing with doubt and even negation all the paths that open onto the supernatural world.

Thus, no more Sacraments, apart from baptism, until Socinianism freed its followers from even this. No more sacramentals, blessings, images, relics of saints, processions, pilgrimages, and so forth. No longer an altar, only a table. No more sacrifice, as in every religion, only the Lord's Supper. No more church, only a temple, as with the Greeks and Romans. No more religious architecture, since there are no more mysteries. No more Christian painting and sculpture, since there is no more sensible religion. In short, no more poetry in a form of worship fertilized neither by faith nor love.

6. The suppression of mysterious elements from the Protestant liturgy inevitably led to the total extinction of that spirit of prayer called unction in Catholicism. A rebellious heart has no love, and a heart without love can at best produce passable expressions of respect or fear, with the haughty coldness of the Pharisee. Such is the Protestant liturgy. One senses that whoever celebrates it applauds himself for not being one of those Papists who bring God down to their level by the familiarity of their vulgar language.

7. Since the Protestant liturgy fancies that it deals so nobly with God, it has no need of created intermediaries. It believes that invoking the intercession of the Blessed Virgin or the protection of the saints would show a lack of respect for the sovereign Being. It rejects all that Papist idolatry that asks of creatures what should only be asked of God. It rids the calendar of all the names of men that the Roman Church so brazenly inscribes next to the name of God. It especially abhors those of monks and other latter-day figures who appear next to the revered names of the apostles chosen by Jesus Christ, by whom the early Church was founded, which alone was pure in faith and free from all superstition in worship and from all laxity in morals.

8. Since one of the main principles of this liturgical reform is to abolish mystical acts and formulas, it necessarily follows that its authors should demand the use of the vernacular in the divine service. This is a crucial point for sectarians. Worship is not a secret thing, they say; the people must understand what they are singing. Hatred of the Latin language is innate in the hearts of all Rome's enemies. They see it as the treasure of Catholics worldwide, the arsenal of orthodoxy against all the subtleties of the sectarian spirit, and the papacy's most powerful weapon.

The spirit of rebellion that drives them to entrust the universal prayer to the tongue of each people, each region, and each age, has produced its fruits, and yet the Reformed cannot but realize every day the Catholic peoples, despite their Latin prayers, appreciate and fulfill the duties of worship better and more zealously than Protestant peoples. At every hour of the day, the divine service takes place in Catholic churches; the faithful who attend leave their mother tongue on the threshold; outside of the times of preaching, they hear only mysterious sounds, and even those cease to resound at the most solemn moment, at the Canon of the Mass. And yet this mystery charms them so much that they do not envy the Protestant's lot, even though the latter's ear hears only sounds whose meaning he grasps. While the Reformed temples struggle to bring austere Christians together once a week, the Papist Church sees its many altars constantly besieged by her devout children. Every day, they tear themselves away from their work to come and hear these mysterious words that must be from God, because they nourish their faith and soothe their sorrows.

We must admit that it was a masterstroke of Protestantism to have declared war on the sacred language; if it could succeed in destroying it, its triumph would be well advanced. Exposed before profane eyes like a virgin who has been violated, the liturgy, from that very moment, has lost its sacred character, and very soon the people would find that it is too much trouble to interrupt their work or pastimes to hear the liturgy spoken as if it were in the marketplace.[2] How long do you think the faithful will go to hear these self-styled liturgists call out: "The Lord be with you," and how long will the people continue to respond: "And with your spirit"? . . . Below, we will make a closer examination of the language of the liturgy.

9. By removing from the liturgy the mystery that humbles reason, Protestantism ensured that it also eliminated the practical consequences, namely freedom from the fatigue and discomfort imposed on the body by the practices of the Papist liturgy. No more fasting, no more abstinence, no more genuflecting in prayer. For the sacred ministers of the temple, no more daily Offices to perform, no more canonical prayers to recite in the name of the Church. This is one of the principal forms of the great Protestant emancipation: to diminish the sum of public and private prayers.

Events soon showed that faith and charity, which are nourished by prayer, were extinguished in the Reformation, whereas among Catholics they never cease to nourish every act of devotion towards God and man, fertilized as they are by the ineffable resources of liturgical prayer performed by the secular and regular clergy, with whom the community of the faithful is united.

10. Since Protestantism needed a rule to identify which of the Papist institutions is the most hostile to its principles, it had to delve into the foundations of the Catholic edifice and find the cornerstone that joins everything together. This heresy's instinct led it immediately to discover the dogma that is irreconcilable with any innovation: papal power.

When Luther wrote on his banner: "Hatred of Rome and of her laws," he was merely promulgating once again the great principle of all the branches of the anti-liturgical sect. From then on, worship and ceremonies had to be abolished *en masse* because they were Roman idolatry. The Latin language, the Divine Office, the calendar, the Breviary, were all deemed abominations of the great whore of Babylon. The Roman Pontiff oppresses reason with his dogmas and the senses with his ritual practices. It must therefore be proclaimed that his dogmas are nothing but blasphemy and error and his liturgical observances nothing but a means of establishing his usurped and tyrannical dominion more firmly. This is why, in its emancipated litanies, the Lutheran Church thoughtlessly continues to sing: "From

---

[2] It is unclear from the French here whether Guéranger is referring to the gathering of a specific Huguenot sect, or if he is imagining a situation where the Catholic Church in France adopts a vernacular liturgy.

the murderous fury, slander, rage, and ferocity of the Turk and the Pope, deliver us, O Lord."

This is the place to recall the admirable reflections of Joseph de Maistre, in his book *Du Pape* (1819), where he shows, with such depth and sagacity, that despite the dissonances that isolate the various sects from one another, there is one quality in which they all unite, that of being *non-Roman*. Imagine any kind of innovation, whether of dogma or discipline, and you will see if it is impossible to advance it without, willingly or not, being labeled non-Roman, or, at best, *less Roman*, if it were less bold. The question remains, what kind of peace could a Catholic find in the first, or even the second, of these two situations?

11. The anti-liturgical heresy, in order to establish its reign forever, needed to destroy, both in principle and practice, all priesthood in Christianity. It understood that where there is a pontiff, there is an altar, and where there is an altar, there is a sacrifice, and hence a mysterious ceremonial. Having therefore abolished the office of the Supreme Pontiff, it was necessary to annihilate the position of the bishop, from whom emanates the mystical laying on of hands that perpetuates the sacred hierarchy. Hence a vast *presbyterianism*, which is but the immediate consequence of the suppression of the supreme pontificate.

From that point on, there are no more priests, properly speaking. For how could simple election, without consecration, make a man sacred? The reform of Luther and Calvin therefore knows only *ministers* or men of God, as one prefers. But it is impossible to stop there. Chosen and installed by laymen, wearing in the temple the robes of a bastard magistracy, the minister is merely a layman furnished with accidental functions. Protestantism is therefore all about laymen — and so it was bound to be, since there is no longer any liturgy; and thus, by the same token, there is no longer any liturgy, since there are only laymen left.

12. Finally, and this is the furthest extreme of degradation, since the hierarchy is dead, the priesthood no longer exists. Consequently, the prince, the only possible authority among laymen, proclaims himself the head of religion. Thus, the proudest reformers, after shaking off Rome's spiritual yoke, will find themselves acknowledging the temporal sovereign as supreme pontiff, and number power over the liturgy among the rights of royal prerogative.

As a result, there will be no dogma, no morality, no Sacraments, no worship, no Christianity, except insofar as the prince pleases, since absolute power has been given him over the liturgy, through which all these things are expressed and applied within the community of the faithful. This is, nonetheless, the fundamental axiom of the Reformation both in practice and in the writings of Protestant doctors. This final point completes the picture and allows the reader to judge the nature of this so-called liberation, achieved with such violence against the papacy, only to give way, necessarily, to a dominion that destroys the very essence of Christianity.

It is true that, in its beginnings, the anti-liturgical sect was not accustomed to flatter the powerful in this way. Albigensians, Waldensians, Lollards, and Hussites all taught that it was necessary to resist and even attack any princes or magistrates in a state of sin, asserting that a prince loses his right to rule from the moment he is no longer in a state of grace with God. But the reason these sectarians taught this is that they were afraid of the sword of Catholic princes and had everything to gain by undermining their authority. But from the very moment that rulers, allied with the revolt against the Church, sought to make religion a national affair and a tool of governance, the abridged liturgy and dogma became confined to the borders of a region and naturally fell under the highest authority of that region. The reformers could then not help but feel deep gratitude towards those who lent the support of so powerful an arm to the establishment and maintenance of their theories.

It is true that preferring temporal over spiritual authority in matters of religion is utter apostasy, but in this case it was a matter of survival. To be consistent is all very well and good, but one must also live. This is why Luther, who so loudly broke away from the Pope of Rome, denouncing him as the promoter of all the abominations of Babylon, did not blush to declare the theological legitimacy of the Landgrave of Hesse's bigamous marriage. It is also why the Abbé Gregoire found within his principles the ability simultaneously to vote to condemn Louis XVI to death at the Convention and to champion Louis XIV and Joseph against the Roman Pontiffs.

Such are the central principles of the anti-liturgical heresy. We assuredly have not exaggerated, but simply noted the doctrine professed a hundred times over in the writings of Luther, Calvin, the Magdeburg Centuriators,[3] Rudolf Hospinian, Martin Chemnitz, and others. Their books are easy to consult—and indeed, the work that resulted from them is before the eyes of all mankind. Here, it seemed useful to outline the main features of this heresy, for it is always of profit to know error. Direct, positive teaching is sometimes less advantageous and less easy. It is now up to the Catholic apologist to refute these errors.

---

[3] That is, the authors of the *Magdeburg Centuries*, a Lutheran work of ecclesiastical history.

15

Catholic Reform of the Liturgy:
THE COUNCIL OF TRENT,
POPE PIUS V

 HE SIXTEENTH CENTURY—IN THE COURSE of which the true liturgical doctrines were subjected to such rude assaults, and which witnessed the misguided reforms of Ferreri and Quiñones—was nevertheless to see the accomplishment of a veritable, solid, and legitimate reform. This task was reserved for the Roman Pontiffs to undertake and ultimately achieve by themselves.

PREPARATORY WORKS — THE THEATINES

As always, the regular clergy played a crucial role in such an important endeavor, but it was no longer the Franciscans. The insufficient efforts of the mendicant orders were now joined by the zeal of a new branch that had only just sprang from the great tree of the religious state, known as "Clerics Regular." The most ancient of these, the Theatines, founded by St. Cajetan of Thiene, made the first serious attempt at a liturgical reform, laying the groundwork for the great achievement later realized by St. Pius V.

Clement VII, the very Pope who ordered Quiñones to work on the new Breviary, had entrusted this same mission to St. Cajetan, as well as to Giovanni Pietro Carafa, who was one of Cajetan's first companions and later became Pope. The Brief of Pope Clement VII that conferred upon them such a distinguished sign of apostolic confidence is still preserved in the annals of the Theatines. The Quiñones Breviary was preferred, doubtless because it was shorter and more elegantly arranged. That of the Theatines, ascribed in part to Carafa, recommended itself only by its retention of certain ancient and venerable usages, purgation of apocryphal histories, correction of the rubrics, and substitution of homilies from heterodox authors with authentic lessons from the holy Fathers.

In 1555, Giovanni Pietro Carafa ascended the Chair of St. Peter under the name of Paul IV. He set diligently to work on the draft of his reformed Breviary. However, since he wished to accomplish by himself this work, which was so important and worthy of a Pope, he was unable to see it through to promulgation, being frequently diverted by the numerous and grave concerns of his supreme office. He died in 1559, after four years of an energetic pontificate, which he had begun at the age of 79.

After the death of Paul IV, his successor Pius IV directed all of his efforts to the continuation of the council opened at Trent in 1545, which had since been suspended at various times.

Pope Pius IV, who always displayed, in the direction of the council through his legates, keen tact and clear understanding of the Church's true needs, wished to enable the council Fathers to accomplish the greatly desired work of liturgical reform according to all canonical proprieties. To this end, he sent them the work of Paul IV. This provided them with the most reliable guideline, since that great Pope had in his reform aimed solely at brining the Breviary closer to its Gregorian sources and to remove the arbitrary or unsuitable additions made in recent centuries.

The council, preoccupied with the serious matters that filled its eighteenth to the twenty-fifth sessions, reached the year 1563 before the commission that it entrusted with the reform of the Breviary had had enough time to complete its work. To avoid further delays, the legates proposed delegating the task of liturgical reform to the Roman Pontiff, which was approved in the twenty-fifth session.

PROMULGATION OF THE RESTORED BREVIARY

By handing over to the Roman Pontiff the reform of the Breviary and Missal, the council did nothing else than proclaim once again the necessity for all of the Western Church to follow the liturgy of the Church of Rome, the Mother and Teacher. The manuscripts of Paul IV and the documents prepared by the council's commissioners in a similar vein were brought to Rome

At the same time, Pope Pius IV summoned commissioners to him and even added several learned men of Rome to their number. But death prevented the Pope from finishing this great work, and so his successor St. Pius V took it into his own hands and also appointed numerous commissioners to hasten its completion.

Here, we will briefly outline the principles that guided the correction of the Breviary. First, Paul IV (Carafa) and his fellow Theatines' fundamental idea — an idea adopted by the Council of Trent and by Pius IV but diametrically opposed to that of Quiñones — was that the only way to reform the liturgy was to bring it closer to the ancient sources, rejecting the distinction between a privately recited Office and a public Office. It was therefore necessary to consult the oldest manuscripts and to restore their order and arrangement, both in the Psalter and in the distribution of scriptural books, responsories, antiphons, and hymns. In this way, the Church remained true to herself.

When all of this was accomplished, St. Pius V issued the Bull promulgating the Breviary. It begins with the words *Quod a nobis*. This is the translation:

Pius, bishop, servant of the servants of God, obliged by the office of Our pastoral charge to put all of Our care into accomplishing, as far as We can, by the help of God, the execution of the decrees of the Council of Trent ... Foremost among these are the sacred prayers, praises, and acts of thanksgiving contained in the Roman Breviary.

This form of the Divine Office, once established with piety and wisdom by the Supreme Pontiffs Gelasius I and Gregory I, and later reformed by Gregory VII, having, in the course of time, departed from its ancient institution, it became necessary to make it conform once again to the ancient rule of prayer.

Indeed, some have disfigured the harmonious integrity of the old Breviary, mutilating it in many places and altering it by the addition of many novel and doubtful things. Many others, attracted by its greater convenience, have eagerly adopted the new and abridged Breviary composed by Francisco de Quiñones, Cardinal-priest of the title of the Holy Cross in Jerusalem. Moreover, this detestable custom had crept into the provinces; namely, that, in churches which originally kept the custom of saying and chanting the Canonical Hours according to the ancient Roman use, together with the others, each bishop made himself a particular Breviary, thus tearing apart, by means of these new Offices — dissimilar among themselves and proper to each bishopric, so to speak — the communion that consists in offering prayers and praises to the same God in one and the same form. Hence, in so many places, the upheaval of divine worship; hence, too, among the clergy, the ignorance of ecclesiastical ceremonies and rites, so that countless Church ministers have performed their duties indecently, to the great scandal of the pious ...

It is with great zeal that We have urged the completion of this sacred work ... and today We have the good fortune to see this Roman Breviary completed at last.

Having had an account given to Us several times of the method followed by those to whom We had assigned this task; having seen that, in carrying out their work, they had not departed from the ancient Breviaries of the most illustrious churches of Rome and of Our Vatican library; that they had, moreover, followed the most authoritative authors in this matter; and that, while excising foreign and uncertain things, they had omitted nothing that makes up the proper whole of the ancient Divine Office; We have approved their work and ordered that it be printed in Rome, and that it be promulgated everywhere.[1]

Such was the first act of the liturgical reform in Rome. This Bull completely abolished the use of Quiñones's Breviary and established in every place the form of the Office contained in the Roman Breviary, but without

---

[1] Pope Pius V, Bull *Quod a nobis* (9 July 1568).

constraining the Churches that had possessed a particular Breviary for over two hundred years to adopt it, instead giving them the faculty to switch to it subject to certain formalities.

Rome could scarcely have applied a more discreet or efficacious remedy to the great disease of liturgical anarchy. All the Western Churches understood this and made it their duty to embrace the views of the Roman Pontiff and the Council of Trent.

PROMULGATION OF THE RESTORED MISSAL

It still remained to publish an equally important part of the reformed liturgy. The Breviary could not be useful without a similarly corrected Missal to which it conformed. The Roman Commission had simultaneously concentrated its efforts on this task, and two years after the Breviary, in 1570, St. Pius V was able to promulgate the new Missal. It was accompanied by the following Apostolic Constitution, *Quo primum*:

> In order that the Missal and Breviary may be in perfect harmony, as fitting and proper — for it is most becoming that there be in the Church only one appropriate manner of reciting the Psalms and only one rite for the celebration of Mass — We deemed it necessary to give our immediate attention to what still remained to be done, viz, the re-editing of the Missal as soon as possible.
>
> Hence, We decided to entrust this work to learned men of our selection. They very carefully collated all their work with the ancient codices in Our Vatican Library and with reliable, preserved or emended codices from elsewhere. Besides this, these men consulted the works of ancient and approved authors concerning the same sacred rites; and thus they have restored the Missal itself to the original form and rite of the holy Fathers. When this work had been gone over numerous times and further emended, after serious study and reflection, We commanded that the finished product be printed and published without delay, so that all might enjoy the fruits of this labor; and thus priests would know which prayers to use and which rites and ceremonies they were required to observe from now on in the celebration of Masses...
>
> In virtue of Our Apostolic authority, We grant and concede in perpetuity that, for the chanting or reading of the Mass in any church whatsoever, this Missal is hereafter to be followed absolutely, without any scruple of conscience or fear of incurring any penalty, judgment, or censure, and may freely and lawfully be used...We likewise declare and ordain that no one whosoever is forced or coerced to alter this Missal, and that this present document cannot be revoked or modified, but remain always valid and retain its full force notwithstanding the previous constitutions and decrees of the Holy See, as well as any general or special constitutions or edicts of provincial or synodal councils, and notwithstanding the practice and custom of the aforesaid

churches, established by long and immemorial prescription, saving only usage of two hundred years' standing...

Therefore, no one whosoever is permitted to alter this notice of Our permission, statute, ordinance, command, precept, grant, indult, declaration, will, decree, and prohibition. Would anyone, however, presume to commit such an act, he should know that he will incur the wrath of Almighty God and of the Blessed Apostles Peter and Paul.[2]

The advent of a reformed Breviary and Missal was a cause of great joy in the entire Church. The disorder that had reigned in the liturgy, which had been a universal source of grievance, had at last been addressed and met with an efficacious remedy. The Missal of St. Pius V had drawn exclusively upon the purest sources of antiquity.

UNIVERSAL ADOPTION

Rome in its entirety immediately adopted the new liturgical books. The Lateran Basilica itself eagerly embraced a Breviary that was no longer simply that of the papal chapel, or even of the Friars Minor, but the Breviary of the Catholic Church. The Vatican Basilica alone adopted the new Breviary with certain modifications, since it preserved the right to retain the use of the ancient Italic Psalter.

The Church of Milan was governed at this time by St. Charles Borromeo. It was with great zeal that this illustrious cardinal preserved the venerable Ambrosian liturgy. Yet he showed himself no less diligent an observer of the Supreme Pontiff's will, by introducing the liturgical books of St. Pius V in all the churches of his city, diocese, and ecclesiastical province, which were obliged, by law or custom, to follow the Roman Office. Exception was made only for the priests attached to churches of an ancient custom for which the Bull had made provision [*i.e., exception was made for churches that used a liturgy of at least two-hundred years' antiquity*].

All of Italy gradually conformed to the Holy See's intentions. The churches of Sicily, for example, which had used their own particular Breviary, yielded early on. By the end of the sixteenth century, the whole Italian Peninsula, outside of Ambrosian territories, was united under the most punctilious observance of the liturgical uses promulgated by St. Pius V.

The Spanish Peninsula, also early on, submitted with absolute obedience to the Bulls of St. Pius V. Its love for unity and zeal for the Faith took precedence over national sensitivities.

The churches of France, at the period of the Bull's publication, had a liturgy that derived from the Roman Rite introduced by Charlemagne with the addition of particular usages. In the eyes of all of Europe, this combination brought honor to these churches, and according to the terms of the

---

[2] Pope Pius V, Apostolic Constitution *Quo primum* (14 July 1570).

Bull this liturgy could have legitimately been preserved. Yet the Church of France immediately recognized the superiority of the reformed liturgical books over those in use throughout the kingdom. And since, at this time, France still enjoyed the right to convene provincial councils, these pious assemblies proclaimed the necessity of submitting to the Bull of St. Pius V. Nevertheless, Lyon maintained the essence of its Office, which was a mix of the Roman and Gallican.

In this way, liturgical unity was restored to France. This event took place in such a striking manner that there is no example of a pontifical constitution having been recognized as binding in so many councils as that of St. Pius V on the Roman Breviary.

More than a third of France's churches were in possession of a Breviary, Roman in essence, but corrected and reformed by diocesan authority for more than two hundred years. Nonetheless, the bishops judged that unity could not be too perfect, and, recognizing the superiority of the new Breviary's text, they had no difficulty whatsoever in adopting it purely and simply, while others had it printed almost in its entirety under the diocesan title.

As far as we are aware, in all of France, Lyon was the only diocese to retain its old Breviary, and even this was not without borrowing a few improvements from the new Roman one.

THE FATE OF POLYPHONY—PALESTRINA

It is time to return to Rome to consider once more the great works the Roman Pontiffs accomplished. The state of chant and ecclesiastical music demanded all of their attention.

We have already seen how much this part of the liturgy had suffered from the spirit of innovation in the fourteenth and fifteenth centuries. The reader cannot have forgotten the famous Bull of Pope John XXII, *Docta sanctorum*.[3] Notwithstanding these efforts, the problem had worsened in proportion to the relaxation of discipline. In most churches, Gregorian chant had almost entirely disappeared. A purely profane music, raucous, convoluted, bursting with worldly reminiscences, and which paid no attention to the meaning of the words, had invaded the most august basilicas.

Such abuses could not escape the solicitude of the Council of Trent. In 1562, in the congregations that prepared the decree on the Sacrifice of the Mass, it was proposed that all music [*excepting Gregorian chant*] should be absolutely forbidden during the celebration of the holy mysteries. However, the majority of the Fathers, especially the Spaniards, defended polyphony as conducive to piety, provided that the content of the chant and the words were suitable to inspire devotion and the meaning of the words could be understood.

---

[3] See above, ch. 13.

Consequently, in its twenty-second session, the council contented itself with prohibiting "all music that contains, whether in singing or in the organ playing, things that are lascivious or impure."[4]

After approving, and thus giving the force of law, to the Council of Trent's decrees concerning reform, Pope Pius IV established a congregation of eight cardinals charged with ensuring their strict observance. From the first year of its institution, this congregation concentrated on correcting liturgical chant and music in the city of Rome, especially in the pontifical chapel.

This reform was particularly important because this kind of music [*i.e., polyphony*] had increasingly usurped the place of Gregorian chant in the capital of the Christian world. The congregation entrusted this affair especially to the two cardinals, Vitellozzo Vitelli and Charles Borromeo, and instructed them not only to ensure the observance of the decrees of the council by banishing worldly pieces of music, but also to demand a greater clarity in the words of the Mass that were incomprehensible when they were chanted polyphonically.

At the request of the two cardinals, the choir of the papal chapel appointed eight of its members to confer with them. Vitelli and Borromeo demanded that thenceforth, Masses mixed with words foreign to the liturgy or set to profane melodies, as well as motets whose words had been invented by the caprice of private individuals, should be banned. The singers had no objections to this.

But when the cardinals demanded that the words sung polyphonically by the choir should always be easily understood, they replied that this was not always possible. The cardinals insisted on this point, and cited as models certain pieces performed in the pontifical chapel, in particular the *Improperia* of Good Friday composed by the maestro Giovanni Pierluigi da Palestrina.

After several meetings, it was agreed that this illustrious composer would be commissioned to write a Mass whose theme, meter, and melodies would contain nothing lascivious or worldly, and in which, despite the harmony and fugues, every word and the meaning of every phrase could be easily understood.

The cardinals promised that if Palestrina met these requirements, polyphony would continue to be permitted in churches. However, they made no secret of the fact that, should he fail to do so, they would be obliged to take whatever measures they deemed appropriate, based on the advice of their colleagues.

Cardinal Borromeo took it upon himself to give the instructions to Palestrina. To save sacred music and prevent an unduly severe resolution

---

[4] Council of Trent, Session XXII, "Decree concerning the Things to be Observed and Avoided in the Celebration of Mass."

that would have deprived the liturgy of one of its most powerful means of expression, Providence had prepared in Rome itself a man of profound liturgical genius, whose abilities were equal to his mission.

Palestrina set to work with the liveliest ardor. He felt that it was a matter of life or death for religious music. Aided by the Holy Spirit, whose help he had implored, the illustrious master composed three Masses in just a few days, under the conditions prescribed for him. On 28 April 1563, a day forever memorable in the annals of sacred music, the singers of the pontifical chapel performed them before the eight cardinals.

The members of this tribunal were unanimous in their judgment of Palestrina's three Masses: all three met the conditions of the program laid down for the composer, but the third in particular struck them as admirable for the simplicity, unction, and richness that the composer had displayed. The meaning of the text was expressed with a precision and clarity that nothing could surpass. The cause was won.

Pope Pius IV wanted to hear Palestrina's masterpiece for himself. It was sung in his presence in the Sistine Chapel, where the Sacred College had gathered around the Supreme Pontiff. The holy Cardinal Borromeo celebrated the Mass, and Palestrina's music, performed by the incomparable voices of the pontifical singers, enchanted all present. At the end of the ceremony, the Pope said, after this Mass by Palestrina, polyphony could no longer be attacked, and that it should not be suppressed, but rather used in moderation.

REFORM OF THE CALENDAR BY GREGORY XIII

After having established the purity of the Missal and Breviary and preserved the Church's traditions respecting sacred music, another great enterprise, both social and liturgical, demanded the Roman Pontiffs' attention. The calendar, which served equally as the foundation of the liturgy and of human relations, had fallen into complete disorder. The responsibility to reform it belonged to the Roman Pontiffs, since, from the Church's foundation, they had been tasked with informing the churches of the date of Easter, the center of the Christian year, and this date was becoming increasingly uncertain.

The Council of Trent had concerned itself with this serious issue, but in the end referred its examination and judgment to the Pope. And indeed, it was a great spectacle to see Europe, or rather the entire civilized world, still in the sixteenth century, asking Rome once again for the lost key to the science of time.

Gregory XIII had the glory of rendering this service to mankind. Surrounding himself with eminent scholars, he formed a commission of the most renowned experts in astronomical studies, two of whom proved particularly influential: Cardinal Sirleto and the German Jesuit Christopher

Clavius. An Italian physician, Aloysius Lilius, although deceased by the time the matter was concluded, played perhaps the chief part in it, by means of a special memorandum he left behind, in which he indicated the easiest and surest method for the much-needed correction. Gregory XIII also consulted a number of learned foreign astronomers, including François de Foix-Candale, a French nobleman. When the Pope had collected all the findings necessary for an informed and legitimate reform, he proclaimed it to the Church and formally established it through a Bull that begins with the words *Inter gravissimas*.

Suffice it to say that all Catholic states immediately adopted the Gregorian calendar, while Protestant nations were more or less reluctant to accept this service to society because it came from a Pope. Nevertheless, they eventually acquiesced, but England only in the eighteenth century.

Here ends our history of the liturgy in the sixteenth century, which, despite its tempests and scandals, should be numbered among those that the Church of Jesus Christ traversed with the greatest glory. What is most important to observe is the Church's reform of herself, "renewing her youth like the eagle's" (Ps. 102:5). How many mighty and wondrous works were accomplished by the Roman Pontiffs Pius V and Clement VIII! What a provident and energetic government created these institutions, upon which rest all the exterior forms of Catholicism to this day!

⊛ Pius IV published the rules of the *Index of Prohibited Books*, as well as the famous "Tridentine Profession of Faith," which upholds orthodoxy within the Church.

⊛ St. Pius V promulgated the Breviary, the Missal, and the admirable synthesis of Catholic dogma known as *The Roman Catechism*.

⊛ Gregory XIII reformed the calendar and published the Roman Martyrology (1583).

⊛ Sixtus V produced a corrected edition of the Vulgate and established the "Roman Congregations."

⊛ Clement VIII published the Pontifical and Ceremonial, and secured the purity of the Breviary and Missal for centuries to come.

II

THE ROMAN LITURGY AFTER THE COUNCIL OF TRENT

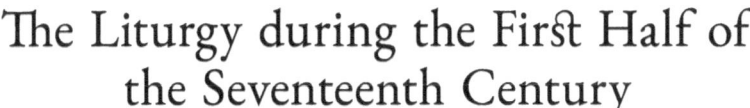

16

The Liturgy during the First Half of the Seventeenth Century

 ITURGICAL UNITY THUS PREVAILED IN the West from this time. Half a century passed before anyone would dare to undermine it. No less faithful than the other Churches to this unity, the Church of France, which had so vigorously executed the stipulations of the Bull of St. Pius V in its various provincial councils, serenely enjoyed this great blessing and zealously labored to perpetuate it.

Before recounting the sad tale of the liturgical revolution that would soon follow, we must at least say that the first half of the seventeenth century was, for the Church of France, its last period of liberty. It was at this time—which passed all too quickly—in the year 1614, that Cardinal du Perron, the voice of the clergy, so eloquently and with such dignity vindicated the ancient public law of Christendom, which the blind undertakings of the Third Estate were threatening with complete destruction.

Later, in 1625, the assembly of the clergy again professed the doctrine of the infallibility of the Supreme Pontiff. Furthermore, in 1653, an assembly of clergy declared expressly that "the judgments pronounced by the Popes, in response to consultations with the bishops in matters of faith, have a sovereign and divine authority through the entire Church."[1] We like to dwell on these pure traditions of the Church of France, for the course of events will soon lead us into a lamentable history. Permit us, then, to delay a little longer.

CODIFICATION OF THE RITUAL

While the liturgy in France was exposed to attacks that were even more threatening for the future than they were to the present, Rome completed the great work of reforming divine worship. The Breviary, the Missal, the Martyrology, the Pontifical, and the Ceremonial had already appeared. It still remained to publish an equally important book, the Ritual.

Until that time, the Ritual had not constituted a separate liturgical book. The various formulas of which it is composed today were either found in Missals or Breviaries. But since the Breviary and the Missal of St. Pius V no longer contained these kinds of details (excepting blessings), and the Pontifical comprised only those rites intended for the use of bishops, it became necessary to publish a special book that met the needs of the clergy.

---

[1] D'Argentré, *Collectio Judiciorum*, 3:276.

Paul V undertook and completed this task. The Brief for the publication of the *Rituale Romanum* appeared on 17 June 1614, and begins with the words *Apostolicæ Sedi*. The Pope first recalls the work of St. Pius V and Clement VIII on liturgical reform, after which he adds:

> With these established, there remained to be published, by authority of the Apostolic See, a single volume containing the sacred and pure rites of the Catholic Church, which must be observed by those with care of souls in the administration of the sacraments and in other ecclesiastical functions, so that, amid such a multitude of rituals, they might perform their ministries following a norm, walking with steady step in harmony under unified and faithful guidance. This matter had been urged a long time ago, but was delayed by the attention given to the printing, by God's grace, of the Greek and Latin editions of the general councils. We have taken it up with vigor to fulfill what we judge to be our duty. In order that the task proceed correctly and orderly as it should, we entrusted it to certain of our venerable brethren, the cardinals of the Holy Roman Church, outstanding for their piety, learning, and prudence, who with the counsel of scholars and having consulted ancient as well as other available rituals ... after mature deliberation and through the divine clemency have compiled the Ritual with suitable brevity. Having seen the received and approved rites of the Catholic Church arranged in order in this Ritual, We deem it right that it be published for the public good of God's Church, under the title of The Roman Ritual. Therefore, we exhort in the Lord our venerable brethren patriarchs, archbishops, bishops, and their vicars, beloved sons of ours, as well as abbots, all parish priests everywhere, and all others concerned, that henceforth, as sons of the Roman Church, they use the Ritual established by the authority of the same Church, Mother and Teacher of all, during the sacred functions, and that in such an important matter they observe inviolately whatever the Catholic Church and the usage of antiquity that she has approved has laid down.[2]

The tenor of this Brief shows that the publication of the Roman Ritual was no less solemn than that of the Breviary, Missal, Ceremonial, and Pontifical. However, it should be noted that Paul V's Brief does not contain an express injunction to use the Roman Ritual to the exclusion of all others. The Pontiff confines himself to a simple but urgent exhortation. The reason for this difference stems from the extreme diversity that had hitherto prevailed in the West regarding the ceremonies accompanying the administration of the sacraments. The violent destruction of local customs in this area would have caused both scandal among the people and murmuring among the clergy.

---

[2] Pope Paul V, Apostolic Constitution *Apostolicæ Sedi* (17 June 1614).

Nevertheless, what was bound to happen did in fact happen: the Ritual of Paul V was soon adopted by the majority of Western Churches. Those dioceses that retained the substance of their customs at least adopted the formulas for the administration of the sacraments, blessings, and so forth. The publication of this book completed the liturgical reform.

NEW REDACTION OF THE HYMNS

The majority of hymns were reworked and brought into conformity with metrical rules by order of Urban VIII. This Pope, who loved literature and successfully cultivated Latin poetry, could not tolerate the numerous inaccuracies found in most hymns of the Breviary. He lamented, as he said in his Brief, that the holy Fathers had drafted rather than perfected their hymns, and he believed that the dignity of divine worship urgently demanded a reform in this respect. Nevertheless, he did not deem it appropriate to undertake the work himself, instead entrusting it to four Jesuits.

The work of these four commissioners was bound to give rise to divergent opinions. If we might offer our own view, we would say first of all that it was a massively difficult task to correct the verses of others, and especially verses whose sense and words resounded in the memory of the whole Christian world. The correctors were asked to preserve the meter and meaning of each verse, to maintain the substance of the expressions, or, in a word, their particular color. In our opinion, they fulfilled this task as well as they could have. There are undoubtedly rare instances where they sacrificed too much for the sake of a classical purity.

Whatever our particular feelings, it cannot be denied that the adoption of hymns corrected in this way provoked considerable opposition. The principal reason for this opposition was the impossibility of correcting the old choir books without ruining them, and the unmusical construction of certain verses. One Belgian prelate, a pious and learned man, said of the reformed hymns: *Accessit latinitas et recessit pietas* ("Latinity entered and piety withdrew").

Roman cantors also quipped that the correctors were more familiar with the Muses than with music. It proved impossible to introduce these corrected hymns into St. Peter's Basilica. Likewise, the religious orders and monastic congregations preserved the old ones.

17

The Beginning of Liturgical Deviation in France

W E ARE NOW ENTERING INTO THE MOST delicate and distressing part of the story we have set out to relate. While the entire Latin Church remained faithful to the liturgical forms established by St. Pius V, in accordance with the wishes of the Council of Trent, a revolution was taking shape in the Church of France. In less than a century, we will see the gravest changes introduced into the texts of the Divine Office.

To fully elucidate the causes of this change, it is necessary to recall the history of France in the seventeenth century. It was during this period, which still displayed such magnificent remnants of ancient Catholic observances, and which saw the rise of so many pious institutions, that the seeds of Protestantism, secretly implanted into French customs, broke through the ground and produced various doctrines of disunion. Some of these, formally heterodox, were stigmatized under the name of Jansenism. Others, less daring, less distinct, and with implications more difficult to unravel, coalesced into a national system of Christianity, subsequently known, more or less accurately, as Gallicanism. The liturgy was to feel the impact of this movement.

THE NEED FOR AN AUTHORITATIVE COMMENTARY ON SCRIPTURE

Above, we identified as one of the characteristics of the anti-liturgical heresy a hatred for everything mysterious in worship, and especially the use of a sacred language unknown to the people.[1]

The French innovators of the seventeenth century were careful not to deviate from such a tried and true line of action. As early as 1660, Joseph de Voisin, a doctor of the Sorbonne, published a work in five volumes entitled: *The Roman Missal according to the Rule of the Council of Trent, translated into French with an explanation of all the Masses*, etc.[2]

The 1660 Assembly of the Clergy of France proved faithful, on this occasion, to those venerable traditions that should never have perished from our country. It condemned de Voisin's translation of the Missal into the vernacular, and to ensure that nothing was missing from the solemn

---

[1] See chapter 14.
[2] Joseph de Voisin, "Le Missel romain, selon le règlement du concile de Trente, traduit en français, avec l'explication de toutes les messes ..." (Paris, 1660).

condemnation of the recent attack against the sacred mystery of the liturgy, a Brief from Pope Alexander VII, dated 12 January 1661, lent its irrefutable authority to the Assembly's sentence.

The Pontiff expressed himself in this way:

> Certain sons of perdition, eager for novelties even unto the loss of souls and contemning ecclesiastical laws and practice, have recently succumbed to the madness of daring to translate into the vernacular French tongue the Roman Missal, written in Latin according to the usage approved in the Church for so many centuries . . . Thus, by their temerarious efforts, have they attempted to degrade the most sacred rites, by lowering the majesty given to them by the Latin language and exposing to the eyes of the vulgar the dignity of the divine mysteries . . . We perpetually condemn, reject, and prohibit the above Missal translated into French, forbidding all Christ's faithful to print, read, or retain it, on pain of excommunication . . . [3]

Today, all the faithful in France are able to subject to scrutiny the greatest mysteries of the Canon of the Mass, thanks to the countless translations that have been widely disseminated. In like manner, the Bible is made available to them in the vernacular from every direction. What are we to make of this state of affairs?

We maintain, along with all the councils of the last three centuries, that the use of translations of Sacred Scripture, if they are not accompanied by a gloss or notes drawn from the holy Fathers and the teachings of tradition, is illicit. So too, with the authority of the Holy See and the clergy of France, we hold that any translation of the Canon of the Mass that is not accompanied by a commentary that resolves difficulties is akin to prohibited versions of Scripture.

Could there really have been no alternative to this pure and simple translation of the Canon of the Mass? Was it necessary to disregard the prescriptions of the Holy See and the Council of Trent, when it would have been so straightforward to attach to the text a commentary anticipating any objections, a gloss preventing the eye of the profane and unlettered reader from piercing the shadows that safeguard the mysteries against his vain curiosity?

PREPARATORY ATTACKS — THE RITUAL OF ALET
The Ritual appeared to the anti-liturgical sect as an effective vehicle for promoting their doctrines. This book seemed particularly well-suited to serve the designs of the Jansenist party. One of the most zealous of its

---

[3] Pope Alexander VII, Bull *Ad aures nostras* (12 January 1661). A translation of the entire Bull by Gerhard Eger may be found at https://sicutincensum.wordpress.com/2018/02/07/lay-hand-missals-damnata-reprobata-et-interdicta/.

leaders, Nicholas Pavillon, the Bishop of Alet,[4] dared to insert into the Ritual that he published for his diocese in 1667 several of the maxims of Saint-Cyran and Antoine Arnauld on the administration of the sacraments.[5] This work was reviewed by Arnauld himself.

Without denying outright the power of the sacraments, the Jansenists succeeded in undermining their proper use by teaching that:

● the Eucharist is a "reward" for an advanced piety rather than a beginner's virtue;

● frequent confessions typically do more harm than good;

● absolution should regularly only be given after the performance of penance;

● it is appropriate to restore public penances.

Now, the doctrines that we have just cited were professed and applied in a hundred places in the Ritual of Alet, although extreme care was taken not to use excessively strong language, so as not to offend the Apostolic See. Nonetheless, Rome did not fail to detect the venom with which the enemies of the true faith had poisoned one of the most sacred sources of the liturgy.

As soon as the Ritual of Alet appeared, Pope Clement IX signaled his apostolic zeal by issuing a solemn condemnation of this pernicious book. In his famous Brief of 9 April 1668, the Pope expresses himself in these terms:

> Last year in Paris, a book was published in the French language under the title: *Roman Ritual of Pope Paul V according to the use of the diocese of Alet, with instructions and rubrics in French,*[6] in which are contained not only many things contrary to the Roman Ritual published by order of Our predecessor Paul V, but also certain doctrines and propositions which are false, singular, perilous in practice, erroneous, opposed and repugnant to the custom commonly received in the Church and to ecclesiastical constitutions . . . We condemn, by the force of the present document, this French book entitled *Roman Ritual.* We reprove and forbid it, and will it to be held as condemned, reproved and forbidden.

THE BREVIARY OF VIENNE

The Breviary of this period that opened the broadest path for the innovators was the one published in 1678 by the Archbishop of Vienne, Henri de Villars. It was introduced to the diocese as an Office that enjoyed great superiority over the ancient one, given that it replaced all the antiphons and Gregorian responsories not drawn from Sacred Scripture with biblical passages that had never before featured into the liturgy. The structures of

---

[4] The old bishopric was near Limoux, in Aude.

[5] The two foremost Jansenist theologians in seventeenth-century France. Saint-Cyran was eventually imprisoned, and Arnauld fled into exile.

[6] *Rituel romain du pape Paul V, à l'usage du diocèse d'Alet, avec les instructions et les rubriques en François* (Paris, 1667).

the novel design had even necessitated the abandonment of many other actually scriptural liturgical pieces which the old Breviary had drawn from St. Gregory's Responsorial. For the most part, the lessons were neither those of the 1522 Breviary of Vienne nor those of the Roman Breviary of St. Pius V.

The work was undertaken outside the diocese, far from Viennese traditions, in Paris. In this city, Henri de Villars delegated the task to Antoine Argoud, the dean of Vienne's metropolitan church, giving him as assistants Jacques de Sainte-Beuve, infamous in the annals of Jansenism, and Sieur Du Tronchet, a canon of the Sainte-Chapelle. These three men had the care and responsibility of the entire enterprise, and after three years their work was ready to be presented to the Archbishop of Vienne, who approved and published it.

Before long, a Missal was issued from the same source. This is not the place to dwell on details. It should be noted, however, that the enthusiasm produced by the new liturgy in the diocese of Vienne was not quite universal, so that twenty years later most ecclesiastics in the diocese of Vienne were still reciting the Roman Breviary rather than that of Henri de Villars.

THE BREVIARY OF HARLAY: PROTOTYPE OF COMING REFORMS
But no Breviary, both in terms of the circumstances of its reform and its governing principles, presents a more instructive history or a more remarkable system than the one given to his diocese by François de Harlay, Archbishop of Paris, in 1680. It is with the publication of this Breviary, far more renowned than that of Vienne, that we must place the true beginning of the epoch which saw the reversal of the work of Charlemagne and the Roman Pontiffs.

It is true that Harlay's Breviary contained a number of passages expressly directed against the doctrine of the "Five Propositions."[7] This archbishop, like many of his fellow prelates, while waging an unrelenting war against the Holy See and its doctrines, professed a strong aversion for Jansen's doctrine on grace. Such prelates could make use of Jansenist party members when they needed to, but they knew how to contain them.

We shall make the following observations about François de Harlay's work:

First, the title of the book was simply this: *Breviarium Parisiense*, without the usual addition found in all editions since 1584: *Ad formam sacrosancti concilii Tridentini restitutum* ("restored according to the form of the holy Council of Trent"). Thus, the link between the diocesan Breviaries of France and the Roman Breviary was broken for the Church of Paris. Before long, they would have a liturgy that was no longer Roman! What

---

[7] The "Five Propositions" constitute the summary of Jansenist doctrine. They are drawn from Cornelius Jansen's book entitled *Augustinus*. Harlay's Breviary was thus hostile to Jansenism, being "directed against the doctrine of the Five Propositions.'"

unknown territory were they about to enter? Truly, this omission on the very frontispiece of this book was telling, and it foreshadowed much of what was to be found within the work.

Indeed, apart from the Psalter, which remained in line with that of the Roman Church, a great number of lessons, homilies, and antiphons were changed in the Proper of the Season. Almost the entire Office of the Holy Trinity was reformed, and the lessons for the octave of the Corpus Christi, so lovely in the Roman Breviary, were replaced by others.

The Proper of the Saints contained even more discrepancies. The Commons had been reworked in a hundred places, and featured many new antiphons and responsories.

Now, if one asks whence these modern texts came from, which replaced St. Gregory's Responsorial after it had been in use for a thousand years, one will find that they were exclusively drawn from Sacred Scripture. The words consecrated by tradition had had to give way to these biblical verses selected by modern and suspect hands. They could not suffer the use of non-scriptural texts even for a two-line antiphon. The sectarians who advocated the exclusive use of Scripture in divine worship had thus gained this initial advantage. With a little more effort and another fifty years of patience, what remained of the traditional texts in Harlay's Breviary of 1680 would disappear as well.

Shall we hear the vain excuse that they made when asked to justify so many audacities? They—who had expunged so many miraculous accounts and extraordinary deeds of the saints (no doubt for the greater glory of these friends of God)—were heard boasting of these amputations. They claimed merit for substituting purely historical and questionable stories with passages from the holy Fathers which, they argued, confirmed the dogmas that were attacked by the heretics, particularly the cult and intercession of the saints. It is a strange preoccupation to consider the Breviary and other liturgical books, not as repositories of pious traditions, but as an arsenal of controversy, a mere supplement to the treatises studied at school.

Considering now the way in which the cult of the Blessed Virgin was treated in Harlay's Breviary, we see that it was greatly diminished. First, the blessings of the Office *De Beata*, which were proper to the Church of Paris, always so devoted to its glorious patroness, had been suppressed. The Little Chapters of the same Office, whereby the Roman Church applies to Mary several passages from the Sapiential Books relating to divine Wisdom—a tradition so ancient and so dear to piety—were also sacrificed.

Henceforth, in the Breviary of Paris, the Office of the Virgin no longer contained this antiphon that was so fearful to all heretics: *Gaude, Maria Virgo, cunctas hæreses sola interemisti in universo mundo* ("Rejoice, O Virgin Mary, for thou alone hast put to death every heresy over all the earth"); nor that other one, no less venerable, in which the Church implores Mary's help to thwart the stratagems of error against the glory of the Queen of Heaven: *Dignare me laudare te, Virgo sacrata; da mihi virtutem contra hostes tuos* ("Vouchsafe that I may praise thee, O sacred Virgin. Give me power over thine enemies").

In most Western and Eastern Churches alike, the solemnity of 25 March, the cornerstone of the liturgical year, was called "the Annunciation of the Blessed Virgin." By this, the Church wished to bear witness to her faith in and love for Our Lady, who gave her consent to the great mystery of the Incarnation of the Word. The commission that produced Harlay's Breviary made bold to oppose this manifestation of faith and of gratitude. No doubt out of fear of "indiscreet devotion," it decreed that this solemnity would henceforth be exclusively a feast of Our Lord under the title: *Annuntiatio Dominica* ("The Lord's Annunciation").

Let us now turn to the authority of the Roman Pontiff. First of all, François de Harlay decreed that the feast of St. Peter should be relegated to the rank of "minor solemnities," which was soon imitated in more than sixty dioceses. The "legends" [*i.e., the traditions*] that recounted the acts of the Roman Pontiffs' authority in antiquity were modified under the specious excuse of preserving the Fathers' own words.

The spirit that animated Archbishop Harlay was particularly evident in the suppression of an ancient and venerable piece, which rightly offended his Gallican sensibilities: *Tu es pastor ovium, princeps Apostolorum; tibi tradidit Deus omnia regna mundi: Et ideo tibi traditæ sunt claves regni cœlorum* ("Thou art the shepherd of the sheep, the Prince of the Apostles; to thee God hast given all the kingdoms of the world: And thus the keys of the Kingdom of Heaven have been given into thy possession").

HARLAY'S MISSAL

After publishing his Breviary in 1680, François de Harlay set about reforming the Missal in the same manner as he had the Breviary. The commission mentioned above continued its work, and in November 1684 the archbishop was able to announce to his diocese, with a pastoral letter, the gift of a new Missal worthy of the Church of Paris.

Before considering this further, let us make some observations that also apply to Harlay's Breviary. We agree that the Archbishop of Paris had the right to make appropriate reforms to the books of his diocese, provided that:

⊛ they were made in the spirit of tradition, which is the principal element of the liturgy;

⊛ in his emendations, the Roman part of these books was respected;

⊛ the reforms were particular applications of the principles followed throughout antiquity in matters of liturgy.

But we cannot help but vigorously protest against the Protestant maxim which had not been admitted in the preface to Harlay's Breviary, but which was finally stated in that of his Missal. There, François de Harlay says: "All the words that are to be chanted we have drawn exclusively from the Holy Scriptures, with the conviction that nothing could be more appropriate."

This was the same principle adopted by Luther in his own liturgical reform, when he said: "We do not blame those who wish to retain the Introits of the Apostles, the Virgin, and the other saints, since these three Introits are taken from the Psalms and other passages of Scripture."[8]

In any case, François de Harlay undertook and completed this work. He expelled from the chanted part of the Missal all those texts — so solemn, moving, poetic, mysterious, and replete with dogma — in which the Church lent her voice of tradition to the faithful, to exalt the majesty of God and the sanctity of His mysteries.

In this general overview of the Harlay's Missal, we are far from having described all its audacities. Beyond them, his Missal also contained the most peculiar contradictions. According to the plan of reform traced out in his pastoral letter, all the chanted parts of the Missal should have been taken from Holy Scripture, yet he retained the proses or sequences, which are indeed among the parts of the Mass meant to be chanted. Moreover, new sequences were composed, such as those for the Ascension, *Solemnis hæc festivitas*, and for the Annunciation, *Humani generis*. It seems, then, that the reformers only feared the "words of men" when they lacked control over them.

In spite of these shameful and criminal injuries inflicted upon the Roman liturgy in the Parisian books, it is certain that these mutilations did not affect even a twentieth part of the Gregorian Antiphonary. One can still say, therefore, that under the episcopates of François de Harlay and his successor Cardinal de Noailles, the liturgy of Paris was and remained the Roman liturgy. The unity established by the Council of Trent and St. Pius V, even though it had suffered, had not yet perished.

However, the attacks François de Harlay levelled against the integrity of the liturgy, along with the pernicious principles that had prevailed in his reform, were all set to bear fruit in the near future. Indeed, there is no stopping on such a path: one must either advance or retreat.

THE BREVIARY OF CLUNY

The Abbey of Cluny and the small congregation dependent upon it, called the Order of Cluny, were chosen by the innovators to test out a comprehensive liturgical reform worthy of France.

At this time, Cardinal de Bouillon was the Order of Cluny's abbot general. This prelate, so regrettably infamous for his laxity of morals and colossal vanity, would become answerable to the Church, among other things, for being the first to eradicate the Roman liturgy in France. He chose the holy

---

[8] Cited through Pierre Le Brun, *Explication de la Messe*, 4:13.

and venerable Basilica of Cluny as the setting for the inauguration of a set of Offices totally foreign to the Gregorian books.

The Order of Cluny had always maintained its ancient liturgical practices. This congregation never adopted Paul V's Monastic Breviary, which had not been made obligatory for all monasteries. We will therefore leave aside the question of legality, while observing that, even if nothing prohibited the reform of the monastic books of the Cluniac Order, the total and violent destruction of the entire corpus of Gregorian Offices can scarcely be regarded as a legitimate reform, and can by no means claim the character and the rights of one.

As we learn from the most eminent Abbot of Cluny's pastoral letter, it was during the Order's chapter held in 1676 that a resolution was passed to reform the monastic Breviary of Cluny. This task was entrusted to the care of Dom Paul Rabusson, underchamberlain of the Abbey, as well as to the treasurer, Dom Claude de Vert. This was precisely the same period in which François de Harlay was carrying out the reform of the Parisian Breviary, and since Harlay's reform was the expression of principles that were then molesting the Church of France, it was natural to expect that some of its applications would be found in this new Breviary of Cluny. According to a contemporary writer, these two Cluniac monks "had close connections, during the course of their work, with the commissioners writing the new Breviary of Paris, and they adopted many things from the latter into their Breviary that they took pride in."[9]

First of all, the principle — so dear to the anti-liturgists, laid down but not fully applied in Harlay's Breviary — of using only Sacred Scripture in the Divine Office, was proclaimed in the pastoral letter and applied in its full extent to all Offices, whether of the Proper of the Season or of the Proper and Commons of the Saints. Thus, a significant part of St. Gregory's Responsorial was eliminated outright, but in order to make the destruction even more complete, the innovators who so ardently sought to make Sacred Scripture prevail over tradition reached the point of sacrificing — without regard for antiquity, and thus at the risk of revealing to the eyes of all their desire for upheaval — nearly all the countless antiphons and responsories that the Gregorian books had drawn from Holy Scripture itself. They replaced them with verses of their own choosing, intending to form a sort of mosaic of the Old and New Testaments, according to the overarching plan their minds had devised. And these men still claimed to honor antiquity, lying to themselves.

After hunting down traditions in the antiphons and responsories, the commissioners of the Breviary of Cluny — still following in the footsteps of François de Harlay, yet moving in such a way as to far surpass

---

[9] Jean-Baptiste Thiers, *Observations sur le nouveau bréviaire de Cluni* (Brussels, 1702), vol. I, p. 94.

them — likewise found a way to discard the legends of the saints entirely. Not a single one was spared, and passages from the holy Fathers with a more or less historical tone were fixed in their place.

Ever faithful to the system they had invented *a priori*, and to which either antiquity or contemporary practices of the Church were made to yield in all cases, they concocted, in order to lower the feasts of the Blessed Virgin, a class of five feasts of Our Lord, which would take the highest place of importance at the head of the calendar. Had they confined themselves to the three ancient feasts of Easter, Pentecost and Christmas, they would have remained within the bounds of ecclesiastical tradition, but in their desire to equate Epiphany and Ascension with the first three, and to place these five solemnities in a class in which no other feast, not even the solemnity of the Corpus Christi, could find a place, they exposed their mania for innovation and at the same time the glaring contradictions with their solemn pretensions to knowledge of antiquity.

The Parisian reform had already had a wide impact, awakening a taste for novelty. But it was left behind the moment the innovators had resolved to cross the limits imposed by tradition. A model was necessary for all the creators of liturgy that this country was about to produce. These champions of liturgical perfection needed a banner. The Breviary of Cluny was everything that they could have desired: everything in it was novel.

THE HYMNS OF SANTEUL

We should already have mentioned Jean-Baptiste Santeul, a canon regular of Saint-Victor, in connection with Harlay's Breviary, for which he provided several hymns, but as he composed a far greater number for the Cluny Breviary, we have postponed mentioning him until now.

We have already cited St. Bernard's famous letter detailing the qualities that must be present in both the composer of a liturgical work and the work itself: "In the august solemnities, it is not fitting to hear new or frivolous things, but rather authentic and ancient ones, which edify the Church and savor of ecclesiastical gravity..."[10]

Woe, then, to those who have expelled from the liturgy the age-old hymns composed by men of authority, such as St. Ambrose, St. Gregory, Prudentius, and the like, to replace their truly authentic works with those that savor of frivolity, to replace their ancient works with novelty, to replace their words which savor of ecclesiastical gravity with echoes of the profane Muse!

The authors of the Cluny Breviary proclaimed, as the fundamental principle of their liturgical reform, the need to banish all human words from ecclesiastical books, replacing them with texts taken from Sacred Scripture.

---

[10] See the end of chapter II.

One might therefore have been inclined to think that the removal of the venerable hymns that the Western Church sang for so many centuries was merely a conscientious application of this rigorous principle, but one would be deceived. The "human words" of the holy Fathers were replaced by the all-too-human words of Jean-Baptiste Santeul. And yet, in their docility or distraction, the public has failed to notice how contradictory is the assertion placed at the beginning of all Breviaries since that of Cluny, that "nothing remains lacking in authority, nothing that is not drawn from the pure sources of the Holy Books."

Furthermore, are we sure that Santeul's hymns are the human words of the canon of Saint-Victor exclusively? If we are to believe Goujet and the infamous Mésenguy, well informed about the fabrication of the novel Liturgies,[11] Nicolas Letourneux, the chief architect of Harlay's Breviary, provided the material and Santeul wrote the verses. Thus these two men — Letourneux, notorious for supporting heretics and the author of a work censured by the Church,[12] Santeul, echoing him — were the figures behind what the Cluny Breviary substituted for the Catholic liturgical tradition . . .

Now, let us see how one of his contemporary admirers, Jean de La Bruyère, portrays Santeul:

> Imagine a man who is easy-going, gentle, accommodating, and approachable; and then suddenly violent, angry, impetuous, and capricious. Picture a simple man, ingenuous, credulous, playful, and flighty, a child with gray hair. But allow him to collect himself, or rather to give himself over to the genius that acts within him — I dare say without his having any part in it, and as if without his knowledge. What verve! What sublime flights! What imagery! What mastery of Latin! You might well ask if I speak of one and the same man. "Yes, one and the same, of Theodas, and him alone."[13] He shouts, he grows agitated, he rolls on the ground and gets up again, he twirls about, he roars, and from the midst of this tempest, a light shines forth that gleams and gladdens. Let us speak plainly: talks like a fool but thinks like a wise man. He speaks absurdly of true things and foolishly of sensible and reasonable things. It is astonishing to see common sense blossom from this bosom of buffoonery, amidst grimaces and contortions.
>
> What more can I add? He speaks and acts better than he knows, as though there were within him two souls unacquainted with one another, independent of each other, acting in turn or performing entirely separate functions. This remarkable portrait would be incomplete if I omitted to add that he is at one and the

---

[11] Both notorious Jansenist clerics. Claude-Pierre Goujet, *Bibliothèque ecclésiastique du dix-huitième siècle* (Paris, 1736), vol. 3, p. 474; François-Philippe Mésenguy, *Lettres sur les nouveaux bréviaires* (Paris, 1735).

[12] Letourneux was a cleric closely tied to the Jansenist milieu, and his liturgical commentary, *L'année chrétienne*, was posthumously condemned by Rome.

[13] La Bruyère's nickname for Santeul.

same time insatiably eager for praise, ready to fly in the face of his critics, and yet at heart docile enough to profit by their censures. I am beginning to persuade myself that I have been describing two completely different people. It might even be possible to find yet a third man in this Theodas, for he is an excellent fellow.[14]

This is not quite how history portrays the hymnographers of the Latin Church, St. Ambrose and St. Gregory, or those of the Greek Church, St. Andrew of Crete, St. John Damascene, St. Joseph, and the like. The Spirit who rested on these divine men had removed from them all resemblance to those human poets inspired by profane frenzy.

Santeul's elegant Latin and classical genius are extolled, and at the same time the degenerate style of the Fathers of the Church and the barbaric language of the mystics and medieval saints' lives are pitied, which shows that some still argue for the superiority of the ancients or moderns. For our part, we believe, along with many others, that the Latin of St. Ambrose, St. Augustine, Prudentius, St. Leo, St. Gelasius, St. Gregory, St. Bernard, and the like, is not the same language as the Latin of Horace, Cicero, Tacitus, Pliny, or Seneca. To attempt to revert the language of the Church to the pagan forms of those writers of the Augustan age is foolishness, if not barbaric impropriety. Santeul's hymns, and those like them, are simply one of a thousand instances that one might cite when recounting the deplorable history of the rebirth of paganism in the morals and literature of Christian societies of the West.

THE MASSES OF HENRI DUMONT

We should not fail to mention a skillful composer of plainchant from the period that occupies us, whose work has acquired a merited acclaim in France. Henri Dumont, born in Liège in 1610, the organist at Saint-Paul in Paris and one of the *maîtres de la musique* of the Chapelle Royale, proved himself a faithful guardian of the ecclesiastical traditions in music. He courageously objected to Louis XIV's order to add orchestral accompaniments to motets, citing the decrees of the Council of Trent. He died in 1684, bequeathing us several Masses in plainchant, one of which, written in the first mode, is chanted in all the churches of France on solemn feasts. At a time when the Gregorian tradition had all but perished, it was difficult to produce greater effects with plainchant than those that Dumont achieved in this composition, which a hundred and fifty years of popularity have not yet worn out.

We limit ourselves to these few lines about ecclesiastical chant in the second half of the seventeenth century. We must mention, however, that apart from the plainchant with which we are principally concerned, a large

---

[14] Jean de La Bruyère, *Les characters* (Paris, 1688), ch. 12.

number of pieces of the kind known as *chant figuré* or *plain-chant musical* were produced at this time, a bastard genre which we will have occasion to mention again, and which constitutes the most deplorable form of music to which a human ear can be condemned.

During the second half of the seventeenth century, the liturgy in France began to be governed by principles entirely opposed to those that had been, and continued to be, upheld in the other provinces of the Catholic Church. These novel principles, introduced under the guise of improvement, are in fact identical to many of those we have identified above as forming the anti-liturgical system.

1. The *disregard for tradition in the forms of divine worship* was evident in the deliberate suppression of ancient Gregorian pieces, the ancient calendar of feasts and saints, and so on, from the Breviary and Missal of François de Harlay and from the books of Cluny, with no regard for antiquity.

2. The intention to *replace formulas in ecclesiastical style with readings from Sacred Scripture* was similarly manifested in the approach of the editors of these same liturgical books, who sought to thoroughly reshape the Divine Office basing it exclusively on biblical passages.

3. Despite this, the correctors of the new Breviaries did not hesitate to *fabricate and introduce new pieces of their own composition.*

4. They *contradicted their own principles*, speaking of antiquity while creating modern pieces, and of the word of God while introducing human words.

5. This innovation resulted in an appalling *diminution of that spirit of prayer* which is called unction, in Catholicism;

6. The weakening of the veneration of the Blessed Virgin and the Saints is, so to speak, the main characteristic and openly admitted goal of the liturgical reform of the seventeenth century.

7. There was a marked movement towards *translating Sacred Scripture and the liturgy into the vernacular.*

8. The changes were introduced into the liturgy with the intention of *undermining the authority of the Roman Pontiff.*

Let us add, for the sake of completeness and clarification, that the Jansenists (and consequently, heretics) found an entry into the sanctuary; that several bishops declared themselves favorable to this work, despite the condemnation of the Holy See; that notorious Jansenists were part of the commissions that wrote the Breviaries of Paris and Cluny.

18

The Liturgy During the First Half of the Eighteenth Century

HE ATTACKS MADE ON THE LITURGY during the second half of the seventeenth century should give the reader a foretaste of the scandals that lie ahead in the period we have just begun to study. The story unfolds entirely in France, the only country that felt the need to challenge the liturgical unity established in the sixteenth century. All the other churches of the West had remained faithful to the traditions of divine worship, and their voices, in unison with those of Rome, their Mother and Teacher, continue to resound with the noble and melodious chants of the Gregorian Antiphonary and Responsorial.

First, there was the great event that resonated throughout the eighteenth century: the publication of *Réflexions morales sur le Nouveau Testament* by Fr. Pasquier Quesnel of the French Oratory. This manifesto of the Jansenist sect inevitably included principles that would affect the liturgy. Indeed, it contained Antoine Arnauld's doctrines on the reading of Sacred Scripture, which had already directly led to the translation of the New Testament into French published in Mons in 1667, as well as those of the Missal by de Voisin and of the Breviary by Letourneux, and indirectly to the audacious project of replacing all the chanted texts in the liturgy with passages from the Bible.

RECITATION OF THE CANON ALOUD

The anti-liturgical sect devised quite an effective way of leading the faithful to desire the use of the vernacular in the Divine Offices: namely, ceasing to observe the secret of the sacred mysteries by introducing the recitation of the Canon aloud. To those who are indifferent or unaccustomed to recognizing the importance of the liturgy, this change may seem trivial, but it contained within it the seed of a total revolution. As soon as the people begin to hear the Canon recited aloud, they will demand that it is read in French, and once they hear the liturgy and the Holy Scriptures read in the vernacular, they will begin to form their own judgments on the teachings of the Faith on controversial subjects.

Indeed, if the people had to choose between Rome and Jansen, the followers of this Bishop of Ypres were confident they could sway them in favor of his doctrine through their influence, preaching, and sophistry. This was precisely the same strategy employed by Luther, Calvin, and their first followers, which had proven highly effective with the masses. Therefore, the Council of Trent saw fit to protect the faithful from such seduction by issuing a twofold anathema, both against the partisans of the vernacular in the Divine Offices and against those who advocated for the recitation of the Canon aloud:

> If anyone says that the rite of the Roman Church, according to which a part of the Canon and the words of consecration are pronounced in a low voice, is to be condemned; or that the Mass ought to be celebrated only in the vulgar tongue; let him be anathema. [1]

Already during the time of the sixteenth-century Reformation, there were certain doctors who — partly motivated by their love of novelty and partly out of a blind and all-too-common hope of attracting the heretics back into the Church by softening Catholic doctrine and practices — believed that they could put an end to the success of the Protestants' brazen preaching by criticizing the venerable custom of reciting the Canon of the Mass in secret. Two of these were Gerhard Lorich and George Cassander. What these two theologians had conceived, with a praiseworthy intention, no doubt, but one that was badly misguided, was exhumed and adopted in the eighteenth century by the Jansenist sect to serve both as a means of external attack against the authority of the liturgy and as a rallying sign among their followers.

It was not long before a major scandal broke out on this subject in the Church of Meaux. François Ledieu, a cathedral canon and one-time private secretary of Bossuet, who was charged to oversee the printing of the new Missal of Meaux, which appeared in 1709, dared on his own authority to settle the issue with the most glaring of innovations. In defiance of the integrity of the liturgy, he introduced a red ℞ [*which means Response*] before the *Amen* at the end of the formulas of the Consecration and communion, and placed the same red ℞ before each occurrence of *Amen* already present in the Canon. His aim, as is easy to see, was to compel the priest to recite the Canon aloud, so that the people, or at least the clerics, could respond *Amen* in the places marked by this ℞. One recognizes, in these subtle and ingenious methods, the cunning of the party of which François Ledieu was then a more or less intelligent representative.

But God had established an orthodox shepherd over the see of Meaux, who wasted no time in repudiating the audacious work that had been associated with his name. Henri de Thiard de Bissy, Bossuet's immediate successor and a steadfast opponent of Jansenism, issued a vigorous decree (dated 1710) forbidding, on pain of suspension *a divinis*, the use of the new Missal published under his name until the corrections that he specified had removed every last trace of the scandalous innovations that had

---

[1] Council of Trent, Session 22, can. 9.

tainted the book. He pointed out that these innovations were "contrary to the immemorial usage, not only of the diocese of Meaux, but of the whole Church, and that they tended to promote the practice of saying the Canon of the Holy Mass aloud."

The rights of orthodoxy were also upheld by Pierre Le Lorrain, better known as the Abbé de Vallemont. In a work that was rather poorly written, but nonetheless notable for the unquestionable learning that the author displayed, he demonstrated with clear evidence the temerity of the innovators who sought to impose their system against one of the most ancient and venerable rules of the Church. His book is entitled *Du secret des mystères, ou l'Apologie de la rubrique des missels.*

But the Abbé de Vallemont's book was not sufficient to end the controversy. It is true that, in the eyes of the Church's faithful sons, the matter had long been settled by the canon of the Council of Trent and the express rubric of the Roman Missal; nonetheless, it was fitting that a well-composed book should be written on a subject of such importance. The opinions of the two most illustrious Benedictine liturgists of the time, Dom Mabillon and Dom Martène, were already well known. They openly excoriated the new system with all the authority of their vast erudition on the subject of sacred rites.

Father Pierre Le Brun, of the French Oratory, who was already renowned for his liturgical scholarship and irreproachable orthodoxy, also entered the fray. In 1725, following his fine work on the Mass,[2] he published a three-hundred-page dissertation on the practice of reciting part of the Mass prayers in silence in all churches and in all ages. The learned Oratorian treated the question from every angle, examining in great detail and discussing with the utmost success the same evidence drawn from antiquity by the defenders of saying the Canon aloud, who alleged that saying it in silence was itself an innovation. Suffice it to say that Fr. Le Brun's work not only won the approbation of scholars, but also of all the orthodox priests in the Church of France at the time.

THE RESPONSE OF LANGUET, ARCHBISHOP OF SENS

Let us speak now discuss a crucial event that occurred only a few years after the publication of the Missal of Meaux. After Jacques-Bénigne Bossuet, Bishop of Troyes,[3] had announced the publication of a new Missal to his clergy and the faithful of his diocese, the Cathedral Chapter assembled and resolved, by a majority of seventeen votes to five, to lodge an appeal for abuse with their metropolitan, the Archbishop of Sens. The see of the illustrious Church of Sens was then occupied by Jean-Joseph Languet de

---

[2] Namely, the *Explication littéral, historique, et dogmatique des prières et des cérémonies de la Messe*, cited above.

[3] A nephew of the more famous Bossuet († 1704), the "Eagle of Meaux."

Gergy, a zealous prelate who stood as a bulwark for the House of Israel, and whose name will forever be a source of consolation for the Church.

The 1736 Missal of Troyes included, among other rubrics, the instruction that the Canon of the Mass was to be recited, not "secretly" (*secreto, submissa voce*), as in earlier Missals, but simply "in a lower voice" (*submissiori voce*) than the other parts of the Mass. The author did not dare to insert the red ℞, which had proven so unsuccessful in Meaux; furthermore, it would have been too bold to formulate an entirely explicit rubric. The party thus chose the words *submissiori voce* to replace *submissa voce*.

The Missal of Troyes had also suppressed the ancient custom of reciting the *Confiteor*, the *Misereatur*, and *Indulgentiam* prayers, and even the priest's words *Ecce Agnus Dei* and *Domine, non sum dignus*, in the administration of communion of the faithful.

Against current Church practice, observed even in the Pontifical Masses, the Missal of Troyes abrogated the rubric that particularly prescribes that the priest celebrating a Solemn Mass must privately recite the prayers and readings sung in choir.

Another rubric of the Missal of Troyes, still more scandalous than those mentioned above, bore witness to the desire to abolish in the diocese's churches the practice of placing a crucifix and candles on the altar. Instead, it established that one should place on the altar only what was required for the sacrifice, i.e., the chalice, paten and host.

Finally, following the example of the Harlay's Missal, the Missal of this Bishop of Troyes suppressed all the chants not taken from Sacred Scripture, replacing them with a manifest Jansenist agenda.

Such was the Missal of Troyes, a work well-suited, as one can readily see, to ignite the zeal of such a steadfast guardian of orthodoxy as Archbishop Languet. He gladly accepted the Chapter of Troyes's appeal and replied with a pastoral letter full of learning and vigor, soon followed by two others, addressed in general to the clergy subject to the jurisdiction of the Archbishop of Sens.

This prelate began by astutely pointing out the twofold tendency of innovators in matters of liturgy: "There are some," he said, "and it is a deplorable thing, who dare to introduce changes into the sacred rites, sometimes to revive (so they claim) the usages of antiquity, and sometimes to give greater perfection to new usages."[4]

Turning to the rubric of the Troyes Missal which favors the recitation of the Canon aloud, the Archbishop of Sens expresses himself as follows:

> There can be no doubt that the author of this Missal intended
> to introduce the recitation of the Canon and orations called
> "Secret" aloud. Although he has not professed this openly, he

---

4 Jean-Joseph Languet de Gergy, *Mandatum et Pastoralis institutio de novo Missali Trecensi*, in *Opera Omnia* (Sens, 1752), vol. 2, p. 1218.

has subtly and skillfully endeavored to insinuate this practice, which, for some forty years now, seems to have been introduced into our churches by certain priests without sanction or authority, and which is particularly prevalent among those who have shown themselves to be indocile and disobedient to the Apostolic Constitutions.[5]

The prelate, after highlighting the troubling nature of the words *submissiori voce*, and denouncing the fact that a large number of priests in the diocese of Troyes took advantage of this rubric to recite the Canon aloud, vigorously combats the Jansenists' principles on this matter.

The Archbishop of Sens then cites all the Missals in use today in the Latin Church and the Roman Pontifical itself, which prescribes the recitation of the *Confiteor* during the administration of communion to all ordinands. He demonstrates that this custom of confessing one's sins with a liturgical formula before receiving communion, although not of the very earliest antiquity, was suggested, at least in spirit, by Origen and St. John Chrysostom. He argues that, in any case, once a custom is established and universally observed in the Church, a Catholic must consider it as instituted by the Holy Spirit.[6] If it were necessary to suppress those things in the liturgy which are not of the earliest antiquity, we would therefore be constrained to abolish the common recitation of the *Gloria in excelsis*, which, in the time of St. Gregory, was recited by the bishop alone; to suppress the use of the Constantinopolitan Creed, which was only introduced into the Roman Church under Pope Benedict VIII; to celebrate Mass at suppertime, as in the time of the Apostles; to restore the Mass to the Rite described by St. Justin in his Second Apology, and so forth.[7]

Languet then turns his attention to another rubric from the Missal of Troyes, which suppresses the longstanding practice in the Latin Church whereby the celebrant of Solemn Mass is required to read at the altar the prayers and readings that take place in the choir.[8] Turning then to the Missal of Troyes's reprehensible attempt to suppress the use of the crucifix and candles on the altar during Mass, Languet denounces the Calvinist instincts so gracelessly expressed in this rubric.

The indefatigable prelate goes on to attack the Bishop of Troyes's changes to the Roman Missal, the suppression of Gregorian formulas, and the

---

[5] Ibid., 1229.

[6] Ibid., 1226.

[7] Ibid., 1227.

[8] In the Tridentine Rite, the priest at Solemn Mass reads all the propers and lessons at the altar in a low voice, even though they are sung by the choir or read by the deacon and subdeacon. The 1960 rubrical reform of John XXIII suppressed the practice of the priest reading the lessons chanted by the deacon and subdeacon; the 1964 reforms eliminated the practice of the priest reading the Introit, Gradual, and other propers sung by the choir. In many places where the Tridentine Rite is still celebrated, the pre-1960 practice has returned.

arbitrary or malicious substitution of certain passages from Sacred Scripture for antiphons formed from traditional words, or even borrowed, from the earliest antiquity, from Scripture itself: "This venerable antiquity," he says,

> which the author of the New Missal prides himself on imitating, he tramples underfoot in the composition of the new Masses he substitutes for the ancient ones. This proves that the author, in the novelties he has sought to introduce, has chosen antiquity as a pretext and not as a rule . . . This author has not understood what confirmation the orthodox faith derives from the antiquity and the universality of our sacred liturgies. And yet the liturgies that from the earliest centuries of the Church, even long before St. Gregory, are read throughout the Church, are so many precious monuments of tradition which support and confirm our belief. It is their testimony that the Catholic faith employs as a weapon against innovators; this faith which is one, perpetual, and universal.[9]

In another pastoral letter on the Missal of Troyes, the Archbishop of Sens writes:

> Is not tradition also a kind of word of God, a rule of faith? But in what monument does this holy tradition appear to us more surely and more effectively than in those prayers composed in the most remote antiquity, employed by the most universal custom, preserved in the most constant uniformity? . . . Can we find in the Holy Scriptures the dogma of the perpetual virginity of the Blessed Virgin as clearly as in the prayers of the Church, and especially in those words which we read in the liturgical books of St. Gregory: *Post partum, virgo, inviolata permansisti* ("After His birth, O Virgin, thou didst remain inviolate")? Is it not in the liturgy that we find proof of the Church's tradition regarding the canonicity of the holy books themselves, and on a great many other points?
>
> Furthermore, it is often the ideas of an individual mind that have been disguised under the texts of Scripture, and it is these that have been substituted for the ancient prayers. Indeed, the words are taken from Sacred Scripture; but their arbitrary *accommodation* to certain feasts, or to the praises of certain saints, is the product of personal ingenuity . . .
>
> But the people who will read these texts in the Mass, who will chant them, who will learn them by heart, who will soon perhaps see them translated into the vernacular, will not have your commentary before their eyes. What is obscure and difficult in these passages will contaminate the minds of the faithful with false principles which will seem to them to be based on the texts themselves, and when it pleases an innovator to mutilate the texts

---

[9] Languet de Gergy, *Mandatum et Pastoralis institutio*, 1251.

in order to spread and confirm his errors, he will find the people already prepared and ready to lend an ear and faithful assent.[10]

RATIONALIST EXPLANATIONS OF LITURGICAL SYMBOLISM

We shall now address the new attack made on the liturgy by the famous editor of the Cluny Breviary: Dom Claude de Vert.

It is a principle in every religion that its ceremonies supplement its texts of worship. The Christian religion, which bases its means of salvation for the faithful on the Sacraments, proclaims the necessity and importance of sacred rites as divinely instituted, containing the grace they signify. It sees in the matter and form of these Sacraments external circumstances not chosen arbitrarily or for convenience, but imposed with the direct aim of signifying and operating at the same time.

Nevertheless, the anti-liturgical sect has gone after nothing more violently than it has this Christian symbolism, which confers mystical value upon a gesture or a material object, spiritualizing visible creation and magnificently accomplishing the goal of the Incarnation, sublimely expressed in that admirable liturgical phrase: *Ut dum visibiliter Deum cognoscimus, per hunc in invisibilium amorem rapiamur* ("As we recognize in Him God made visible, we may be rapt up through Him in love of invisible things").[11] When this heresy has been able to act directly, it has crushed every kind of symbolism.

It was easy to foresee that the same movement which had overturned tradition in the Missals and Breviaries of Paris, Cluny and Troyes, which had nearly corrupted the Canon of the Mass in the Missal of Meaux, which was pushing for the translation of the Bible and liturgical books into the vernacular, which led a large number of priests to violate the secrecy of the mysteries in the celebration of Mass, would tend, in this universal secularization of the liturgy, to materialize the ceremonies whose ancient mysticism stood in too flagrant contradiction with this entire system of naturalism . . .

Generally speaking, our Catholic doctors were too exclusively on the defensive against the so-called Reformation. They softened dogma, pruning from worship everything that seemed difficult to defend against their adversaries. They wanted to avoid offending the Protestants, and even, if possible, to satisfy their reason. They granted them small victories, tacitly agreeing that the Reformation had certain grievances against the Church, which had erred through exaggeration. This was an imprudent tactic that success has never justified.

Dom Claude de Vert, the treasurer of the Abbey of Cluny, took it upon himself to "naturalize" the ceremonies of the Mass. On a trip to Rome

---

[10] Ibid., 1374.
[11] From the Preface for the Feast of the Nativity.

around 1662, during which he witnessed the pomp of the ceremonies practiced in the capital of the Christian world, far from delighting in their mysteries, he conceived the idea for a book in which, disdaining to explain the symbols of the liturgy on *mystical* grounds, as had hitherto been the entire tradition of the liturgists in the Eastern and Western Churches, he would seek only the *physical* grounds, by means of which he promised to explain everything.

Dom de Vert's doctrine is all the more dangerous for its apparent innocence. According to his thinking, the Church, in instituting her ceremonies, did not aim at the instruction and edification of the faithful. Mystical reasons should not be wholly rejected, even if they are arbitrary in themselves. But the essential thing to bear in mind is the natural cause of each sacred rite, and to be careful not to claim that these rites are performed to represent moral or mystical truths to us.

So it was, in the eyes of the treasurer of Cluny, that "baptismal immersion originated in the custom of washing children at the moment of birth, for physical reasons."[12] A newly baptized Christian receives the anointing of chrism when he emerges from the water; Dom de Vert tells us that

> this anointing was not a practice peculiar to the Church. We know that all nations, especially the Jews and Orientals, since water dries out and wrinkles the skin after washing and bathing, were careful to rub oil on the parts that had been wet, which is why anointing is almost always attached to baths in Scripture. It is for this reason that women in many places, after doing the laundry, immediately rub their hands and arms with oil, to prevent, as they say, the skin from wrinkling.[13]

The sacramental rites of Extreme Unction are subjected to this same system of rationalist explanation. "Since in praying for the sick," writes Dom de Vert, "the people always asked for their ailments to be soothed, so they could hardly have failed to use lenitive medicines at the same time, and indeed to soothe the sick parts by *anointing them with oils*."

In like manner, when the priest puts on the sacred vestments to celebrate the Holy Sacrifice, he crosses the stole over his chest, "so that the two bands, which meet at the top of the chest, can cover the alb at the point where the opening of the chasuble leaves a gap, ensuring that everything is uniformly adorned."

Moreover, at the end of each Nocturn, the choir, which was seated during the lessons, rises at the *Gloria Patri* of the last Responsory, not, as St. Benedict says in his Rule, *ob reverentiam sanctissimæ Trinitatis* ("to give reverence to the most holy Trinity"), but because they are about to

---

[12] Dom Claude de Vert, *Explication simple, littérale et historique des cérémonies de l'Église* (Paris, 1710), vol. 2, p. xvi.
[13] Ibid., 386.

exit the choir, since they used to leave at the end of each Nocturn. Such examples could be multiplied indefinitely.

One can imagine the effect that the appearance of such a work must have had in the early years of the rationalist century. It went through several editions, and although it was itself no more than the result of the doctrines of the seventeenth-century French school, it exerted a decisive influence over the period in which it appeared. Henceforth, one could no longer pay attention to the symbolism of the liturgy without running the risk of being seen as bereft of knowledge, or as a man attached to the mystical imaginations of the darker centuries.

We shall, however, point out as adversaries of Dom Claude de Vert and the naturalism of which he was the apostle, the illustrious prelate Joseph Languet and Fr. Pierre Le Brun of the French Oratory, in his superb *Explication de la Messe*.

THE NEW MASS OF THE CURÉ JUBÉ

Dr. Nicolas Petitpied, the very man who was later to put his liturgical knowledge at the service of the Bishop of Troyes, returned from Holland and settled in the village of Asnières, just outside Paris. Jacques Jubé, the parish priest and a zealous Jansenist, welcomed the doctor with enthusiasm, and together they devised a plan for a new liturgy which — while retaining the advantages of the books of Harlay's edition in terms of distancing from Rome — would offer a living model of the revolution that was being planned.

In Jubé's church there was a single altar, called the Sunday Altar, because it was used exclusively on Sundays and feast days. After Mass, this altar was immediately stripped, as are all altars in the Latin Church after the morning Office on Maundy Thursday. When it was time to celebrate the sacred mysteries, it was covered with a single cloth, and even then there were neither candles nor crosses. When the priest advanced to the altar, he was preceded by a large cross, the same one carried in processions and the only one left in the church. At the foot of the altar, he said the opening prayers, to which the people responded aloud. Then he would sit in an armchair on the Epistle side, and there he would intone the *Gloria in excelsis* and the *Credo* without reciting either of them, nor the Epistle or the Gospel. He said only the Collect; in general, he did not pronounce any of the texts sung by the choir.

The bread, wine and water were ceremonially offered to the celebrant with a procession. There is nothing reprehensible in this, since the custom had been maintained until that time in many French churches. However, in addition to this offering of the matter for the Sacrifice, seasonal fruits were placed on the altar, despite the impropriety of this practice.

After the Offertory procession, the chalice was brought from the sacristy without a veil. The deacon held it aloft with the priest and uttered the words of the Offertory with him, according to the custom of Rome and Paris. However, they both pronounced the formula aloud to signify that they made the offering in the name of the people. The entire Canon was likewise recited aloud, as one would expect. The celebrant left the *Sanctus* and *Agnus Dei* to the choir. The blessings accompanying the words *Per quem hæc omnia, Domine, semper bona creas, sanctificas*, and so on, were said over the fruits and vegetables placed on the altar, rather than over the sacred gifts. The people's communion was no longer preceded by any of the prayers ordered by the current discipline. The subdeacon, although he was vested in a tunicle, received communion with the laity.

However, the church in Asnières did not venture to inaugurate the vernacular into the liturgy. Instead, before Vespers, a sort of deaconess publicly read the day's Gospel in French.[14]

Such was the bizarre parade played out by the Jansenists, in the center of France, thanks to the tolerance of a corrupt archbishop, Cardinal de Noailles.

Let us pause here to summarize the principles that the anti-liturgical sect applied in their various undertakings described in this chapter.

1. *Hatred of tradition*, manifested in the suppression of most of the Masses of St. Gregory in the Missal of Troyes, and in Dom Claude de Vert's contempt for the doctrine of the Fathers on the mystical meaning of the ceremonies.

2. The *substitution of passages from Scripture*, selected according to individual insight and for heretical purposes, in place of texts in the ecclesiastical style. The Missal of Troyes presents innumerable applications of this principle.

3. The *fabrication and introduction of new formulas*, full of poison. This is one of criticisms made by Languet against the Missal of Troyes.

4. The *contradiction of one's own stated principles*. Indeed, the Missal of Troyes, like the Missals and Breviaries of François de Harlay and Cluny, speaks of nothing else than the restoration of true antiquity, while it is replete with novelties.

5. The *removal of all ceremonies and formulas from divine worship that express mysteries*. Dom de Vert conceded, it is true, that the people should be allowed the ceremonies, but only after they have been completely emptied of the mystical element of which they were only the form. Furthermore, the Church of Troyes, reformed according to the parish of Asnières, soon had only a table for an altar.

6. The *total extinction of the spirit of prayer*, called unction in Catholicism. Read the work of Dom Claude de Vert, and experience what a

---

[14] Pierre-François Lafitau, *Histoire de la Constitution Unigenitus* (Besançon, 1820), 423.

spirit of faith and prayer will remain in your heart when you assist at the ceremonies of the Mass or the other Sacraments, as interpreted with the help of his commentary.

7. The effort to *diminish the marks of devotion to the Blessed Virgin.*

8. The *call to use the vernacular in the divine service.* Quesnel, for instance, expressly demands it.

9. *Attacks on the authority of the Apostolic See.* Thus, in the Missal of Troyes, the suppression of orations for the Pope and the mutilation of the Mass of St. Peter.

10. The *authority of the temporal ruler in matters of the liturgy,* recognized by the clergy. After Languet found himself unable to restore his suffragan bishop to sound liturgical doctrine, the king intervened and compelled the Bishop of Troyes to retract some of the scandals of his Missal; however, the king deemed that some of the outrages contained in the Missal did not have to be disavowed.

19

The Liturgy of Vintimille

N THE PRECEDING CHAPTER, WE recounted the open efforts of the Jansenists to seize control of the liturgy, and in particular their proclivities towards the use of the vernacular in the Offices, towards the stripping of the altars, and their Calvinist habits in worship.

As long as the French court showed a firm resolve to support the apostolic constitutions against Jansen and Quesnel, their sect could only hope to enjoy at rare intervals and in very restricted localities those moments of freedom when it would be possible to test its damnable theories at its leisure.

This left the Jansenists with only one resort: to fracture liturgical unity by stealth, and to attempt for the whole of France what they had already achieved in Paris under François de Harlay. If they succeeded in constructing the framework of a national liturgy, or at least in dividing the robust body of orthodoxy formed by the one hundred and thirty dioceses of the Church of France, then the heretics would have good reason to hope that it could no longer be crushed by those liturgical formulas that the Roman Church imposes on the particular churches, at times in which the faith is in great peril.

The Jansenists had already prepared this work of division through perfidious systems on the Church's constitution and on the prerogatives of the French nation. They consummated it by flattering the bad literary tastes of the time, by exaggerating the faults that historical criticism could discover in the old books,[1] and finally, it must be said, by pointing out the advantages of an Office that was not so long to recite, promising to shorten the length of the priest's prayer time, and this at a time when the Church was threatened with the greatest evils.

SCHEMES FOR NEW BREVIARIES: FOINARD AND GRANCOLAS
It was easy to judge how far things had gone in the forty years since Harlay's liturgical reform when, in 1720, a work appeared in Paris with the title "Plan for a new Breviary, in which the Divine Office, without changing its ordinary form, will be composed particularly of Sacred Scripture, being instructive, edifying, of a natural order, without cross-references or repetitions, and very brief, with some observations about the old and new Breviaries."

---

[1] Namely, criticism of the historical accuracy of lives of the saints contained in Matins lessons, and sometimes in proper antiphons and responsories.

The author was Frédéric-Maurice Foinard, formerly parish priest of Calais, known for several works including an *Explication de la Genèse* ("Explanation of Genesis"), which was suppressed due to the hazardous and peculiar ideas it was found to contain. Foinard was not content with exposing his theory to the public eye, but took the trouble to add example to precept, and published, in 1726, a Breviary executed according to his plan, in which the entire liturgy of the Divine Offices had been reworked and subjected to the crucible of his particular genius.

Along with that of Cluny, Foinard's Breviary forms the storehouse from which most of the materials used in the eighteenth-century Breviaries were drawn. This book failed to find a publisher outside of Amsterdam. The following year, 1727, Jean Grancolas, a doctor of the Sorbonne, also included a special chapter on the "Plan for a New Breviary" in his *Commentaire du Bréviaire romain.*

Here are men who wanted to persuade the Catholic Church, in one of its greatest and most illustrious provinces, that it was deprived of a liturgy in keeping with its needs, that it knew less about the things of prayer than a couple of professors from the Sorbonne, and that its faith lacked a suitable expression.

Furthermore, these presumptuous men, having weighed the Church and scrutinized her needs, not only claimed that her liturgy had sinned by defect, or by excess in certain details, but they went as far as to present her to the people as lacking a suitable system in the entirety of her worship. They set about drawing up a new plan for the Offices — new both in terms of the materials to be used in their composition and in terms of their general and particular outlines.

For these heretics, the books of St. Pius V, which are quite simply those of St. Gregory, are not even worth naming anymore. Even those of François de Harlay, despite their substantial innovations, were still too Roman. A complete system must emerge from an individual mind and be printed, for the benefit of the churches that are to produce a new edition of the Breviary.

Let us listen to these two great legislators of our sanctuaries. Foinard is the most explicit in his desires. The title of his book deserves our attention first of all:

Plan for a New Breviary. Thus, the Breviary is, among the institutions of the Catholic Church, the only one that has no need of antiquity, and can be recast, after centuries, according the plan devised by a private individual.

For a new Breviary, in which the Divine Office, without changing its form. So he agrees to retain in this Breviary Matins, Lauds, the Little Hours, Vespers, and Compline, with the same number of psalms, hymns, and so on. There will still be a Psalter, a Proper of the Season, a Proper and a Common of the Saints.

In which the Divine Office will be composed particularly of Sacred Scripture. Until now, the Church used her own voice to celebrate her mysteries. She believed herself entitled to speak to her Spouse; the traditional element seemed to her as divine as Scripture itself. And indeed, the ancient Breviary, with its antiphons, responsories, and versicles, was nothing other than tradition. Dr. Foinard, well aware that a private individual cannot create a tradition, proposed to cram his work with biblical phrases that he himself would select at his leisure and according to his preferences.

Instructive. So tradition teaches us nothing. The Church, in her works, does not know how to instruct us, she who has the words of eternal life. Rather, to receive instruction, we must turn to certain priests of dubious doctrine, who will initiate us into doctrine.

Edifying. If the Church instructs us poorly, she can hardly edify.

Of a natural order, without cross-references. No more of those convoluted rubrics which oblige the priest to make a serious study of the Divine Office. Besides, such rubrics are themselves traditions, and it is only right that they should disappear.

Without repetition. It is unfortunate that those who pray to God are made in such a way that they feel the need to repeat their requests often.

And very brief. Behold, the key to its success! The sum of the prayers will be reduced, and in order to rouse desire for this *New Breviary* with the full understanding, the commitment to making it *very brief* is expressed in black and white in the title of the book, which was destined to spread such wonderful news everywhere! The stated aim is to restore the Church of France to the Breviary of Quiñones. St. Pius V, the councils of the sixteenth century—all of these are forgotten and scorned. "We want a Breviary composed of Sacred Scripture, and, above all, a *brief* Breviary; oh, we shall have it; there will be Jansenists to write it."

REDUCED RECOURSE TO THE INTERCESSION OF THE SAINTS
With a self-assurance that defies belief, Foinard proposed a new ranking of Christian feasts to be followed henceforth. Here is how he envisioned regulating the harmony between these noble elements of the universal liturgy in the future. He first proposed creating a superior class of feasts of Our Lord, in which no feasts of the Blessed Virgin or of the saints could be included, unlike the Roman Breviary, which so inappropriately includes both in the same rank. Such was the idea of Foinard and Grancolas, and both of them dared to exclude the feast of Corpus Christi from the list of major feasts of Our Lord!

Foinard and Grancolas nonetheless agreed not to allow Corpus Christi, the Assumption, and the feast of the patron saint to fall below the second class. However, in exchange, St. John the Baptist and Sts. Peter and Paul, not being deemed worthy to stand at this second level, were relegated to the third, which they called "solemn minor." Thus did these doctors wish to extend the impudent reforms of Letourneux and Dom de Vert to the whole of France.

One of their main principles, the sanctity of the Sunday, meant the day could not be so degraded as to consecrate it to the feast of a saint, or even of the Blessed Virgin. It could only give way to a solemnity of Our Lord. From now on, Sundays were to be privileged even over the Assumption of the Blessed Virgin, All Saints' Day, and so forth. With even greater reason, major and minor doubles — which so pleasantly diversified the monotony of Sundays for the faithful by reminding them of God's friends, their virtues and their protection — were to be forever relegated to weekdays, on which their feasts would pass silently and unnoticed.

Furthermore, to give the Lenten season a somber tone in keeping with what he believed to be the spirit of the early Church, Foinard proposed removing all the feasts of the saints that fall during this period, even the Annunciation. The calendar would henceforth be purged, and since the avowed aim of Grancolas and his accomplices was to make the clergy prefer the ferial Office to that of the saints, one cannot deny that he chose an excellent means of ensuring this preference by confining the Office of the Saints within such narrow limits.

But what a lamentable spectacle it is to see our churches infiltrated with maxims tainted with Calvinism, so grossly opposed to those of the Apostolic See, which has not ceased for two centuries to strengthen the Church's calendar with the addition of new protectors!

Now, if one were to ask by virtue of what right these tinkers thought they could justify such an upheaval of divine worship, Foinard points out that in the sixth century St. Gregory wrote to St. Augustine, the apostle of England, telling him that he was free to admit into divine service the customs of either the Gauls or any other Church, if their fusion with those of the Roman Church could facilitate and confirm the conversion of the Anglo-Saxons.[2]

This was a very strange diversion. In his letter, St. Gregory was not referring to the Divine Office proper, which was always that of Rome in the Anglo-Saxon Church, but simply of certain customs and observances of secondary importance. Moreover, the power that the Pope conferred on St. Augustine was legitimate, specific, and personal.

By what stretch of logic could one have claimed such power in France, after so many centuries, after the destruction of the Gallican Rite, after the establishment of the Roman Rite, after the Council of Trent and the Bull of St. Pius V, and after the French councils accepted this Bull? Moreover, is it reasonable to equate the liturgical usages of the Gauls and other ancient Churches of apostolic foundation with those that Foinard or his ilk conjured up in their own minds?

---

[2] Frédéric-Maurice Foinard, *Projet d'un nouveau Bréviaire* (Paris, 1720), 174.

THE BREVIARY OF DE VINTIMILLE

The Church of Paris was on the brink of replacing en masse the Gregorian Offices it had been singing since the eighth century with a new set of unknown and unheard-of Offices, freshly concocted by three private individuals — a priest, an acolyte, and a layman. This event was to lead to the complete ruin throughout most of France of the work of Charlemagne and the Roman Pontiffs.

Around 1725, François-Nicolas Vigier, a priest of the French Oratory and the superior of the Seminary of Saint-Magloire, who had also undertaken the composition of a Breviary in keeping with the new ideas, was in a position to share the fruits of his labors with the public. This obscure figure was to become the instrument of the greatest liturgical revolution that the Church of France had seen since the eighth century.

God, in His inscrutable way, allowed this man to find a patron in Charles-Gaspard de Vintimille, who had just succeeded Cardinal de Noailles in the see of Paris. De Vintimille, who had successively occupied the sees of Marseille and Aix, reached the see of Paris around his seventy-fifth year. A man of gentleness and tolerance, he tried to strike a balance between the appellants and the supporters of the Bull.[3]

Charles de Vintimille had allowed himself to be persuaded that the Church of Paris should not lag behind the many other churches throughout France that had embraced a new liturgy. He had heard of Fr. Vigier's work; it had met with his favor, and this Oratorian was chosen to endow the Church with a new set of Offices. Only two men were appointed to assist him, men whose names alone recall the greatest scandals of the period. The first, François-Philippe Mésenguy, was a notorious rebel against the decrees of the Church. Although an ordained acolyte, he had never wished to receive the subdiaconate. His *Exposition de la doctrine chrétienne*, which was placed in the Index in 1757, was also condemned by Clement XIII in a solemn brief dated 14 June 1761. His writings against the Bull *Unigenitus* and in favor of "the appeal" made him one of the Jansenist party's most celebrated champions.

The second of Vigier's collaborators was a mere layman: Charles Coffin, Rollin's successor in the administration of the Collège de Beauvais in Paris, and an "appellant" like his predecessor. Coffin had taken on the task of composing the hymns required for the new Breviary. The hymnographer behind this new Breviary might have surpassed Santeul in terms of true genius for sacred poetry, but he offered even fewer guarantees in terms of

---

[3] The Bull, Pope Clement XI's *Unigenitus*, dated 8 September 1713, condemns 101 propositions extracted word-for-word from Quesnel's *Réflexions Morales sur le Nouveau Testament*. Those who refused to accept this pontifical judgment and made an appeal to a general council were named the "appellants." Opposed to them were the "partisans," who were faithful to Roman orthodoxy.

orthodoxy. Coffin, a serious and contemplative character, was a notorious heretic. So it was that the Church of Paris, and so many others after it, were to receive their sacred hymns from a man outside the Catholic Church. The poems of an obdurate Jansenist were to replace the hymns of the Roman Church, which François de Harlay and Cardinal de Noailles had at least retained almost in their entirety.

The commission appointed by Charles de Vintimille to provide the Church of Paris with a worthy Breviary was thus made up of these three individuals, Vigier, Mésenguy, and Coffin. Only one was a priest, and of the other two, one was a mere acolyte, and the other a layman. Many consequences follow from this fact...

Finally, 1736 saw the introduction of the new liturgy. The Breviary, which had been announced to the whole diocese by a mandate from Archbishop Vintimille, was headed by a pastoral letter from the prelate.

"The first pastors," the pastoral letter reads,

> set themselves the special task of bringing together in the whole of the ecclesiastical Office the materials necessary for priests to more easily instruct the peoples entrusted to their care in the science of salvation. Such was the service rendered by the three illustrious prelates, our immediate predecessors. Following their example, a large number of bishops in this kingdom have published new Breviaries with praiseworthy success.[4]

Thus, these three archbishops—Péréfixe, Harlay, and de Noailles—should be regarded as the authors of the liturgical revolution. It was in Paris that the idea emerged of transforming the Breviary into a mere book of priestly studies, of stripping it of its popular character and no longer viewing it as a repertory of texts consecrated by tradition. Until then, it had been regarded as a collection of prayers and readings meant to resonate within the congregation of the faithful, and everything it contained was ordered towards divine worship. Henceforth it was reduced to a book for private study.

The pastoral letter then goes on to detail the improvements introduced by the new Breviary:

> In the arrangement of this work, with the exception of the hymns, orations, canons,[5] and a certain number of lessons, we have deemed it necessary to draw all the parts of the Office from Sacred Scripture; convinced, with the holy Fathers, that these prayers will be more pleasing to the Divine Majesty, since they reproduce not only the thoughts, but the very words of God.[6]

The sole "holy Father" he cites is St. Cyprian, who, incidentally, does not say at all what he is made to say here. The holy Fathers continually

---

[4] Charles-Gaspard-Guillaume de Vintimille du Luc, *Lettre pastorale* (3 December 1735).
[5] Read at Prime in the use of Paris.
[6] Ibid.

emphasized the authority of tradition, and there is not a single passage in their writings in which they have said or implied that it would be appropriate to remove ecclesiastical formulas from the Divine Office and replace them with verses from Scripture.

NUMEROUS BUT SHREWD INSERTIONS

The execution of the Breviary did not betray these promises. Everything, or nearly everything, was new. But novelty alone did not define the character of this liturgy. It invited entirely legitimate objections and was, indeed, worthy of its authors.

On the issues raised by Jansen and Quesnel—issues that had already been settled by the Church—the Breviary of 1736 often subtly hinted at the doctrines of Vigier, Mésenguy and Coffin through veiled language. Numerous omissions were also made in order to get rid of inconvenient authorities. For example, in order to undermine the dogma of the Jesus Christ's death for all men, the antiphon taken from St. Paul was eliminated from the Office of Good Friday: *Proprio Filio suo non pepercit Deus, sed pro nobis omnibus tradidit illum* ("God spared not even His own Son, but delivered Him up for us all").

Numerous additions and insertions were made in the new Parisian Breviary with a Jansenist intent, but in general they were circumspect and took precautions, at least to some extent, against Catholic objections. It is characteristic of heresy to proceed through ambiguity, retreating into the twists and turns of deceptive language.

Of course, we do not want to take the trouble, nor do we wish to bore the reader, with a complete enumeration of the controversial passages in the Breviary of Vintimille, but we should draw attention to at least one more: the Office of Vespers and Compline on Sundays, a popular Office if ever there was one. Let us see how the Jansenist sect managed to give it a completely new color in line with its views. In the Roman liturgy, the solemn reading of the Little Chapter at Vespers after the psalmody is intended to collect the prayers of thanksgiving of the faithful on the Lord's Day, a day whose rest is at the same moment a religious act and a consolation. What could be more moving and more apt to inspire confidence in God than these beautiful words of St. Paul: *Benedictus Deus et Pater Domini nostri Jesu Christi, Pater misericordiarum et Deus totius consolationis qui consolatur nos in omni tribulatione nostra* ("Blessed be the God and Father of Our Lord Jesus Christ, the Father of mercies and the God of all comfort, who comforts us in all our tribulation").

Is it not evident that the choice of these divine words could only have been made by our merciful Mother, Holy Church, who always seeks to nourish and deepen our abandonment to our heavenly Father? She does not approve of frightening the faithful by placing too often before their eyes the terrible mysteries of predestination and reprobation, mysteries through which many have suffered shipwreck in their faith.

The Jansenist sect, on the contrary, sees only one thing in religion. It speaks solely of predestination, the efficacy of grace, the nullity of human will, and God's absolute power over that will. Here, then, is how the heretics fraudulently replaced the sublime Chapter we have just read: *Benedictus Deus et Pater Domini nostri Jesu Christi, qui benedixit nos in omni benedictione spirituali in cœlestibus in Christo, sicut elegit nos in ipso ante mundi constitutionem, ut essemus sancti et immaculati in conspectu eius in caritate* ("Blessed be the God and Father of Our Lord Jesus Christ, who has blessed us with every spiritual blessing in the heavenly places in Christ, and He chose us in Him before the foundation of the world, that we should be holy and unspotted in His sight in charity").

The sinner who hears this second Chapter read out and who feels that at this moment he is neither *holy* nor *immaculate*, where will he find strength to lift himself up again? He is told that, in order to attain salvation, he must have been *chosen in Jesus Christ before the creation of the world*. What guarantee will he have of this election for himself? In his uncertainty, he will not respond to the promptings of grace in his heart. He will shake off the yoke of a religion which brings despair rather than consolation. It is now widely acknowledged that such predestinationism, which was more or less triumphant in the pulpit, as well as moral rigorism, were significant causes of irreligion in the eighteenth century.

These are precisely the words of Scripture[7] that the Jansenists use against us in order to establish their system on the irresistibility of grace. We know that Scripture is the word of God, but we also know that it is a double-edged sword that can either deal death or defend against it, depending on the hand that wields it.

NEW REDUCTIONS TO THE CULT OF THE SAINTS

If we now consider the way in which the new Breviary had treated the cult of the saints, one might say that its authors took it upon themselves to surpass the audacity of François de Harlay.

We have already seen how the system that gave Sunday precedence over all concurrent feasts diminished the solemnity of the cult of the saints, and how, under the guise of restoring the customs of antiquity, it stood in contradiction with the Roman Church, whose duty it is to instruct the other Churches by her own customs. Not content to establish a rule so

---

[7] The editor of the 1977 edition has omitted the text that Guéranger is here referring to, a passage from St. Paul (Heb. 13:21) that was adapted to the Lector's Blessing at the Office of Prime: *Deus pacis aptet nos in omni bono, ut faciamus eius voluntatem, faciens in nobis quod placeat coram se* ("May the God of peace adapt us to every good, that we might do His will, doing within us that which is pleasing in His sight").

unfavorable to the cult of the saints, the calendar also underwent substantial reductions at their hands . . .

By accepting the new Breviary, the Church of Paris deprived herself of a large number of protectors, and it is difficult to express what advantage it thought to gain from such a strange purgation of the calendar. Among the various saints sacrificed to Jansenist hostility, most originated from the Roman calendar, but a number belonged exclusively to France, such as St. Albin, St. Eutropius, and St. Theobald, and yet these were also shamefully expelled.

As for the way in which the cult of the Blessed Virgin — a cult which theologians call *hyperdulia*, owing to its pre-eminence — was treated in the new Breviary, we can only speak of it with a deep sense of sorrow. It can be said that this is the greatest flaw of the new Breviaries, and all men of goodwill are obliged to agree that the editors had the express intention of diminishing the manifestations of Catholic piety towards the Mother of God. [*Coffin, the reform commission's hymnographer, altered the wording of three hymns*—Ave maris stella, Memento salutis auctor, *and* Virgo Dei Genitrix—*to give them a Jansenist sense.*]

In the case of feasts of the Blessed Virgin themselves, one could see the plans of the Jansenist sect unfold on a larger scale. [*The Office of the Circumcision, in the Octave of the Nativity, consecrated by antiquity almost entirely to the Mother of God, disappeared together with its venerable antiphons composed at the time of the Councils of Ephesus and Chalcedon; the name of the Blessed Virgin completely disappeared in the title of the feast of the Annunciation; the Office of the Assumption was mutilated; the Office of the Nativity of Mary was stripped of its melodious antiphons.*]

THE EPISODE OF THE INSERTS

Let us now show what these men had done against the authority of the Apostolic See. First, until the publication of the new Breviary, the Church of Paris celebrated, along with the whole Church, the feast of the Chair of St. Peter in Rome on 18 January, and feast of the Chair of the same apostle in Antioch on 22 February, to honor the supreme pontificate which had had its seat successively in these two cities. It was too much for Vigier and Mésenguy to devote two days of the year to the profession of a dogma as odious to the Jansenist sect as that of the papal supremacy. Accordingly, they brought the two feasts together on the same day, thus breaking with Rome and all the churches that follow her.[8]

---

[8] The Invitatory of Matins for the Chair of St. Peter was suppressed because it expressed St. Peter's prerogatives too forcefully. One particular stanza of Coffin's hymn for this feast provoked objections for containing a phrase that was seen as favorable to Arianism. The feast of St. Peter was despoiled of its octave. Many passages from the holy Fathers affirming the prerogatives of the Prince of the Apostles were also suppressed.

In the new Breviary, the Proper of the Season did not include a single Office that had not been remade, generally in its entirety. The feasts of Christmas, Easter, and Pentecost were no longer celebrated with the same chants. Advent, Lent, and Easter saw the sacrifice of their innumerable responsories, antiphons, verses, and lessons; scarcely a hundredth of them was preserved. But what was gravest of all, and at the same time most distressing for Catholic piety, was the fact that the Office for the last three days of Holy Week had been completely remade. Thus, the Triduum presented an entirely different appearance from that imposing body of psalmody and chants dating back to the first centuries.

The Proper of the Saints, as one may have already concluded from what we have said, presented a no less distressing aspect. The reductions made to the calendar had impoverished it to the same extent. The legends were stripped of many of their miracles and pious narratives;[9] the old proper Offices of the Holy Cross, All Saints, St. Andrew, St. Lucy, St. Agnes, St. Agatha, St. Lawrence, St. Martin, St. Cecilia, St. Clement, and so on, were suppressed despite their ineffable melodies. The octaves, not only of St. Peter and St. Paul, but also of St. John the Baptist and St. Martin, were also eliminated. Most of the Offices were reduced to three lessons, in order to make the Office shorter. These are just a few of the serious innovations that were immediately apparent in the new Proper of the Saints.

With the new Breviary as we have just described it, its appearance could not fail to excite an uproar among the portion of the clergy formally opposed to the new errors. The seminary of Saint-Sulpice — which had in 1680 renounced the Roman Breviary and accepted that of François de Harlay only after conscientious resistance and on the archbishop's express orders — protested against the new liturgy with a candor worthy of the inviolable orthodoxy it had always upheld. The seminary of Saint-Nicolas-du-Chardonnet expressed the same objections. Many parish priests likewise voiced their indignation. Even the archbishop's council was divided. This prelate's two vicars general spoke with one voice against the Breviary.

Charles de Vintimille, disquieted by the complaints of the two vicars general, and also moved by the admonitions of Cardinal de Fleury, resolved to do justice, at least in some measure, to the complaints that reached him from all sides. The archbishop was advised to adopt a half-measure which consisted in maintaining the Breviary but placing inserts with corrections in the places that had most incensed the supporters of the Bull [*"Unigenitus," which condemned the Jansenist propositions*]. This advice was accepted.

---

9 Today, the word "legend" primarily evokes an imaginary story, an invented episode. Dom Guéranger here employs the term in the sense of a biography. In the Breviary, the legend of a saint is simply the account of his life. The change of this word's meaning derives from the abuse of criticism, which has accustomed us to the idea that every account of a miracle is necessarily a later and mythical addition.

In any case, only about fifty inserts were made, and the corrections were few in number. The most notable of these was the deletion of the *Ave, maris stella* arranged by Coffin and its restoration to its original form. It was clear that these slight changes, intended to offer some satisfaction to Catholics, did not address the core issues of the Breviary itself, and even left uncorrected several of the passages which had given rise to particular complaints. It was impossible to obtain anything more.

THE MISSAL OF VINTIMILLE

With the Breviary now introduced, Vintimille felt it was necessary to promulgate a new Missal that reflected this same system. It was clear that the Missal of Harlay, after being revised by Cardinal de Noailles, was too closely aligned to the Roman liturgy to accommodate the calendar and the other innovations of the modern Breviary.

The new Missal needed an editor. The acolyte Mésenguy was chosen for this great enterprise. He had been partly responsible for the new Breviary, and when a commission was formed to address the complaints provoked by this new book, he was notably not invited to participate. Doubtless, his status as an "appellant" and a notorious heretic had demanded that at least this tribute be paid to public decency. However, now that a book even more important and sacred than the Breviary was at hand, the Missal, the Sacramentary of the Church of Paris, this man was sought out, a heretic who was not even ordained as a priest.

It seems that Mésenguy had already begun work on the Missal several years earlier, since the book was ready for publication in 1738, and it was announced in a pastoral letter from Archbishop Vintimille dated 11 March of that year. Detailing the changes introduced in this book, the archbishop spoke as follows: "Almost no changes are to be found in the Gospels and Epistles for Sundays and ferias, nor in the same Propers for feasts that are holy days of obligation for the people. More changes have been made in the pieces chanted at the Masses in the Proper of the Season."[10]

Charles de Vintimille here freely admits to one of the gravest violations made against the liturgy in terms of the popular character of divine worship. Without even mentioning the Graduals, Alleluia verses, Offertories and Communions [*i.e., the chanted pieces mentioned in the letter*] chosen by St. Gregory and his predecessors, which should never have been lost—especially at a time when men prided themselves so much on their enlightened zeal for antiquity—was it not a grave mistake to dare to violently change, in a large number of Masses, the Introits themselves, which from time immemorial served to distinguish between the various Sundays of the year?

---

[10] Charles-Gaspard-Guillaume de Vintimille du Luc, *Missale Parisiense* (Paris, 1738), 5–11.

How can one now read and understand our national chronicles, the charters and diplomas of our ancestors, in which Sundays are constantly referred to by the opening words of this solemn antiphon? Will it come to the point that the priest himself will no longer be able to explain these historical documents unless he equips himself with a Roman Missal in order to understand things that the common people themselves once knew? And yet, how sad it is to see the zeal with which, in those days, men embraced anything that could create a rift between the present and the past!

The pastoral letter continued:

> We have chosen those passages of Scripture which seemed to us the most suitable for arousing piety, the easiest to set to chant, and the most in keeping with the sacred readings at Mass. However, we did not so strictly shackle ourselves to any particular method that we neglected, above all, to seek what could raise the heart to God and help it to conceive the sacred fire of faith, hope, and charity.[11]

St. Gregory also set himself the same goal when choosing the pieces for his Antiphonary, and it was even agreed that he had succeeded. It is astonishing that the eighteenth century should have claimed such an abundance of unction and the spirit of prayer, and that a Jansenist like the acolyte Mésenguy should have been called upon to become, for the Church of Paris, the instrument of the Holy Spirit.

Vintimille's pastoral letter goes on:

> The same reasoning has led us to add several proper Prefaces that were lacking, namely, for Advent and certain more significant solemnities, such as Corpus Christi, the Dedication, All Saints' Day, and others. Thus, we have endeavored to draw closer to the ancient custom of the Roman Church, which once had almost as many proper Prefaces as Masses, as is still the practice today in the Churches of the Ambrosian rite.[12]

Why, then, did they not take the Prefaces of Advent, the Dedication, All Saints' Day, and even St. Denis from the old sacramentaries? Why have such long and cumbersome Prefaces been newly written by professors of the Sorbonne, whose style bears so little resemblance to the refined and cadenced phrasing of St. Leo and St. Gelasius? Why, above all, give the honor of composing such sacred prayers to a heretic like Dr. Laurent-François Boursier, who was expelled from the Sorbonne in 1720 for writing against the Council of Embrun? It is to such a man that the Church of Paris owes its All Saints' Day Preface. In this Preface, Boursier tells God that, by crowning the merits of the saints, He crowns His own gifts (*eorum*

---

[11] Ibid.
[12] Ibid.

coronando merita, coronas dona tua): a very Catholic expression in one sense, and very Jansenist in another.

We will not here dwell on the specifics of this new Missal. It will suffice to have outlined its plan according to the pastoral letter that serves as its preface. In any case, this book was in itself less reprehensible than the Breviary. The complaints of Catholics had at least managed to repress the audacity of the Jansenist sect, which had been on the verge of triumphing through the liturgy. Nevertheless, whether through weariness or discouragement, the resistance gradually subsided. The Breviary and the Missal of Vintimille took deep root, and it marked the end of the Roman liturgy in the Church of Paris.

Furthermore, this same Church, which God, in His inscrutable counsels, had thus subjected to the harsh humiliation of seeing heretical hands elaborate the Divine Offices that she would henceforth celebrate, had the lamentable honor of leading many other Churches in the kingdom down the infelicitous path she had been pushed down. The example it had set in the time of François de Harlay had already been contagious; the example it set during the time of Charles de Vintimille had many additional consequences.

Thirty years after the appearance of the Breviary of 1736, the Roman liturgy had disappeared from three-quarters of French cathedrals, and, of this number, fifty or more had adopted the work of the Vigier and Mésenguy. The Holy Church of Lyon was among them. What an event, then, was the appearance of Vintimille's books! How is it that it has not left a greater mark in history?

Let us now draw the conclusions that result, for liturgical doctrine, from the events set out in this chapter. First of all, of the twelve characteristics we have defined in the works of the anti-liturgical sect, many are visible in the various schemes of the great revolution we have just recounted.

1. A *departure from traditional formulas*. As in the "Plan for a New Breviary," and Vintimille's Breviary and Missal of Paris of 1736. Everywhere, it is clamored that "we must pray to God with His own words": *Deum de suo rogare*.

2. Consequently, *ecclesiastical-style formulas were replaced by passages from the Bible*. The intention was expressly stated and put into practice. It was the essence of the entire work.

3. The *fabrication of new formulas*. Coffin's hymns, Boursier's Preface for All Saints, and so on. An immense quantity of new proses [*i.e., sequences*].

4. The *contradiction of their own principles in their works*, made manifest by the thousands of novelties introduced by men who spoke only of restoring venerable antiquity, and who not only fabricated new hymns,

new proses, new orations, and new Prefaces, but also rid the Breviary and Missal of an immense quantity of their Gregorian pieces, which were not only ancient, but also drawn from Sacred Scripture itself.

5. The *weakening of that spirit of prayer called unction in Catholicism*. It is widely agreed that the new Breviaries, despite all their art, do not match the old books in terms of piety. Vigier and Mésenguy were constantly at pains to introduce biblical phrases with a double sense into their work, like watchwords for their heretical party; it would have been a great miracle if much unction had survived this.

6. The *reduction of the cult of the Blessed Virgin and the saints*. A glance at Foinard's and Grancolas' "Plan for a New Breviary," which was realized in the new calendar and Proper of the Saints of the new Parisian Breviary, confirms that this was the ultimate intention. Predictable results followed, and this should hardly astonish us.

7. *Abbreviation of the Office and reduction of public prayer*. We have seen how shamelessly Foinard vaunted this goal, even in the title of his book. In the new Breviaries, nothing has been spared to achieve this.

8. *Attacks on the authority of the Holy See*. One need only recall the merging of St. Peter's two Chairs into one, or the suppression of the octave of the feast of the Prince of the Apostles, and so forth.

9. The *expansion of presbyterianism* in this liturgical innovation, which was the work of simple priests, in which mere acolytes and even laymen played a significant part: a subject of great disrepute for the hierarchy, and soon for the entire ecclesiastical order.

At the end of this chapter, we may include in the short list of those who protested against this wanton destruction of every liturgical tradition, alongside Languet and Saint-Albin, the names of Belzunce, Bishop of Marseille; de Fumel, Bishop of Lodève; the seminaries of Saint-Sulpice and Saint-Nicolas-du-Chardonnet; Abbés Regnauld and Gaillande, and above all that courageous Jesuit, Fr. Hongnant, who, despite the wrath of Parlement, confessed the pure Roman traditions from which his Society, ever faithful to the teachings of St. Ignatius, has never strayed.

20

New Liturgies in Reaction to the Jansenist Spirit

HE READER HAS ALREADY SEEN SOME manifestations of the Catholic spirit in France in response to the innovations assailing the liturgy on all sides. However, it is surprising that these same protests, inspired by such upright intentions and endowed with all the necessary zeal, did little more than slow down the march of innovation without halting it.

Deviation from ancient Catholic customs was universal in the doctrines accepted by the majority of French Catholics, and liturgical innovation, destined to become such a powerful means of intensifying this deviation, was at the same time a consequence of it. In the back of their minds, both semi-Jansenists and sincere Catholics held the same convictions: that the Church of the first centuries had enjoyed a perfection that the following centuries lacked; that the ecclesiastical institutions of the Middle Ages were the result of less pure principles than those of the early Church; that something had to be done to bring religious practices more into harmony with the needs of society; and, finally, that Rome, though still to be followed, was lagging behind the movement that eighteenth-century France had conceived and set in motion.

This presumption in judging the Church's current institutions weakened, in the eyes of many, not only the authority of the Holy See, but even that of the broader Church that rendered judgment alongside Rome in the cases of Jansen and Quesnel. This explains how even non-Jansenist bishops, such as François de Harlay and Charles de Vintimille, publicly entrusted Jansenists with missions of the highest importance, such as reworking the liturgy.

It is true that the Church of France included bishops who were firmer in their orthodoxy. However, even among these there were some who, while declaring that no heretic would ever receive from them a commission to work on the liturgy, and while refusing to admit the Breviary of Paris into their dioceses, were nevertheless considering a renewal of the liturgy. They failed to ask themselves whether this would undermine the principle of tradition that is the sole strength of the Church, thus breaking one of the last external links that bound the Church of France to the Apostolic See.

It goes without saying that the Breviaries revised by prelates genuinely zealous for the doctrine of the Bull *Unigenitus* would contain an emphatic profession of the dogmas attacked by the new Jansenist errors, and thus that they would contrast sharply with the new Parisian books. Yet, once again, what a strange contradiction it is to break with tradition on so many liturgical points in order to make it triumph over a single point of doctrine!

A NEW AND ANTI-JANSENIST BREVIARY (AMIENS)

The first Breviary distinguished by this bizarre quality is that of Amiens, published in 1746 by Bishop Louis-François d'Orléans de La Motte. This venerable prelate, who was always so zealous for the purity of the faith in his diocese, where he set an example of all virtues, had also succumbed to the universal love of liturgical novelty that swept his century. While the Jansenists were striving to eradicate the Roman forms from the liturgy, since they found them incompatible with their doctrines, this bishop perceived a danger in a certain prayers of the Roman Breviary, due to the errors of the time, and, without consulting the Holy See, or rather forgetting that texts based on tradition are inviolable, he dared, in his zeal, to suppress a large part of the Collects for the Sundays after Pentecost. This proscription targeted orations which mentioned the power of grace. The prelate feared that these might be misinterpreted among his people. Despite his always upright intentions, the bishop was nonetheless giving an indirect lesson to the Roman Church. It was the first time in the Church's history that the truth was defended by a means analogous to those that heretics have so often used to fight against it.

In the new books of Amiens, an attempt was made to conceal the intentions that had led to the suppression of these Collects we are talking about by drafting the Missal according to a new plan. The basis of each Sunday Mass was the Gospel lesson in the Roman Missal; for the rest, the aim was to conform all the other texts to the Gospel's lesson, which thus became the focal point of every Mass. Introits, Graduals, Offertories, Communions, even Epistles — all was overturned and renewed as needed. As a result of this arrangement, one can readily see how the Collects could have been sacrificed so readily.

As for the general appearance of the new Amiens books, it was similar in every respect to that of the new Parisian ones. The Psalter had been reformed along the same lines. The calendar, the Proper of Season, the Proper of the Saints, the Commons, in a word, everything presented the same surface similarities. Upon closer examination, admittedly, one could find many marks of the Catholic intentions that had guided the selection or redaction of the different parts. Ultimately, these books were as good as they could possibly be — provided that due condemnation is passed on the fact of their existence and the deplorable results that they were destined to produce, no less than the other books, in helping to destroy traditions in divine worship, and, by the same token, in the erosion of ancient Catholic customs.

URBAIN ROBINET AND HIS *BREVIARIUM ECCLESIASTICUM*

The year 1744, two years before the publication of the new Breviary of Amiens, was remarkable in the history of the French liturgy for an event of the same kind as the one we have just described, and which had even more far-reaching consequences: the publication of Dr. Urbain Robinet's *Breviarium ecclesiasticum*. The intentions that led him to follow in Foinard's footsteps were undoubtedly pure. He wanted to establish a liturgical corpus, composed from a wholly Catholic perspective, to place in opposition to the Breviary of Vigier and Mésenguy, which he had vigorously opposed.

Nevertheless, here again the same notions towered over the general principles of liturgical innovation: the obsession with reshaping the Church's language to suit a particular age or the ideas of a particular scholar; the use of Sacred Scripture as the sole material for antiphons, versicles and responsories; the reduction of the Breviary to a more abbreviated form. But despite these reservations, we must recognize that Dr. Robinet was one of those well-meaning Catholics caught up in the trends of his age. He clearly saw the importance of embracing and submitting to the Holy See's judgments on new errors, but failed to understand the harm in breaking from unity and universality in a matter so close to the heart of Catholicism as the liturgy.

Here, we will highlight only a few features of Robinet's Breviary, and recount its fate. It never reached the prominence of that of Vigier and Mésenguy's Breviary, which was a work of the Jansenist party, and moreover, since it was presented to the public as the Breviary of the Church of Paris, it seemed destined to win a greater esteem.

As for the relative merits of these two Breviaries, it is our estimation that, while Robinet's may have possessed sounder doctrine and a broader range of learning, Vigier and Mésenguy's had fewer peculiarities, more harmony, and better taste. The *Breviarium ecclesiasticum* enjoyed only moderate success, being adopted solely by the dioceses of Le Mans, Cahors, and Carcassonne.

DEUM DE SUO ROGARE

Let us see now whether these modern liturgists achieved happier results in terms of content than they did in form. It is well known that their aim was to ensure that, henceforth, the people would only "pray to God with God's own words": *Deum de suo rogare*. This meant that henceforth, all responsories, antiphons, and versicles would be taken from the Bible.

Regarding the mysteries whose fulfillment is recorded in the Holy Scriptures, one might still manage, with some difficulty, to find a sufficient number of texts to fill the various parts of the liturgy, while banishing the magnificent pieces of ecclesiastical style that expressed the mysteries much more precisely, having often been composed specifically to counter heresies.

But, when it comes to the Office of the Saints, could the Bible provide in sufficient abundance? Would it not often be silent on such occasions, leaving no other recourse but to resort to accommodate the interpretation of certain passages? Can such forced interpretations, which are based only in the words themselves and not the sense, be truly considered "the word of God"? Is this *Deum de suo rogare*?

The innovators sensed this inadequacy of their system and began to compose Offices with texts that seemed to make allusion to the events they wished to celebrate, but which in reality had nothing to do with them. Here are a few examples drawn from Robinet's Breviary, which, as we have said, was used in three churches in France.

On the feast of the Assumption of the Blessed Virgin, the antiphon for First Vespers reads: *Magna eris et nomen tuum nominabitur in universa terra* ("Thou shalt be great, and thy name shall be renowned throughout all the earth"). It seems like a very beautiful phrase, and one is stirred to seek out its source to admire its wonderful aptness more closely. So, let us consult the Book of Judith, chapter 11, verse 21, as Robinet himself suggests. Is it the praises of the elders of Bethulia to the city's liberator, Judith? No, it is Holofernes who speaks, and he tells the pious widow, to reward her for what he considers to be her betrayal of the Israelites: "Thou shalt be great *in the house of Nebuchadnezzar*, and thy name shall be renowned throughout all the earth!" Certainly, if the application of these words to the Blessed Virgin is not blasphemous, then one must conclude that the word of Holofernes is the word of God, and the house of Nebuchadnezzar the Kingdom of Heaven. Let the admirers of these new liturgies explain how this should be understood...

In the Common of an Abbot or a Monk, this is the Little Chapter for Terce: *Descenderunt multi quærentes iudicium et iustitiam in desertum, et sederunt ibi* ("Many sought after justice, and judgment, went down into the desert, and abode there"), with the reference to 1 Maccabees 2:29. What a fine text, evidently a prophecy about the monastic life! However, if we look up the passage indicated, we find first of all that Robinet has been no more sincere here than he was in that of the Book of Judith, for we read: "And they abode there, *they and their children, and their wives, and their cattle.*" What strange monks with their children, wives, and cattle! Once again, this is not a scriptural passage about the monastic state; it is nothing but a misplaced deceit.

Let us turn to an even worse passage, where Robinet plunges into a serious heresy without realizing it. This is from the fifth Responsory for the Office of Sts. Peter and Paul.

℣. Urbs fortitudinis nostræ Sion: Salvator ponetur in ea * Murus et antemurale.
("Zion, the city of our strength: a savior shall be placed therein, * A wall, and a bulwark.")

℞. Tu es Petrus et super hanc petram. * Murus et antemurale.
("Thou art Peter, and upon this rock I shall build my Church. * A wall and a bulkwark.")

Thus, Zion is the city of our strength, while the Savior is its wall and rampart; St. Peter is the stone, and on this stone is the wall and rampart. Jesus Christ is therefore supported by St. Peter, and not St. Peter by Jesus Christ. If the Responsory does not mean that, then it means nothing at all. And all of this is called *Deum de suo rogare*!

Now we shall collect a few contemporary opinions on these new French liturgies, and show that the illustrious prelates Languet, de Saint-Albin, de Belzunce, de Fumel, and so on, were not the only ones in the eighteenth century to raise their voices in favor of tradition and to harshly criticize the work of the reformers.

The first witness we present is, surprisingly enough, Foinard himself. In his "Plan for a New Breviary," when explaining his thoughts on the new liturgical experiments attempted before 1720, he condemns them with remarks that apply just as well to the Breviaries of the following years. "It does not appear," he says, "that unction prevails in the new Breviaries. There has certainly been a great deal of effort put into appealing to the intellect, but it seems that there has been far less effort for the heart."[1] Further on, he adds these remarkable words: "Could it not be said that most of the antiphons in the new Breviaries have been created solely to be read with the eyes, out of curiosity and outside the Office?"[2]

Let us also listen to Abbé Robinet. Here is an admission that is not without significance: "Those who composed the Roman Breviary," he says, "knew the spirit of prayer and the words appropriate to it better than we do today."[3]

---

[1] Foinard, *Projet d'un nouveau Bréviaire*, 64.
[2] Ibid., 93.
[3] Urbain Robinet, "Lettre d'un Ecclésiastique à son Curé sur le plan d'un nouveau Bréviaire," 2.

21

The Legend of Saint Gregory VII

EDITOR'S SUMMARY: *The word "legend" is here used in the old sense of "historical biography," and not in the more recent sense of a fable, that is, an imaginary tale.*

Dom Guéranger devotes this seventy-page chapter to a study of the introduction of the feast of St. Gregory VII into France. Nevertheless, this historical episode pertains more to canon law than to the liturgy proper, which is why we will limit ourselves with a brief summary of this chapter.

Gregory VII was the eleventh-century Pope who not only excommunicated the German Emperor Henry IV, but also deposed him. He then compelled Henry to come prostrate himself before him in Canossa in 1077. The emperor feigned submission but soon turned against the Pope again, and Gregory was forced to leave Rome and ultimately to die in exile in Salerno, where he was buried.

The prolonged devotion at his tomb on the part of the Italian people justified, many years later, the insertion of Gregory VII's name into the Roman Martyrology, although he had never been the object of a formal canonization. This type of canonization, without the preliminary procedure, is known as "equipollent canonization." It is a perfectly regular process, particularly at that period.

Subsequently, the Holy See composed an office for St. Gregory VII for use in the Roman basilicas. It was later extended to Cistercian and then Benedictine monasteries. Finally, on 25 October 1728, Pope Benedict XIII ordered the insertion of the feast of St. Gregory VII into the Missal and Breviary throughout the Catholic world.

The Parlement of Paris, in agreement with the royal court, rejected this insertion, declaring to find in it a troubling precedent against "the rights of the Gallican Churches." Were they about to raise to the altars a Pope who claimed the right to depose kings?

This controversy, which occurred some years after the controversy over the French king's jura regalia, and which stoked the same rivalries, caused a great storm among the French clergy. The Jansenists and the Gallicans joined forces to stand in opposition to Rome, and they effectively prevented the insertion of the "legend of St. Gregory VII" into the diocesan Missals and Breviaries. It was not until the Restoration that this feast would be celebrated in the Church of France.

Dom Guéranger attaches a great importance to this matter because he believes that, in the seventeenth and eighteenth centuries, the liturgy suffered attacks from the Gallicans as well as the Jansenists. The Parlement and the court reserved for themselves the right to authorize or reject the publication of papal decrees within French territory. As a result, a fair number of decisions of the Apostolic See (particularly on the liturgy) never became known and thus were never enforced in France, because they had not been "registered" by the Parlement.

22

The Work of the Supreme Pontiffs on the Roman Liturgy

N THE COURSE OF THE FOUR CHAPTERS we have just devoted to the history of the liturgy in the first half of the eighteenth century, we have had to focus on France. This country alone was the scene of the unhappy revolution whose desolate picture we have had to retrace.

The rest of the Catholic world remained faithful to ancient traditions and the Roman unity of the liturgy. The Apostolic See continued to regulate the forms of worship there. Its decrees were received with obedience, and the Gregorian books continued to serve as an expression of the piety of the clergy and faithful.

But during the fifty years of this half-century, the Roman liturgy was not without its own valuable developments. While the Gallican Church was proceeding by the way of destruction, the Roman Pontiffs, so jealous to preserve the ancient deposit of St. Gregory, continued to enrich it with new offices and new feasts.

THE WAY OF ENRICHMENT

The great and pious Clement XI, in his solicitude for the temporal needs of the Christian people, filled an important lacuna in the liturgical books. Among the prayers that the Church addresses to God in various calamities, the preceding centuries had offered none to avert the dreaded scourge of earthquakes. In the year 1703, with Italy having been devastated by numerous disasters of this kind, Clement XI composed and placed in the Missal the three magnificent prayers under the heading: *Tempore terræ motus* ("In the time of earthquake"). In the Breviary, he added this new invocation to the Litany of the Saints: *A flagello terræ motus, libera nos, Domine* ("From the scourge of earthquake, deliver us, O Lord").

It was this same Pope who extended to the universal Church the solemnity of the Most Holy Rosary, under double major rite, in commemoration of the victory at Lepanto.

Pope Innocent XIII instituted the feast of the Most Holy Name of Jesus.

Pope Benedict XIII, in addition to the feast of St. Gregory VII that we have already discussed, also instituted the feast of the Seven Sorrows of the Blessed Virgin Mary, as well as that of Our Lady of Mount Carmel.

No Pope has surpassed Benedict XIII and few equaled him in his zeal for the sacred rites. He solemnly dedicated hundreds of altars, both in Benevento while he was archbishop and in Rome during his papacy. St. Peter's Basilica alone contains twelve altars consecrated by him. The number of churches that he dedicated is no less astonishing.

Finally, Benedict XIV ascended to the Apostolic See. It was inevitable that he would turn his attention to divine worship, since his learned writings placed him at the forefront of the liturgists of his time. Deeply versed in the customs of antiquity, this Pontiff was not indifferent to the serious changes that the calendar of the Roman Breviary had undergone since the time of St. Pius V. The number of ferial days had been greatly reduced by the addition of over a hundred new Offices. The problem of the multiplication of saints' feasts had been exploited by the French innovators. Should Rome, then, continue to allow the persistence of a pretext that had allowed the French sectarians to make their divorce from the Roman books tolerable to many people?

This Pontiff began by making a resolution to which he remained faithful throughout his eighteen-year pontificate: not to add any new Offices to the Breviary. He did, however, confer the title of doctor on St. Leo the Great in a solemn Bull, but this saintly Pope had already been on the Roman calendar for many centuries. It is satisfying to see this appeal in favor of ancient customs and this reluctance to enter into new ways, both of which are characteristic of the operations of the Holy See.

The Roman Martyrology was a particular focus of Benedict XIV's work. He prepared an edition which appeared in Rome under his authority in 1748.

THE SILENCE OF ROME ON THE FRENCH REFORMS

It is not uncommon to hear serious people express astonishment that these same Pontiffs, so zealous for the preservation of liturgical traditions, did not fulminate against the novelties that were taking place in the French churches during that time. We have even observed that many seemed inclined to regard this silence as a kind of approval.

However, if these people were to take the trouble to peruse the printed collections of the decrees of the Congregations of the Council of Trent and of Rites, they would find numerous proofs of the Holy See's constant intentions regarding the observance of the Constitutions of St. Pius V for the Breviary and the Roman Missal. All questions addressed to Rome on this subject have been and always will be resolved in this way.

Innovators have long attempted to justify their bold opinions or practices by invoking the Holy See's silence. But they have always been told that they ought not to cite the Holy See's silence as a mark of approval. The Roman Pontiff has received the mission of teaching; he is the doctor of all Christians. When he has spoken, the matter is settled (*"Roma locuta est:*

causa finita est"). As long as he has not spoken, the faithful must refrain from arguing anything based on his silence.

Let us therefore admit, on the one hand, that the Pope offered no clarification on the new French liturgies. But let us agree, on the other hand, that he missed no opportunity to declare that the Churches bound by the Breviary and Missal of St. Pius V were not at liberty to adopt another Breviary or Missal.

If we wish to seek the reasons for the great reserve shown by the Holy See in the matter of the new liturgies, we need only recall the fundamental maxim of ecclesiastical government, a maxim suggested by the strong and merciful God: "The bruised reed he shall not break, and smoking flax he shall not quench" (Isa. 42:3). Does this mean that Rome should approve of the dimming of the flame in the lamp that should always shine with splendor, or that she should rejoice in the brazen splintering that has compromised the solidity of the reed?

When Benedict XIV tells us, while discussing Bossuet's *Défense de la Déclaration de 1682*, that it would be difficult to find a work so opposed to the doctrine universally accepted regarding the rights of the Roman Pontiff, and that nevertheless Rome has refrained from censuring it, what reasons does the Pontiff give to explain this tolerance? He undoubtedly emphasizes the respect due to the memory of the great Bishop of Meaux, who, like so many other prelates, "merited religion so well"; but the decisive reason was the hope of avoiding new causes for discord.

When the French Parlement and the Assembly of the Clergy of 1730 agreed, each in their own way, to suppress the cult of St. Gregory VII, would we say that the silence maintained by Benedict XIII meant that he renounced his universal decree for the cult of this holy Pontiff? Or that he considered the five writs he had issued against opponents of this decree to be abrogated? One must admit that this is not the case, since the famous "legend" has been maintained in the Roman Breviary, as a strict precept, for 25 May.

23

Last Efforts Against the Roman Practices

N ANOTHER FORTY YEARS, THE REMNANTS of traditional French society will be scattered like debris across the land. Madness has gripped every mind; even those who seek to preserve something of the past yield in other respects to the crazed fashions of the day.

THE LITURGY OF RONDET

While waiting for the day when laymen would present the "Civil Constitution of the Clergy" to the Constituent Assembly, another layman, a disciple of Jansen and an apocalyptic visionary, Laurent-Étienne Rondet, found himself at the head of the liturgical movement. This man was summoned by ten different dioceses to oversee the publication of the new liturgical books they wished to adopt. He was everywhere; churches called him to their aid, seeing in him the same spirit that had animated men like Letourneux and Mésenguy.

The shepherds of the faithful, whose duty it was to teach through the liturgy, having renounced the ancient Gregorian tradition, made obeisance to a layman, an avowed follower of dogmas that they condemned, and more or less hand delivered the prayers of the altar over to his judgment.

It should be noted, however, that all the Breviaries and Missals in whose publication Rondet took part have two particular characteristics that distinguish them from the Parisian books of Vigier and Mésenguy. The first is the decision to use only the current Vulgate edition of Holy Scripture, eliminating phrases, words and even syllables that, deriving from the Vetus Latina,[1] still recalled the Gregorian origin of some responsories and antiphons. The question of whether the texts of the Vetus Latina should be retained in the liturgy had been debated in Rome since the sixteenth century. But early on, Pope Clement VIII settled every uncertainty, declaring that the older text should be maintained in all the chanted pieces.

The second characteristic of the liturgical books issued from Rondet's hands was that they had a "Common of Priests." This addition to the

---

[1] The *Vetus Latina* ("Old Latin") is the ancient Latin translation of the Bible used in the Church before the Vulgate, the Latin edition prepared by St. Jerome at the end of the fourth century which became the canonical version.

Commons also produced yet another deplorable disruption of liturgical traditions in modern Breviaries, namely, the complete elimination of the title of *Confessor*, without which it is impossible to understand anything about the hagiological system of the Catholic Church.

THE INNOVATIONS OF LYON

However, none of the innovations we have just mentioned were as lamentable as that which, in 1776, devastated the holy Church of Lyon, the first see of the Gauls. Since then, it can be said that she lost her ancient beauty, widowed both of the apostolic hymns of her Irenaeus and the Gregorian melodies imposed on her by Charlemagne. She has nothing left to offer the pilgrim still attracted by the memory of her glory, apart from the still-imposing spectacle of the famous rites she performs in the solemnity of the Sacrifice.

The oriental splendor of these rites might still, no doubt, be enough to delight the Catholic traveler, if not for the cruel contrast that suddenly shatters the illusion — the jarring noise of novel words, the din of modern chants, unknown to the vaulted ceilings of the august primatial cathedral of the Gauls before the day that it saw Antoine Malvin de Montazet take his throne, and heresy with him, in the center of its apse.

The illustrious chapter of this primatial Church, by a capitular act of 13 November 1776, accepted the substitution of the liturgy of Lyon, the last remnant of our holy Gallican traditions, by that of Paris. It thus humiliated the Church of Lyon before that of Paris, just as the Church of Paris had humiliated herself before Vigier and Mésenguy.

The Church's ceremonies remained, it is true, but the chants and texts had changed. Thus, the face of this Church, which once prided herself on knowing nothing of novelties, was disfigured. But in France, deviation would be universal, for everywhere the rule of tradition was scorned.

Nevertheless, as is always the case, the innovations met with courageous, albeit feeble, opposition. A minority in the primatial chapter voiced its objections. There even appeared a document entitled: "Reasons for Rejecting the novel liturgy of the Lord Archbishop of Lyon."[2] But soon the Parlement of Paris condemned the book to the fire, and after the sentence of this secular court — which had become the final arbiter of liturgical questions in the Church of France — silence fell over all. The Breviary and Missal of Archbishop Montazet were accepted without further resistance. To complete his project, Montazet had a theology textbook drawn up for the use of his seminary, a work which remains one of the most dangerous heretical writings of the eighteenth century.

---

[2] Primatial Chapter of Lyon, *Motifs de ne pas admettre la nouvelle Liturgie de M. l'Archevêque de Lyon* (Lyon, 1776).

THE NEW RITUAL OF PARIS

Although Archbishop de Juigné did not revise either the Missal or the Breviary, he nevertheless undertook a very significant liturgical reform in the diocese of Paris: the publication of a new Ritual. We are not referring here to the *Pastoral de Paris*, a dogmatic and moral compendium, that pertains only to the duties of the holy ministry. The Ritual properly speaking is what concerns us.

The new edition of this book displays a boldness which, in one respect, surpassed anything seen before. While the Jansenists, the authors of the new liturgical books, had taken pains to insert innovations into the entire liturgy, at least they had not ventured to tinker with the style of the ancient texts they decided to keep. The prayers for the administration of the Sacraments had not suffered any variations. Until this time, the eighteenth century had not presumed to give Latin lessons to St. Leo and St. Gelasius. But in the Parisian Ritual of 1786, the clergy found that all these venerable formulas had been rewritten, under the pretext of introducing a greater elegance!

Thus, it was no longer just the hymns, antiphons, and responsories that lacked dignity and had to be remade at the expense of tradition, which cannot be remade. It was the dogmatic teaching of the first centuries — the purest, the gravest, the most universal doctrines — which had to vanish to make way for the more or less pompous phrases of Louis-François Revers, canon of Saint-Honoré; of one Abbé Plunkett, professor of the Sorbonne; and finally, of one Abbé Charlier, secretary to the archbishop.

One more step, and the Canon of the Mass would have had its turn, disappearing to make way for novel prayers, thus finally ridding Protestants of the invincible weight of its age-old testimony.

Still another step, and the reason for not admitting the vernacular into the liturgy — based on the necessary immobility of the sacred formulas — would have disappeared forever. Such events were needed to reveal the strange deviation the anti-liturgists had been working within the minds of French Catholics. More than fifty years would pass before any serious thought was given to restoring the ancient forms of tradition in the Parisian Ritual.

LITURGICAL MULTIPLICITY

We will not prolong this incomplete survey of the liturgical deviations in our Churches. In the midst of so many innovations, it will suffice for us to select a few characteristic features in order to introduce the reader to the principles that produced them all, and to expose the kind of men who were their promoters and executors.

By 1791, over eighty of the one-hundred and thirty Churches in France had renounced the Roman liturgy. No province other than Avignon was unanimous in retaining it, and it perished entirely from the ecclesiastical provinces of Besançon, Lyon, Paris, Reims, Sens, and Toulouse.

Of the dioceses that had not adopted the Roman Breviary at the time of St. Pius V's Bull, but simply reformed their Franco-Roman Breviaries according to its example, not one had retained this magnificent liturgical form. The innovators had therefore hunted down the French elements in the liturgy with the same rigor they had displayed against the Roman elements, because both of these were traditional.

Only the distinguished collegiate church of Saint-Martin in Tours dared to reprint its beautiful Franco-Roman Breviary in 1748, thus giving a lesson to even the most famous cathedrals of France, and this church alone, on the day of disaster, succumbed with the glory of not having renounced her traditions.

THE ANTI-LITURGICAL HERESY AND ITS DEVELOPMENTS

We have outlined elsewhere the theory according to which the anti-liturgical heresy — that is, the enemy of religious form — has operated since the earliest centuries, and the facts we have presented throughout this history should have fully exposed the intentions of the followers of this accursed doctrine.

One must have observed that the principal characteristic of this heresy is to proceed with cunning, never hesitating to embrace the contradictions that the system inevitably leads to. Destined by its very nature to cling like a canker to the religion of the people, it knows how to advance or to conceal its progress in proportion to the risks that it might run of being extirpated by the hand of the faithful and their shepherds. Often, it is content to survive as a hidden virus, waiting for the chance to erupt. In other cases, however, it suddenly dares to break out without restraint.

Thus, in France, it crept in under the guise of perfecting the prayers of the liturgy, of paying even more just homage to Sacred Scripture in the divine services, and of a better appreciation of the value of historical criticism. It flattered the nation's self-love and diocesan pretensions, and within a century this heresy had found a way to destroy the unity of the Roman prayers in three-quarters of France, to annihilate the work of Charlemagne and St. Pius V, to infiltrate false doctrines into the altar books, and finally, to have men, whose maxims were condemned by the universal Church as heretical, as editors of public prayer.

These were undoubtedly significant results, but were only achieved gradually under the pretext of literary as well as religious perfection. It had been necessary to conceal the aim, to speak constantly of antiquity while violating it, and above all to avoid alerting the people through too obvious external changes of visible objects.[3] For the French nation has been

---

[3] Vestments, altar vessels, the basic "choreography" of the Mass, the *ad orientem* stance, the use of incense — all these external things were untouched by the reforms. The obvious visual difference between the Novus Ordo Missæ and the Traditional Latin Mass did not exist between the Traditional Latin Mass and neo-Gallican uses described by Guéranger.

and always will be Catholic above all else, and the more repressed it feels in terms of religious expression at a given time, the more it will return to them with fervor as soon as the obstacle is removed.

LITURGICAL TRANSFORMATIONS IN GERMANY

It was an entirely different story in Germany. In the sixteenth century, Luther's Reformation had been welcomed with enthusiasm across large portions of this vast land, since it was seen as a liberation of the body from the merely external and burdensome practices imposed by Catholicism.

In the regions that had remained Catholic, the zeal of the eighteenth-century anti-liturgists drew inspiration from these favorable beginnings, and when they sought to attempt an uprising, they were careful not to waste precious time falsifying Breviaries and Missals. Instead, they directly and openly applied their perfidious efforts at reform to the very visible forms of Catholic worship. They knew that German rationalism was less subtle than the French spirit, and quickly realized that they could leave the Roman Breviary intact in the hands of a clergy whom they could gradually lead to no longer wanting to recite any Breviary at all.

The first signs of this anti-liturgical spirit, even in the midst of the Catholic faithful, had already emerged in the canons of the infamous Council of Cologne of 1536. But it was another thing altogether when, towards the end of the eighteenth century, Joseph II set out to use his imperial authority to promote the anti-liturgical schemes suggested to him by the triple coalition of the forces of Protestantism, Jansenism, and modern philosophy.

Catholicism had already been undermined in a large section of the German clergy by dissolving the fundamental notion of the Church — the authority of the Roman Pontiff — through the poisonous writings of Febronius, and later Eybel.

In 1781, Joseph II turned his attention to practical matters, issuing a series of regulations on ecclesiastical matters. He began, as has always been done, by declaring war on the religious orders, stripping them of their exemptions and means of self-perpetuation while awaiting the opportunity to attack episcopal jurisdiction itself.

However, the real way to strike at the Catholic faith among the people was to reform the liturgy. The emperor did not hesitate to do so, and soon promulgated his infamous decrees on the divine service, whose meticulous detail led Frederick II to refer to Joseph as "my brother the sacristan." The situation, however, was far from amusing.

On 8 March 1783, an imperial order was issued that forbade the celebration of more than one Mass at a time in the same church. On 26 April, the emperor promulgated a very extensive regulation abolishing numerous feasts, banning processions, dissolving confraternities, reducing expositions of the

Blessed Sacrament, enjoining the use of the ciborium instead of the monstrance in most Benedictions of the Blessed Sacrament, prescribing the order of Offices, determining which ceremonies were to be retained and which were to be abolished, and even going so far as to specify the number of candles to be lit at each service. Shortly afterwards, Joseph issued a similar decree ordering the removal of the images most venerated by popular devotion.

THE SYNOD OF PISTOIA

But what was most astonishing during this period was the appearance of the same scandals in Italy, where everything seemed poised to resist, or even prevent, the slightest sign of the anti-liturgical heresy.

Before daring to reform Catholicism in the part of Italy that was unfortunately under his control, Leopold, Grand Duke of Tuscany, sought support from a prominent ecclesiastical figure within his realm. This figure was Scipione de' Ricci, Bishop of Pistoia and Prato, a faithful disciple of the French "appellants" and fanatical admirer of all their works, especially of their ambitious liturgical experiments.

On 18 September 1786, under the auspices of the Grand Duke, that infamous synod opened in Pistoia, whose proceedings caused scandal in the Church, but one, it should be said, that was very quickly quelled.

It is not our purpose here to lay out the shameful agenda that the Synod of Pistoia, in its sacrilegious insolence, sought to impose on the entirety of Catholicism. We will focus on the liturgical aspects of its proceedings, which are the only ones we have the leisure to present to our readers.

The faithful interpreter of Scipione de' Ricci, the editor of his *Memoirs* and a disciple of Voltaire, de Potter, describes the Bishop of Pistoia's liturgical plans as follows: "His friends in France, among them Maultrot, Leroy, and Clément, and the Italians who shared their principles, hastened to communicate to him their ideas and insights for carrying out a complete reform of the Breviary and Missal."[4]

Furthermore, Ricci's predilection for this liturgical school is clearly evident in the choice of books that the synod prescribed for parish priests. They were careful not to omit Nicolas Letourneux's *Année chrétienne* or Mésenguy's *Exposition de la doctrine chrétienne*. These two masterpieces by the infamous compilers of the Breviaries of Cluny and Paris figure prominently in the catalogue alongside Alet's *Rituel* and Quesnel's *Réflexions morales*.

Let us first observe that the "Fathers of the Diocesan Council," as they called themselves, were of the opinion that churches should avoid "overtly ornate and costly decorations, since they captivate the senses and lead the soul to a love of lesser things."

---

[4] De Potter, *Mémoires de Scipion de Ricci, évêque de Pistoie et Prato, réformateur du catholicisme en Toscane, sous le règne de Léopold* (Paris, 1826), vol. 2, p. 220.

In the chapter on the reform of the religious orders, they expressed the wish that these orders "should not have churches open to the public; that their Divine Offices should be reduced; and that only one or, at most, two Masses a day should be celebrated, with other priests confining themselves to concelebrating."[5]

In the same session, it was the pleasure of the Fathers "to abolish the processions that took place to visit some image of the Blessed Virgin or of a saint," and to prescribe to parish priests of the countryside "to restrict as much as possible the length and duration of the Rogation processions." The purpose of these suppressions, they say, is "to prevent tumultuous and indecent gatherings, as well as the banquets that tend to accompany these processions."

As for feasts, the Fathers complain that their abundance is an "occasion of idleness for the rich and a source of misery for the poor," and they address His Serene Highness the Grand Duke to seek a reduction in the number of days devoted to religious duties.[6]

"With respect to the external practices of devotion to the Blessed Virgin and the other saints," say the Fathers, "it is our will that every hint of superstition to be removed, such as attributing a certain efficacy to a determinate number of prayers and salutations [*i.e., the Hail Mary*], most of which are recited without taking heed of their meaning, and generally to any external or material act or object."[7]

After this insult against the Rosary and the various chaplets approved and recommended by the Holy See, the reformers of Pistoia would naturally turn their attention to images. Therefore, immediately afterwards, they enjoined the

> removal from churches of all images that represent false dogmas, such as those of the Sacred Heart of Jesus, and those that are an occasion of error for the simple, such as images of the incomprehensible Trinity. Likewise, those images in which the people seem to have placed a particular confidence, or in which they recognize some special virtue, should be removed.

The Synod also ordered the uprooting of "the pernicious custom of distinguishing certain images of the Virgin Mary by particular titles and names, most of the time vain and childish."[8]

For the Synod, the reform of the devotion to the Blessed Virgin and the saints was only a consequence of the reform to which, following Joseph II's lead, it had felt it necessary to subject the devotion to the Blessed Sacrament and the Sacrifice of the Mass.

---

[5] *Atti e decreti del Concilio Diocesano di Pistoia* (1786), Session VI, 238–39.
[6] Ibid., 207–9.
[7] Ibid., 201.
[8] Ibid., 202.

Thus, the Fathers of the diocesan Council of Pistoia decreed that the ancient custom of having only one altar in the same church should be restored. Neither reliquaries nor flowers were to be placed on this altar.[9]

"Participation in the victim," they say a little further on, "is an essential part of the Sacrifice." However, they were not willing to condemn as illicit Masses in which those present do not receive sacramental communion.[10] Indeed, such boldness would have seemed too Lutheran; but the Fathers declared that, except in cases of grave necessity, "the faithful may only receive communion from the hosts consecrated at the Mass at which they have assisted."[11]

As for the language to be used in the celebration of the sacred mysteries, the Synod's intentions are revealed in these expressive words: "The Holy Synod desires that the rites of the liturgy be reduced to a greater simplicity; that it be celebrated in the vernacular, and that it always be proclaimed aloud."[12]

"For it would be contrary to apostolic practice," the Fathers add with their patron Quesnel, "and to God's intentions, not to provide the simple people with the easiest means of uniting their voice to that of the whole Church."[13]

Elsewhere, they taught that it is a condemnable error to believe that the celebrating priest can apply the special fruit of the Sacrifice to whomever he wishes.[14] [*This provision is directed against Mass intentions.*]

As for the veneration to be paid to the mystery of the Eucharist, the Synod ordered that the exposition of the Blessed Sacrament should be restricted to the feast and octave of Corpus Christi, except in the cathedral, where exposition will be permitted once a month. In other churches, on Sundays and feast days, only Benediction with the ciborium will be given.[15]

As for the mystery of the Passion, the Synod stated that, while it should particularly engage our piety, we must also free that piety from "all the useless and dangerous material aspects" that superstitious devotees of recent centuries have sought to impose on it. The spirit of compunction and fervor certainly cannot be attached to a fixed number of Stations, or to a series of reflections that are arbitrary and often false.[16] [*In short, the Synod formally discouraged the practice of the Way of the Cross.*]

SCIPIONE DE' RICCI'S FIFTY-SEVEN *ECCLESIASTICAL POINTS*
As early as 26 January 1786 [*eight months before the Synod of Pistoia*], in an effort to secure the clergy's cooperation in the religious reform he was

---

9 Ibid., Session IV, 130.
10 Ibid., 140.
11 Ibid..
12 Ibid., 131.
13 Ibid., 206.
14 Ibid., 132.
15 Ibid., 126.
16 Ibid., Session VI, 199.

planning, Ricci sent all the prelates of the duchy fifty-seven articles for consultation.

The main articles focused on the necessary reform of the Breviary and the Missal; the abolition of all stipends for Masses; the reduction of luxury in churches; the prohibition of celebrating more than one Mass a day in each church; the critical examination of all relics; the unveiling of covered images; the administration of the Sacraments in the vernacular; instruction for be given to the people concerning the communion of saints and suffrages for the dead; the urgency of subjecting regular clergy to their ordinaries; and so on.

In particular, the articles insisted upon the need for diocesan synods, through whose support Grand Duke Leopold hoped to instill the principles that he so longed to see adopted by his bishops into the second-order clergy.

These "Ecclesiastical Points" (*Punti ecclesiastici*) along with the responses from the archbishops and bishops of Tuscany were published in Florence in 1787. The book's frontispiece features a portrait of the Grand Duke supported by Renown and surrounded by allegorical figures of Justice, Commerce, Abundance, and Time. Below is a putto holding an open book, on which is written the word *Encyclopédie* in large letters and in French. This was undoubtedly enough to reveal the ulterior motives of the anti-liturgists.

RECAPITULATION OF THE ANTI-LITURGICAL DEVELOPMENTS

Let us pause to consider the grievous affront that the adorable mystery of the Eucharist suffered within several Catholic nations. Here, Satan's malice is most evident.

We have shown elsewhere how the Albigensians and Waldensians managed to circumvent the divine mercy of the Savior present under the Eucharistic species by preaching everywhere that if a priest is not in a state of grace, he cannot consecrate. From this, it follows that, since God alone knows the heart of man, the faithful could only believe in the presence of Christ in the host they received at communion if they were privy to God's own knowledge.

Later anti-liturgists did not dare to deny the divine Eucharist either. Nevertheless, since this Sacrament is the object of the believer's faith, the propitiatory sacrifice for the salvation of the world, and the life-giving nourishment of the Christian on earth, they found it necessary to attack the Eucharist under this threefold character.

Indeed, if they had been truly zealous to see public piety give honor to the Savior of men in the mystery of His love, then why these edicts and synodal decrees against the exposition of the Blessed Sacrament? Why extinguish the candles that burned on the altar as a popular sign of joy and love? Why command that Benediction of the Blessed Sacrament be performed with the ciborium, which conceals the host, rather than the monstrance, which displays and surrounds it with a radiant crown, a true triumph for piety?

Why were there so many writings and regulations in various countries hostile to the rite of the exposition of the Blessed Sacrament? Why have so many of the new Breviaries and Missals degraded the feast of Corpus Christi, which until then had ranked among the greatest solemnities, to a lower rank? What an age, and what men, who regarded this as an excess!

As for the Eucharistic sacrifice itself, what have the anti-liturgists not done to diminish its significance in people's minds? The altar vexes them; they would like to see nothing more than a table. They remove the crucifix and candlesticks, as they did in Troyes and Asnières; the relics and flowers, as in Tuscany; thus chasing out Christ and His saints, leaving God's altar as bare and cold as their hearts.

Upon this altar, august, apostolic, even Mosaic rites are performed over the sacred gifts. They retain some of them, but only after having purged them of all symbolism, so that they are nothing more than customary practices devoid of meaning.

A sacred language enveloped, like a cloud, the majesty of this altar and the mysteries it bears. Yet preparations were made towards the abolition of this venerable usage, by introducing the vernacular into the deepest wonders of the sanctuary through translations, while the priest was invited, in the chimerical name of antiquity, to break the silence of the Canon, until, in certain times and places, some men finally dared, like Calvin, to admit their desire that the vernacular replace the sacred tongue.

Has it not by now been agreed that the Bible alone should provide the material for divine services, at the expense of tradition? Has the liturgy not yet been cut to pieces with a pair of scissors to fashion a mosaic, with which we can depict whatever figures we desire?

But, to return to the divine sacrifice, observe with what insistence the truth that *the people offer with the priest* was repeated. This statement, incontestable in itself, was easily abused in that age of Calvinism to support a laicism akin to the presbyterianism that appeared a few years later, with such a dazzling triumph, in the "Civil Constitution of the Clergy."

If we turn to the Eucharist, the nourishment of Christians, we find it just as relentlessly pursued by the anti-liturgists. Here, as always, the theories are conceived in France, while their brutal and audacious application occurs in other countries. Antoine Arnauld's book *Frequent Communion* and the Ritual of Alet[17]—two of the anti-liturgical sect's productions which have exerted, and exert even still, such a profound influence on sacramental practice in France—adopted, as their fundamental maxim, that communion is the reward of advanced piety, and not of beginner's virtue.

---

[17] See chapter 17.

Who could possibly calculate the extent to which this maxim alone has led to desertion of the holy table! Yet the innovators in Italy did not stop there; they applied themselves to wearing down the piety of the faithful by decreeing that they should only receive communion with hosts consecrated at the very Mass they attended, or at least that communion should no longer be administered outside Mass. This double tactic, if well executed, would have effectively deprived a large number of the faithful of communion, given the numerous complications and excuses that can easily be claimed in a large church.

DEVOTION TO THE SACRED HEART

Great was the Jansenists' wrath upon learning that all their efforts would fail against the faithful's confidence in their Savior's Heart. These sectarians, who sought to perfect man by tearing out his heart, seeing that the Heart of the God-Man, both the symbol and organ of His love, was receiving the adoration of all Christendom, resorted to denying the heart within man, and then denying it in Christ Himself.

Perfect charity casts out fear, said the beloved disciple (1 Jn. 4:18), who reclined upon the Savior's Heart at the Last Supper. Thus does the devotion to the Sacred Heart of Jesus cast out the dreadful *Fate,* that implacable idol that the Jansenist sect had substituted for the gentle image of Him who loves all the works of His hands and wants all men to be saved.

The feast of the Sacred Heart of Jesus was first revealed to a humble religious sister, and this revelation was a secret of the cloister before becoming the great news in the universal assembly of the faithful. The venerable Order of the Visitation, founded by St. Francis de Sales, was specifically chosen by God to make known the work of His gentle power by means of the Venerable Mother Margaret Mary Alacoque, as well as to thereby further glorify the doctrine of the holy Bishop of Geneva,[18] so radically different from the Pharisaism of the Jansenist sect.

Let us relate the key events that marked the triumphal march of devotion to the love of Jesus Christ for mankind. France, the main stronghold of Jansenist machinations, was both the place of origin and the main stage for the establishment of the new feast: a happy portent of the divine intentions that had destined this kingdom to triumph, at the appointed time, over the iniquitous virus that seized its heart.

In 1688, Charles de Brienne, Bishop of Coutances, established the feast of the Sacred Heart of Jesus in his diocese. Six years later, in 1694, the pious Antoine-Pierre de Grammont, Archbishop of Besançon, ordered that the proper Mass for this feast be inserted into the Missal of his ecclesiastical province. In 1718, François de Villeroy, Archbishop of Lyon, prescribed the

---

[18] Namely, St. Francis de Sales, who promoted devotion to the Sacred Heart of Jesus. Margaret Mary Alacoque was subsequently beatified in 1864 and canonized in 1920.

celebration of the feast in his illustrious primatial see. As one would expect, this feast disappeared with Montazet's Breviary. The remarkable circumstances are well known under which Henri de Belzunce, Bishop of Marseille, established the celebration of the Sacred Heart of Jesus in 1720, when his city was struck by the plague. This prelate's confidence was rewarded by the instant abatement, and soon the total cessation, of the scourge.

However, the Apostolic See, despite being petitioned for a long time, was slow to sanction the establishment of the new feast. Unexpected obstacles within the Sacred Congregation of Rites stood in the way of its approval, which had been proposed as early as 1697.

In 1726, the Bishop of Krakow addressed a petition to this effect to Benedict XIII, which soon received the support of Frederick Augustus, King of Poland. Famously, it met with a solemn refusal notified by the Congregation of Rites on 30 July 1729, which was a painful blow for adorers of the Sacred Heart of Jesus, and for the Jansenists a misguided victory.

The intensity of the controversy on this matter, the novelty of the devotion, and the absence of a serious examination of the revelations which had accompanied and led to its establishment, were more than enough to motivate the Sacred Congregation's resolution.

Providence chose, to bring this work to fulfillment, the pious Cardinal Rezzonico. He was called by the Holy Spirit to ascend the chair of St. Peter, where he demonstrated such strength of character under the name of Clement XIII. This holy Pontiff received new petitions from the bishops of Poland, who were almost unanimous in requesting that Christendom be allowed to honor with public worship the Heart of the Redeemer of mankind.

A number of French bishops had, it is true, taken the initiative in establishing the feast; but, whatever their power in the matter, this was nothing more than a praiseworthy gesture, and the Catholic Church was still awaiting Rome's judgment.

It was finally given on 6 February 1765, and the reasons for the decree stated that

> it was well known that the cult of the Sacred Heart of Jesus was already widespread in all parts of the Catholic world, encouraged by a large number of bishops, and enriched with indulgences by thousands of apostolic briefs for the erection of confraternities, which had become innumerable. [19]

The Sacred Congregation declared its withdrawal of the [*restrictive*] resolution that it had taken on 3 July 1729, and deemed it necessary to condescend to the supplications of the bishops of the Kingdom of Poland and

---

[19] "Instantibus plerisque Reverendissimis episcopis regni Poloniæ," *Decreta authentica Congregationis Sacrorum Rituum* (Rome, 1898), vol. 5, n. 4175.

of the Roman archconfraternity. Finally, the Congregation announced its intention to make provisions for the Office and the Mass, which had become necessary to solemnize the new feast.

Both were soon issued, and indeed they were worthy of their sublime purpose, which was, in the words of the decree, "to symbolically renew the memory of that divine love, by which the Only-begotten Son of God clothed Himself in human nature, and, having made Himself obedient unto death, declared that He gave mankind the example of being meek and humble of heart."[20]

THE LITURGY OF THE CONSTITUTIONAL CHURCH OF FRANCE

It does not fall under our present purpose to recount the history of the constitutional schism. We will hasten directly to the year 1797, which is famous in the chronicles of Jansenism due to the clandestine meeting held at Notre-Dame in Paris by the sad remnants of the "intruder clergy," decimated by apostasy, execution, and even the conversion of several of its members. They numbered twenty-nine bishops, not counting six procurators for absent bishops, and the deputies of the second order, all under the presidency of Citizen Claude Le Coz, metropolitan Bishop of Ille-et-Vilaine.

Convoked to rebuild the ruins of the failed Church of 1791, the assembly of the "Reunited Bishops" (as they styled themselves in their own proceedings) inevitably had to address the progress of the liturgy. As we have seen, Ricci [*in Italy*] had done the same at his Synod of Pistoia, a worthy precedent for the so-called councils [*in France*] of 1797 and 1801.

Already, in the Jansenist sect's journal, there had been talk of uniting France under a single liturgy, and the books by Vigier and Mésenguy had been put forward as eminently suitable for serving as an expression of the religious needs of the regenerated Gallican Church.[21] The council of 1797 had also demonstrated its veneration for the authors of the recent Parisian liturgy by recommending, like Ricci, among the books most instructive for faith and morals, Letourneux's *L'année chrétienne* and Mésenguy's *L'exposition de la doctrine chrétienne.*[22]

However, the "Reunited Bishops" did not confine their solicitude to solemnly commending the memory and writings of the Parisian liturgical reformers; they also drew up several decrees on the subject of divine worship. The first began as follows: "The national council, considering that it is important to remove from public worship abuses contrary to religion, and constantly to remind pastors of the observance of the holy rules, decrees: *Article I.* Simultaneous Masses are forbidden." We have just shown the

---

[20] Ibid.

[21] *Annales de la Religion* (9 Messidor, an 3), vol. 1, pp. 206–12.

[22] "Lettre synodique aux pères et mères et autres chargés de l'éducation de la jeunesse" (Paris, 1797), p. 18.

purpose of this prohibition in the plan of the anti-liturgists. Let us simply note here the remarkable zeal of the republican bishops to imitate Emperor Joseph II and Grand Duke Leopold. The second decree reads: "*Article III. In the drafting of a uniform Ritual for the Gallican Church, the administration of the Sacraments will be in the French language. The sacramental formulas will be in Latin.*"[23]

Three years later, in 1801, on the eve of the famous Concordat, the Church of Notre-Dame once again hosted the bishops of the Constitutional Church for their second and last council. Among the other concerns of the prelates, the project of a universal liturgy for the Gallican Church arose once more, and the Abbé Grégoire read a long report on the subject. In his usual manner, he filled it with an immense number of grotesque anecdotes and superficial details bearing no relation to one another, all calculated to display that shallow and poorly digested erudition that characterizes all his writings.

The Abbé Grégoire did not fail to insult, as unseemly, devotion to the Sacred Heart of Jesus, the invention of which he attributed to a Protestant;[24] he railed against private Masses;[25] he exclaimed, in reference to St. Gregory VII: "For the repose of the world and the honor of religion, may heaven preserve us from such saints!";[26] he called for the Canon to be recited aloud;[27] he proposed the admission of the Chinese tam-tam to replace the organ,[28] and so on, and so on.

THE BULL *AUCTOREM FIDEI*

Let us turn our gaze away from this ignoble spectacle and consider the Roman Pontiffs, faithful guardians of the age-old deposit of the Roman liturgy, who oversaw the developments that it underwent during the last fifty years of the eighteenth century.

Reference must be made to the Bull *Auctorem Fidei*, by which Pius VI, on 28 August 1794, forever condemned the Synod of Pistoia, its acts, and its doctrine. It is devoutly to be wished that explicit knowledge of this Bull, an incontestable judgment of faith, be more widespread than it is. One would far less often hear persons, even well-intentioned ones, repeating and maintaining, in a good faith that strains one's belief, many of the propositions irrefragably condemned by this constitution, which can be said to have truly cut the error to the quick.

With respect to the doctrines and assertions of the anti-liturgists of Pistoia, Pius VI explicitly condemns the following propositions:

---

[23] *Journal du Concile National de France* (Paris, 1797), pp. 165, 167.
[24] *Actes du second concile national de France* (Paris, 1801), vol. 2, p. 158.
[25] Ibid., 401.
[26] Ibid., 410.
[27] Ibid., 413.
[28] Ibid., 447.

● the 28th, which suggests that Masses in which none of the faithful receive communion lack an essential part of the Sacrifice;

● the 30th, which describes as an error the belief in the priest's power to apply the special fruit of the Sacrifice to a particular person;

● the 31st, which declares the practice of having only one altar in each church to be both appropriate and desirable;

● the 32nd, which forbids the placing of saints' relics or flowers on altars;

● the 33rd, which expresses the desire to see the liturgy reduced to a greater simplicity, and also to see it translated into the vernacular and recited aloud;

● the 61st, which affirms that adoration addressed to the humanity of Jesus Christ, and even more to a particular part of this humanity, always constitutes a divine honor rendered to the creature;

● the 62nd, which numbers devotion to the Sacred Heart of Jesus among the novel and erroneous, or at least dangerous, devotions;

● the 63rd, which claims that devotion to the Sacred Heart of Jesus can only be exercised insofar as the most holy flesh of Christ, or one of its parts, or even His entire humanity, is separated from the divinity;

● the 64th, which describes as superstitious the efficacity of a determinate number of prayers and pious salutations. [*This proposition was directed towards turning the faithful away from the recitation of the Rosary*];

● the 66th, which affirms that it is contrary to the practice of the apostles and to the designs of God not to provide the people with the easiest means of joining their voice to the voice of the whole Church. [*This proposition was intended to introduce the vernacular into the entire liturgy*];

● the 69th, which places the images of the Most Holy Trinity among those to be removed from churches;

● the 70th, which disapproves of the particular veneration that the faithful are accustomed to render to certain images;

● the 71st, which forbids distinguishing images of the Blessed Virgin by titles other than those alluding to the mysteries described in Sacred Scripture;

● finally, the 74th, which states that regular clergy should not be raised to holy orders, except for one or two at most per monastery, and that only one or two Masses at most should be celebrated each day in their churches, with other priests confining themselves to concelebration.

We must content ourselves with this brief overview of the Bull *Auctorem Fidei* considered from the point of view of liturgical doctrine, while omitting a large number of other features directed against the whole damnable system of which the liturgical revolution of the eighteenth century was but one of the results.

24

First Efforts Towards Restoration

S THE EIGHTEENTH CENTURY DREW TO a close, the cruel persecution that the Church of France was forced to endure for ten years came to an end. By 1799, public oratories and even churches were reopening everywhere. Priests were showing their faces with greater confidence and the stripped altars saw a faint revival of their former splendor. At last, the faithful began to bring out the few sacred vessels, vestments, and reliquaries, precious remnants of the Church's former opulence that had been concealed from the avarice of the persecutors by the manly courage of Christians who risked their lives in doing so. Nothing was as sublime as these first glimpses of the restored symbols of the faith of our fathers and as those Masses celebrated at the heart of our cities, in churches that had been devastated, violated and yet still chaste, and thrilling to behold the sweet sacrifice of the Lamb again after the orgies of the feasts of Reason and the utterances of Theophilanthropy.

The love of sacred pomp is deeply rooted in the hearts of the French, and the alliance of faith and poetry, which forms the foundation of the Catholic liturgy, holds such a strong appeal for them that there is no suffering nor political upheaval that they would not forget in moments when such noble and profound emotions course through their souls.

How guilty, then, or reckless were those who, for an entire century, had the dismal audacity to pursue every possible means to make the people forget religious chants and lay ruin to the pious traditions that are the lifeblood of faithful nations!

THE GENIUS OF CHRISTIANITY

The Concordat of 1801 had great liturgical implications.[1] It guaranteed the exercise of Catholic worship and was received as an immense blessing by a nation that had rejoiced at the return of its priests. Nothing could describe the enthusiasm of Parisians when, on 18 April 1802, the Concordat was finally promulgated amidst a religious and civic ceremony. It was the day of Easter itself, so that the faithful celebrated at the same time the passage of the Lord when the Israelites came out of Egypt, Christ's triumphant Resurrection, and the miraculous restoration of a religion that, nine years

---

[1] The Concordat of 1801 was an agreement between the Holy See and the First French Republic, represented by Pius VII and Napoleon Bonaparte respectively, which restored much of the civil status of the Church in France in order to resolve the hostility of French Catholics to the revolutionary state.

earlier, a sacrilegious decree had declared abolished. The consuls made their way in solemn procession to Notre-Dame, and French flags were seen once again swaying around the sanctuary. Giovanni Battista Caprara, a cardinal of the Holy Roman Church and apostolic legate, celebrated a Pontifical Mass under those now-reconciled vaults.

A very significant book published at the time did much to prepare men's minds for such a wonderful return: Chateaubriand's *The Genius of Christianity*, published in April 1802. This work, which sought to prove that Christianity is true because it is beautiful, did more to reconcile the French with their ancient worship than a hundred refutations of Rousseau's *Émile* or Voltaire's *Dictionnaire philosophique*. Undoubtedly, the new poetic vision revealed by Chateaubriand was not within the reach of all the book's readers; it could even be said that it left something to be desired. Yet the liturgical dimension of *The Genius of Christianity*, that is, the descriptions of feasts and ceremonies, and the vivid depictions of medieval cathedrals and cloisters, formed the most popular part of the work.

And perhaps too there was, in this solemn declaration of Christianity as the eminently *poetic* religion, a fertile reaction to Boileau, who, faithfully echoing the anti-liturgists of his Port-Royal, saw in the Christian faith only "terrible mysteries," and in poetry only "cheerful ornaments."[2] It was indeed in their capacity as classical men of letters that men like Foinard and Grancolas had articulated the fine theories that we have seen, mercilessly hunting down all those outmoded responsories and antiphons composed in a Latin so different from that of Cicero, and cramming all of their new works with pastiches in the style of Horace.

By establishing as a fact the poetic nature of Christianity considered in itself, *The Genius of Christianity* exerted a vast influence, and its impact will one day make for a long story. Among its many advantages, this book had that of arriving at the right time. Napoleon's eagle eye perceived its full significance from the outset, and he sought to attach himself to the author. Pius VII expressed his satisfaction in the most dazzling manner. Dussault, de Fontanes, the great philosopher de Bonald, and the Abbé de Boulogne all joined together to celebrate the importance of this victory won over the enemies of the religious form.

THE *ORGANIC ARTICLES*

Yet in the midst of this triumph, as tribulations always faithfully accompany the Church's successes in this world, unforeseen obstacles tempered the joy of the Roman Pontiff and the Church of France. To be sure, the Concordat had been proclaimed at Notre-Dame, but only a few days earlier,

---

[2] Nicolas Boileau, "Chant III," in *Œuvres poétiques* (Paris, 1872), vol. 1, p. 227, ll. 199–200: "De la foi d'un chrétien les mystères terribles / D'ornemens égayés ne sont point susceptibles ... "

seventy-seven articles had also been decreed under the name of *Organic Articles*. Many of these had been designed to mitigate the influence of Catholicism, and to halt the development of its resurgent institutions. We will confine ourselves to highlighting a few of the provisions under its Title III, entitled: "Concerning Worship."

The first of these, despite its brevity, had immense implications. It was worded as follows: "There will be only one liturgy and one catechism for all Catholic churches in France." Leaving aside the catechism, let us focus our attention on the liturgy. It is not difficult to see that, as a result of the newly drawn map of her dioceses, the Church of France found itself in a deplorable state of confusion with respect to the liturgy.

Numerous dioceses had been reduced by more than half, and new bishoprics had been formed, in whole or in part, from the territory of three or four of the old dioceses. As a result of the changes that had taken place in the eighteenth century, the liturgy of several cathedrals, far from uniting the other churches of the diocese under its forms, found itself vying for ground with five or six other rival liturgies. Such an outlandish spectacle was clearly unheard of in the Church. Never at any time or in any country had the communion of public prayers been so strangely anarchical.

A commission was appointed to draw up new books for the Church of France, but the results of its work were not made public. All that is known is that some of its members pushed for the liturgy of Paris, others for that of this or that diocese, and others still for an amalgam of them all. Meanwhile, that great man [Napoleon], who spoke of "his predecessor Charlemagne," failed to rise to the height of the vision of that illustrious founder of European society.

PIUS VII'S SOJOURN IN FRANCE

Napoleon's coronation had been a great liturgical act, but, in this very aspect, it highlighted the distance that separated the new Charlemagne from the old.

One could certainly understand that the liturgy is the truest expression of religion in a country, when witnessing the Roman Pontiff—who had hastened in an act of utmost devotion to lend his ministry to such a great ceremony—waiting, in pontifical vestments, on his throne in Notre-Dame for a whole hour before the eyes of the whole of France, for the arrival of the new emperor. Napoleon himself took the crown instead of receiving it from the Pontiff, and then crowned with his profane hands the forehead of a princess on which (we may recall) the diadem did not fit. The "bishop from outside" (*l'évêque du dehors*),[3] after being anointed

---

[3] This title was regularly attributed to the French kings, who, following the examples of Constantine and Charlemagne, embodied a conception of sacred kingship that involved safeguarding the interests of the Church.

with holy oil, abstained from participating in the sacred mysteries — a terrible omen of the decree which, five years later, was to cut him off from Catholic communion. All of this was achieved by violating the most precise rules of the liturgy.

Nothing else could capture the enthusiasm of the faithful in Paris and the provinces during the four months that Pius VII spent in the capital of the Empire. Yet there was nothing official or ceremonial about the crowds that flooded the churches where the Holy Father celebrated Mass. The faithful crowded around the holy table by the thousands, in the hopes of receiving the host of salvation from the very hands of the vicar of Jesus Christ. It was an ineffable spectacle to behold this multitude chanting with one voice the *Credo* intoned by the parish priest, surrounding the pious Pontiff as if in a cloud of faith as he celebrated the eternal sacrifice in deep contemplation, giving thanks for finding such devotion still alive in the hearts of the French.

A fine book could be written about Pius VII's sojourn in France at this time, but perhaps nothing would be more moving to recount than the Pontiff's visits to those churches that still bore the scars of the devastation they had suffered. There he celebrated Mass with the angelic reverence so admirably imprinted on his noble and touching figure. The Parisians, who adored Pius VII, used to say of him that "he prayed like a Pope."

LITURGICAL CONFUSION

The year was 1806, and the project for a national liturgy was still on everyone's lips, but the Commission established for this purpose produced no results. The famous project therefore came to nothing, and all that remained of it were the *Organic Articles*.

On the other hand, however, with Napoleon now emperor — and an emperor consecrated by the Pope — it became necessary for him to have an imperial chapel, and also for that chapel to celebrate the Divine Office according to some established liturgical rules. The old court had observed the Roman use since Henry III. Napoleon, so eager to revive all aspects of the etiquette of Versailles, departed from it in this respect. He abolished the Roman liturgy and decreed that only the Parisian books would be used in his presence. This was certainly a great honor for the likes of Vigier and Mésenguy, but it was further proof of the great man's antipathy for anything that might hinder his dreams of a national Church.

Napoleon, who had refused the role of Charlemagne, fell before his time, and the churches could breathe again. However, the Church's freedom was not restored until the return of the House of Bourbon. Upon his return, Louis XVIII re-established the use of the Roman liturgy in the royal chapels. Etiquette alone required this, and we shall not attempt to ascribe to this act any greater value or significance.

The era of the Restoration, unlike that of the Empire, was marked by a significant number of liturgical undertakings. Numerous Breviaries, Missals and Rituals were reprinted, corrected, revised, and even created anew. As for our opinion of this new crisis, we shall say, with all due respect to our contemporaries who still use these books, that it seems to have done nothing but increase the already existing confusion. That said, we should also note that amidst this confusion, signs of a return to sounder theories emerged from all sides. But indeed, it was impossible to devise successful liturgies in the nineteenth century, since knowledge of the liturgy had evidently disappeared in France.

This led to (and we shall continue to avoid naming living persons) cases where a Breviary underwent two or three revisions in the same diocese in a space of twenty years. Venerable usages, maintained by one administration, were suppressed by the next, and restored with modifications by a third. Ceremonies were transplanted indiscriminately from one diocese to another without any concern for the respective dignity of the churches, which forbids such borrowings. Breviaries were reprinted which contradicted the Missal, while Missals were at odds with the Breviary, and choir books lacked any concord among themselves. Outlandish rubrics appeared, as well as feasts without precedents. Almost everywhere, the canonical Office ceased to be sung in cathedrals.

France's error, if there was one, was that it did not shake off quickly enough the yoke bequeathed by the seventeenth and eighteenth centuries. If the liturgy is today a science to be created anew, it is because it has collapsed under the blows of our predecessors. All of the ills of our present situation thus stem from them.

The observations that we have made so far relate to dioceses which, at the beginning of the present century, already had a new [*and therefore non-Roman*] Breviary. The case is entirely different when the Roman Breviary and Missal have been violently expelled, an offense that has occurred several times since 1815 in dioceses where this liturgy had survived all other calamities.

We do not hesitate here to declare ourselves as the champion the Roman liturgy. Such was also the conviction of the holiest prelate of our time, Charles-François d'Aviau, Archbishop of Bordeaux, who so zealously upheld the Roman liturgy in his diocese. Unfortunately, this has not been the case everywhere. It is all too clear that several other dioceses have taken the opposite step. There are even some where the use of Roman books has been outright forbidden.

When a parish priest mounts the pulpit to give his Sunday sermon, instead of the beautiful catalog of patron saints offered each week by the Roman calendar, he states in a few brief words the bare details of the few saints that have been retained; when the monotonous series of Sundays after Pentecost stretches on for five or six months without the eyes of simple men getting to see the varied colors of confessors and martyrs, or to hear chanted the *Iste confessor*, a hymn that they all knew and loved so well, with its sometimes pastoral, sometimes triumphal air—then the faithful begin to ask their rectors what benefit there could possibly be in all of these changes to the way God is honored.

THE NEED FOR IMMUTABILITY

Yet Divine Providence will bring good even out of the furthest excess of evil, and the return to pure traditions will come through the disgust and weariness that was increasingly inspired by these individual works. Already, it cannot be denied, there is a widespread feeling of unease about the liturgical situation among the ranks of the clergy. Attention is beginning to turn in this direction, and it is hard to believe that men will continue to consent to remain so indebted to the eighteenth century for much longer. The continual revisions, the inconsistency between liturgical books, the return to traditional studies, the inability of building a coherent science on such unstable foundations, the difficulty of answering the questions of the faithful—all things betoken a crisis.

There is a universally recognized need to be in harmony with the Roman Church, a need that grows ever stronger and before which the resistance of our so-called Gallican principles fades day by day. After all, it is only natural to prefer to hold to the liturgy of St. Gregory and his successors rather than to that of an obscure and suspect eighteenth-century priest. Everyone understands that, if the law of faith derives from the law of prayer, then the law of prayer must be immutable, universal, and promulgated by an infallible authority.

Moreover, French piety is increasingly freeing itself from the cold and abstract forms with which the seventeenth and eighteenth centuries had encumbered it. It has become, as it was before the Reformation, more expansive and demonstrative. There is a stronger belief in miracles and extraordinary paths to sainthood. The veneration of relics is also seeing renewed popularity, and the faithful rejoice to see Rome, delving ever more deeply into her catacombs, drawing forth the bodies of holy martyrs that it sends to France from time to time to replenish the devastated treasuries of its churches.

FIRST STEPS TOWARDS A ROMAN RESTORATION

A great and solemn example has just been given by Monseigneur Pierre-Louis Parisis, Bishop of Langres, who simply restored the pure Roman liturgy in his diocese. It is a courageous measure which history will remember, and which the prelate explains in a pastoral letter:

You are not unaware, dearest brethren, of the liturgical divergences that affect the celebration of Divine Offices in this diocese. You have often complained about the contradiction and opposition of rites between neighboring parishes, which has led the faithful, after seeing the variations in chants and ceremonies in every church, to wonder whether these temples — where the rites of Religion are celebrated in such diverse ways — are even consecrated to the same worship . . .

You can easily understand the harms this causes to Holy Church, the Bride of Jesus Christ, the one who must have neither spot nor wrinkle (cf. Eph. 5:27), especially in these times of turmoil brought on by impious doctrines . . .

Indeed, among the marks of the true Church, and even above all the others, the mark of Unity must shine forth and make her distinguishable from dissident sects. Hence when the people, who judge the essence of things only by appearances, witness these contradictions, they begin to wonder whether the Catholic Church is truly one throughout the whole earth, when it seems so divided within the limits of a single diocese . . .

Afflicted for a long time by the inconveniences of such an infelicitous and perilous situation, after having reflected day and night and implored the help of the *Father of lights* (Jas. 1:17), we sought how we might unite all the parishes of our diocese in the unity of ceremonies and Offices that is so holy, so desirable, and so conducive to the unity and edification of the faithful. Finally, after much uncertainty, having weighed and examined all these things with the greatest care, it seemed to us that we should return to the liturgy of the Roman Church, our Mother, which, being the center of unity and firmest pillar of truth, will guarantee and defend us and our people against the whirlwind of deviations and against the temptation of change.

But in order to avoid the harm that could arise from the very use of the remedy we are applying, and so that all may gradually submit to the same rule, not by violence, but voluntarily, it is necessary to consider that the greater part of our diocese was previously subject to the Roman Rite, while the other parts, detached from various dioceses [*during the territorial reorganization of the dioceses of France and the suppression of a large number of bishoprics*], have remained unfamiliar with the aforementioned Roman usages . . . Having made these distinctions, we declare and order the following:

1. From the first day of the year 1840, the Roman liturgy shall be the liturgy proper to the diocese of Langres . . .

We therefore entreat all of you, who are our fellow laborers in the Lord, to bring to the execution of this great work all the zeal of which you are capable, so that, just as among us there is only *one Lord, one faith,* and *one baptism* (Eph. 4:5), there will also be among our people only *one tongue* (Gen. 11:1).

Given at Langres, on the Feast of St. Teresa of Ávila, 15 October, in the year of our Salvation 1839.

Who could fail to admire in this truly pastoral letter the zeal for the house of God, tempered by that discretion so recommended by the Apostle (cf. Rom. 12:3), and of which St. Pius V gave such a shining example in the sixteenth century, even as he promulgated this same great principle of liturgical unity?

The more they are at the same time firm and moderate, the more effective will be the results of all the acts of this kind that our century may witness in the Church of France, for we do not believe we can heal a diseased member by wounding it roughly and mercilessly.

However, it must be acknowledged that the return to the liturgical traditions of the ages of faith is now underway and growing more visible by the day. It is even possible to foresee that it will remain one of the characteristics of the present era. The revival of historical scholarship, which has enabled us to take a disinterested look at the morals and customs of the early centuries of faith, and the justice finally rendered to the monuments of medieval Catholic art, have contributed to this restoration, or rather they have rapidly advanced it.

In the meantime, the true friends of the science of sacred rites will rejoice in reading these lovely words, in which Monseigneur Affre, Archbishop of Paris, in his pastoral letter on "ecclesiastical studies," expresses the need to revive a science whose very name seems for too long to have been obliterated:

> The liturgy contains symbols, marvelous summaries of our belief, a dual object of faith and love, which, with the help of a chant both pious and melodious, are engraved in the memory and in the heart. The well-demonstrated antiquity of these symbols, as well as their universality, make them irrefutable witnesses to the apostolicity and catholicity of our faith.
>
> Furthermore, the liturgy contains prayers which presuppose or express in detail each of our dogmas, mysteries, and Sacraments. Like the symbols, they do not have unity of expression, but the very variety of their forms, combined with the unity of doctrine, provides a further demonstration of the immutability of Catholic teaching.
>
> Finally, the liturgy is made up of rites. Together with symbols and prayers, they constitute external worship, a kind of worship that is necessary for a being who, although created in the image of God, is subject to the dominion of the senses. Without these external rites, inner worship would inevitably perish.[4]

And so, let us wholeheartedly welcome the dawn of better days promised to the Church of France, and let us have no doubt that, in the more or less near future, the liturgy of St. Gregory, of Charlemagne, of St. Gregory VII, of St. Pius V, in a word the liturgy of the ages of faith, will again triumph in our churches.

---

4 Monseigneur Affre, *Lettre Pastorale sur les études ecclésiastiques* (Paris, 1841), pp. 11–12.

III

LITURGICAL BOOKS

25

The Importance of Liturgical Books

ATURALLY, NOT ALL OUR READERS WILL have at their ready disposal the liturgical monuments of ancient times and of foreign Churches. Nevertheless, aside from the fact that we shall do our utmost to remedy this deficiency by providing analyses and excerpts, we hasten to assure our readers of the value of their own liturgical studies, even if they confine themselves to a serious study of the six books of which the Roman liturgy is composed: the Breviary, Missal, Ritual, Pontifical, Martyrology, and Ceremonial of Bishops.

These monuments contain such a plenitude of doctrine that anyone who has a thorough command and acquired understanding of them will always be in a position to engage with the scholar whose investigations have embraced the documents of antiquity, of which these six books are a powerful and harmonious summary.

All priests should therefore possess these invaluable books in their libraries and read them continually. They shall find more solid instruction in them than in the vast number of mediocre and unauthoritative volumes which the ecclesiastical book industry churns out daily, with ruinous prodigality, and which generally fail to impart to their readers a single idea per volume.

In the past, diocesan statutes required priests to have the books of the liturgy in their possession. Accordingly, in the ninth century, we find Walter, the Bishop of Orléans, formulate this provision in the seventh article of his Capitulary: "Priests shall have, for their own instruction and that of others, the ecclesiastical books, namely: the Missal, the Evangeliary, the Lectionary, the Psalter, the Antiphonary, the Martyrology, and the Homiliary." [1]

Let those who aspire to the science of divine worship first apply themselves to the assiduous reading of these sacred documents. Let them familiarize themselves with both the formulas and the rubrics. Let them seek, until they have found, the mysterious link that unites all the parts of this sublime whole. Let them not be discouraged either by the apparent aridity of this study or by the repugnance that absurd prejudices might have instilled in them. They will soon reap the rewards of their labor.

Their first careful reading [*of these liturgical books*] will initiate them into the concrete aspects of the divine service and begin to open before them glimpses of its mysteries, which are the joy of the heart and the light of the mind.

---

[1] Walter of Orléans, *Capitula* (*Patrologia Latina* 115:119).

A second reading, fortified by careful research in the fields of theology, mysticism, canon law, ecclesiastical history and antiquity, will renew these initial impressions, and bring them ever greater illumination. Their faith will be nourished by a heavenly manna, their intellect will be conformed to these divine teachings of the Church, and their speech will take on a degree of authority that it had not previously known. And indeed, this light, this warmth, this life will continue to grow for as long as the disciple remains faithful to the lessons the Church imparts through the liturgy. This study will be wedded with that of the Holy Scriptures, which are the priest's daily bread, and with that of tradition, which provides the key to the Scriptures, and of which the books of the Roman liturgy are one of the richest treasures.

It is to the absence of these indispensable aids that we must attribute the almost total eclipse of the science of sacred rites among us. Amid the changes and reconstructions that they underwent, these liturgical books were gradually despoiled of their authority.

It was after the days of liturgical confusion, caused by the ease with which new books for divine service proliferated, that St. Pius V, with the publication of the Breviary and Missal; Gregory XIII, with his edition of the Martyrology; Clement VIII, with those of the Pontifical and Ceremonial; and Paul V, with the inauguration of the Ritual, re-established the sacred rites with a renewed brilliance, ensuring their stability through uniformity. These great Pontiffs thus remedied "the disruption of divine worship that had occurred in so many places, and put an end to the ignorance of ecclesiastical ceremonies and rites among the clergy, which was causing countless Church ministers to perform their duties unworthily, to the great scandal of the pious faithful."[2]

Nevertheless, this reform of liturgical habits would be slow to take effect. In France, we owe it to the books of the Roman liturgy decreed by the Council of Trent and to the zeal of the men whom God raised up to ensure the application of the rules prescribed in these books. What St. Charles Borromeo had achieved for the reform of divine service in his councils of Milan was accomplished in Paris, and from there throughout France, by three priests who had received from on high the mission of regenerating the clergy: St. Vincent de Paul, Jean-Jacques Olier, and Adrien Bourdoise. All three of these men dedicated themselves to restoring the liturgy through the use of the Roman books:

● St. Vincent de Paul, through his Congregation of the Mission, which earned the honor of being officially entrusted by the popes with the duty of ensuring that the traditions of the Holy Sacrifice are maintained, even in Rome itself;

---

[2] Pope Pius V, Bull *Quod a nobis* (9 July 1568).

● Jean-Jacques Olier, through his society of priests of Saint-Sulpice, as well as through his writings, in which we find such a profound and exquisite knowledge of liturgical texts and the mysteries they contain;

● Adrien Bourdoise, through his seminary at Saint-Nicolas-du-Chardonnet, one of whose principal aims was to revive the traditions of divine service.

One will recall the resistance mounted by the communities of Saint-Sulpice and Saint-Nicolas against the introduction, under Archbishops Harlay and Vintimille, of the Parisian liturgy into their churches, where the Roman liturgy, so precisely observed, had exerted such a salutary influence on the whole Church of France.

The uncertainty of liturgical books, their instability, and their variations came to deprive them of that solidity, that gravity, that doctrine, and hence, that consideration which a text that is called to serve as the basis of a science must bring together. What could one hope to determine from books whose permanence could not be guaranteed?

By contrast, by relying on age-old and authorized texts and by diligently consulting the ancient and inviolable books of the Roman liturgy, one will soon come to conform one's thinking to that of the Church in the worship she renders to God.

The administration of the Sacraments, performed with the emotion inspired by all the mysteries that accompany it, and having become more fruitful for the people's edification of the people, will repay with interest the care that the minister will have taken to nourish himself with the sacred formulas of the Ritual, through the graces and spiritual strength it will confer him. No one should ascend to the altar without a full possession of the Canon of the Mass, which so authoritatively contains the doctrine of the Christian Sacrifice.

The mysteries of the great Sacrifice, the Sacraments, the sacramentals, the phases of the Christian cycle so rich in grace and enlightenment, the ceremonies, the sublime language with which the Church speaks to God before men — all these marvels, in a word, will once again become familiar to the faithful.

26

The Antiquity of Liturgical Books

INCE LITURGICAL BOOKS ARE RECOG-
nized as the foundation of liturgical science, it is only nat-
ural to consider the question of their antiquity. When was
the liturgy first committed to writing? Whatever answer
one gives to this question, it has no practical application
on the present day, since we live in an age when the Church has recorded
her traditions of divine worship in books. Even so, the answer could have
some bearing on the authority of the books that are in use today, if one can
establish that their earliest form dates back to the beginnings of the Church,
and that, despite the various modifications they might have undergone, we
must recognize in their contents a permanent foundation that has endured
through the centuries.

APOSTOLIC ORIGIN OF THE GREAT RITES

We are happy to concede that the liturgical books were not written by the
apostles themselves. The only apostolic liturgy that bears serious marks of
authenticity is that of St. James, but it has undergone so many alterations
that it would be difficult to rigorously determine its original form.

Accordingly, we readily grant that the apostles left us no written liturgies, provided, however, that it likewise be granted that they established
in the Churches that they founded all the rites we find universally spread
throughout all Churches, without any record of their origins or of the
developments that led to their adoption. This, as we know, is the great
Catholic rule formulated by St. Augustine concerning the nature of ecclesiastical institutions.[1]

The apostles, who were entrusted with the task of organizing Christian
society, had to concern themselves not only with the essential aspects of
the rites, but also with suitable customs. This is what St. Paul expresses
in his first Epistle to the Corinthians, where, after having regulated the
essential forms of the Holy Sacrifice, he announces that, on his return,
he will "dispose of the rest" (1 Cor. 11:34: *Cetera cum venero, disponam*).

But these various rites necessarily entailed formulas, and these formulas
necessarily tend to become stable. Otherwise, one can imagine the abuses

---

[1] Guéranger seems to be thinking of Augustine's assertion, in *De baptismo contra
Donatistas* (bk. 5, ch. 23, 13), that "there are many things which are observed by the whole
Church, and therefore are fairly held to have been enjoined by the apostles, which yet
are not mentioned in their writings."

in speech, the irreverence toward the mysteries, and the peril for doctrine, if these formulas had been left to the improvisation of the sacred minister. Moreover, the Apostle, in laying down the rules we are discussing, reduces them all to one fundamental principle: that "everything be done decently and according to order" (1 Cor. 14:40: *Omnia honeste et secundum ordinem fiant*).

But how could this decency and order be maintained if the formulas are not established in fixed terms? There can be no doubt, then, that liturgies of some sort were established from the outset to meet the needs of divine worship, a point even our opponents readily concede. But these solemn and sacrosanct formulas must have been, and in fact were, extensive in their content. The majesty and dignity of the mysteries demanded it, and we have irrefutable testimony to that effect. St. Paul, in defining the different forms of liturgical prayer for the Sacrifice, names "supplications, orations, intercessions, and thanksgivings" (1 Tim. 2:1).

St. Justin Martyr, in his first Apology which describes the Christian Sacrifice (ca. 139 AD), plainly affirms that the priest pronounces a *thanksgiving* in many words (*prolixe*), in which he gives glory to the Father of all things in the name of the Son and the Holy Spirit.[2]

Are we to believe that the memory of the priests alone was entrusted with such weighty prayers? The Church today prescribes that her ministers, when offering the Holy Sacrifice, keep their eyes fixed on the prayers of the Canon on the altar card; she forbids them from relying on their memory in the Action of so tremendous a mystery. Would she have shown less wisdom in those early centuries? Would she not, even then, have required that at least one book — be it kept in the innermost recesses of the sanctuary — should serve to refresh the memory of the holy formulas from time to time?

Let us imagine that all the copies of the Canon of the Mass preserved in churches today were suddenly destroyed, and all priests were henceforth reduced to reciting the prayers of the Sacrifice from memory. Can one seriously suppose that, fifty years later, the formulas would still be pronounced at the altar with the same accuracy?

Let us add that it would not only have been a matter merely of memorizing the prayers of the Sacrifice. It would also have been essential to possess, in addition to the form of the Sacraments, the formulas that accompany their administration: the exorcisms of Baptism, the varied orations for the conferral of orders, the prayers particular to the feasts of apostolic institution — in a word, everything that we find preserved in the same style in all of the most ancient liturgies.

Undoubtedly, such a powerful and unshakable memory may have occurred from time to time. Indeed, it remains within the realm of possibility even today, albeit very rarely. Nevertheless, it is dangerous to entrust the liturgy

---

[2] St. Justin Martyr, *Apology* 1, 65.

to memory, and, let it be said again, the spirit of the Church is opposed to holy functions being performed without the help of liturgical books.

This has ever been true; but in the first three centuries of the Church — a period marked by the emergence of so many subtle heresies, cloaked in clever wording, as all heresies are — what means was there to halt the progress of error — which takes pains to conceal itself, and whose discourses, in the words of St. Paul, spreads creepingly like a canker (cf. 2 Tim. 2:17) — if a faithless priest or pontiff, veiling his novelties under the words of an unwritten text, had given himself over to pernicious improvisations? How could other priests or bishops have confronted him, if they could not place before his eyes the inviolable and orthodox text of the liturgy?

Never has the Church has carelessly exposed the deposit of faith to such danger, nor has she suffered holy things to be treated without the dignity and reverence they demand. Even if we had no other proof of the existence of liturgical books before the fifth century than the compelling considerations we have just set out, we would nevertheless have every reason to affirm, on the grounds of the Church's own wisdom, that these books did exist.

CONCRETE EVIDENCE

We will now turn to the concrete evidence which, despite the loss of so many documents from this primitive age, still demonstrate the position contrary to that of Pierre Le Brun. According to this learned Oratorian, the liturgies were not committed to writing until the fifth century.

An episode drawn from the history of the Church of the Gauls in that very same fifth century already compels us to push this arbitrarily designated date further back. St. Gregory of Tours reports that St. Sidonius Apollinaris, Bishop of Clermont, had been invited to the monastery of St. Cyriacus for the dedication of the Basilica, but some malicious hand suddenly removed the book of the liturgy from the altar. Unperturbed by this disruption, the holy bishop completed the entire service for the feast [*from memory*], which aroused such awe among those present that they thought it was not a man, but an angel who had uttered the words.[3] Now, St. Sidonius Apollinaris ascended to the see of Clermont in 471. If the practice of celebrating the liturgy without a book and simply from memory continued into the fifth century, would the holy Bishop of Clermont's deed have caused such astonishment among the people? And would St. Gregory of Tours have found it remarkable enough to include in his history of the Franks? It is difficult to believe.

But let us bring forth direct evidence for the existence of liturgical books from as early as the fourth century. In 379, St. Basil of Caesarea died. Among his many labors for the service of the Church, he compiled a liturgy

---

[3] St. Gregory of Tours, *Historia Francorum*, bk. 2, ch. 22: "Nec putaretur ab adstantibus ibidem locutum fuisse hominem, sed angelum."

which may have differed from that which the Greek Church still preserves under his name, but which was nonetheless recognized as his work in the following century. On this point, we have the testimony of St. Gregory of Nazianzen, a contemporary and friend of the holy doctor.[4] St. Proclus, successor to St. John Chrysostom over the see of Constantinople, expresses himself in the following terms in his treatise on the Divine Liturgy: "The great Basil, realizing that the length of the liturgy had occasioned tedium and aversion among those present, redacted it in a more concise form for the use of the Church."[5] Can one really imagine that the ancient liturgy, which was so long that it had to be shortened in the fourth century, could have rested solely on the memory of priests?

The year 368 marked the death of St. Hilary of Poitiers. St. Jerome, in his catalogue of ecclesiastical writers [*De viris illustribus*], informs us that, during his episcopate, this great man had written a book of hymns and a book of mysteries.[6] This book of mysteries (*liber mysteriorum*) was the Sacramentary or Missal of the Gallican Church, which St. Hilary undoubtedly reordered and enriched with prayers of his own composition, as St. Ambrose had done in Milan in the same century, and as the Popes St. Gelasius and St. Gregory the Great did in Rome in the following centuries.

But were there liturgical books during the persecutions? We shall prove it beyond any shadow of doubt by producing incontestable documentary evidence that has not been put forward in this debate until now. The persecutions of the Church ended in 312, when Constantine granted her peace. The texts we are about to cite must have been composed no later than during Diocletian's persecution, which began in 284, so we will find ourselves in the third century.

First, we will reproduce the text of a Preface from a famous sacramentary of the Roman Church improperly called the Leonine Sacramentary, a collection of liturgical formulas which derive in large part from the earliest days of Christianity. This Preface, undated, appears under the month of April:

> It is right to give thanks to thee, O God, whose Church is at this time mixed with true and false confessors, so that we must always fear the fickleness of human weakness, and yet never despair of the conversion of any man. It is therefore with so much more insistence that we thy suppliants entreat thee, without whom devotion cannot but collapse, to grant perseverance to those who are firm and a restoration of wisdom to those who have been weak.[7]

---

4 St. Gregory of Nazianzen, *Oratio xx de laudibus Basilii*: "Ordinationes sacrarum precum ad altare composuit."
5 Proclus, *De Liturgiæ divinæ traditione*: "Basilius magnus, cum hominum Liturgiæ prolixitatem fastidientium oscitantiam et propensionem perspiceret, redactam in compendium Ecclesiæ recitandam exhibuit."
6 St. Jerome, *De viris illustribus*, ch. 100: "Est eius...et liber hymnorum et mysteriorum alius."
7 *Sacramentarium Leonianum*, April, n. 20: "Vere dignum, cuius ecclesia sic veris confessoribus falsisque permixta nunc agitur, ut tamen et fragilitatis humanæ semper cavenda

Is this not a prayer for the "fallen,"[8] and must not this Preface belong to the days of persecution?

In his great treatise on the Sacrament of penance, Fr. Jean Morin of the French Oratory, within his analysis of certain orations used in the ancient Sacramentaries for the imposition of penance, writes as follows:

> The language, the phrasing, and the style of the orations and the other principal rites contained in these Sacramentaries clearly bear witness to a more ancient time; indeed, they cannot be posterior to Popes Sylvester and Julius...The principal contents of these ritual formulas, both with respect to diction and style, is wholly reminiscent of the times that preceded Constantine's reign.[9]

In the middle of the second century lived the philosopher Celsus, who wrote against Christianity and was later refuted so logically and forcefully by Origen. Liturgical books had been written down as early as the time of this subtle Epicurean, whose work we now possess only in fragments. Indeed, Celsus maintained that he "had seen in the hands of certain [Christian] priests barbaric books, in which the names and deceits of demons appeared."[10] Evidently, the philosopher is referring to the exorcism formulas used on catechumens and the possessed. In his reply, Origen does not deny the existence of these books in the hands of priests, but simply answers that, protected by their prayers, Christians are mightier than sorcerers and demons.[11]

We are now approaching the apostolic age, and we readily admit that we lack direct evidence for the existence of liturgical books at this stage. However, the same dearth of documentary testimony is equally felt in questions of far greater importance than the one we are now discussing.

Let us conclude this discussion with one last witness: the philosopher Lucian, who lived in the second century. In his dialogue *Philopatris* — whose attribution has sometimes been contested, but which can be traced back to the first century of Christianity — the author hurls forth, among his other diatribes against the new religion, mockeries of liturgical prayer. One of the speakers describes a Christian assembly, and after various details, mentions one of the prayers uttered there. This prayer "began with the name of the Father, and ended with a chant in which a large number of names were recited."[12] It is easy to recognize in these words an allusion to the forms

---

mutatio et nullius sit desperanda conversio: quo magis supplices te rogamus, ut, quia sine te non potest solida constare devotio, et firmis perseverantiam et resipiscentiam largiaris infirmis."

[8] The "fallen" (*lapsi*) were Christians who had temporarily renounced their religion for fear of persecution, but who subsequently returned to it.

[9] Jean Morin, *De disciplina in administratione sacramenti Pœnitentiæ* (Venice, 1702), bk. 9, ch. 30, p. 695.

[10] Origen, *Contra Celsum*, bk. 6, n. 40.

[11] Ibid.

[12] Lucian, *Philopatris*, n. 12: "Precationem incipientem a Patre, et in hymno multorum nominum finientem."

of the early liturgy, which opened with the Lord's Prayer and ended with long prayers in which the names of those for whom the Sacrifice was offered were recited. Observe, then, that there was unquestionably a fixed order, a stability of formulas, and a promulgation of rites, all of which necessarily presupposes an established text.

Anyone can see that there is but a short step from a fixed liturgical form to a written one. We shall, therefore, conclude our investigation into the existence of liturgical books in the first four centuries. The reader can judge for himself the strength of the case.

THE SECRECY OF THE MYSTERIES

Pierre Le Brun bases his argument for the purely oral transmission of the liturgy in the early Church on Tertullian's *De corona militis*, which states that we know the formulas of the Sacraments and the manner of administering them only through unwritten tradition. Tertullian enumerates various rites, and concludes as follows: "If, for these and other such practices, you seek a written law, you will find none. Tradition supplies the want, custom confirms it, and faith enforces it."[13] Hence our learned author concluded that there were no written liturgical books; otherwise, Tertullian would have mentioned them.

To this we respond that the term "written law" (*legem scripturarum*) used here by Tertullian does not refer to liturgical formulas committed to paper. Tertullian's entire argument clearly shows that, in this passage, he is dealing with tradition in comparison with Sacred Scripture. The liturgy, written or unwritten, remains a matter of tradition, and Tertullian's reasoning holds true even if the liturgies of that time had been written down.

The argument drawn from the words of St. Basil may appear more formidable, but it is no less flawed. Here are the words of that holy doctor:

> Which of the saints has left us in writing the words of invocation which are pronounced when the bread of the Eucharist and the chalice of blessing are confected? We do not content ourselves with what the Apostle or the Gospel has recorded; but we recite, both before and after, other words, as having great importance for the mystery, and these words we have received from tradition, without writing. We consecrate the water of baptism, the oil of anointing, and the very person who is baptized: but from what writings? Do not these rites come from a silent, secret tradition? What written passage teaches us about anointing with oil? To make three immersions, from what Scripture is this drawn? The other things done at baptism, such as renouncing Satan and his angels, where do we have this in Holy Writ? Do we not receive it from that unpublished and

---

[13] Tertullian, *De corona militis*, n. 4: "Harum et aliarum eiusmodi disciplinarum, si legem expostules scripturarum, nullam invenies: traditio tibi protetendetur auctrix, consuetudo confirmatrix, et fides observatrix."

secret tradition, from that doctrine which our fathers safeguarded
by an unbroken and never indiscreet silence?[14]

We readily admit that this text from St. Basil is a noble witness to the
existence of divine and apostolic tradition, which complements the teaching
of Scripture on the Sacrifice and the Sacraments. However, this passage in
no way proves that these traditions — which were not left to us in writing
by "the saints," that is by the writers of Sacred Scripture — had not been
written down since then, without thereby losing their traditional character.
Today, with Missals and Rituals in print everywhere, we can still describe
them in the same terms.

As for the secrecy that surrounded liturgical formulas in St. Basil's time
and shielded them from contact with the profane, the same practice still
existed in France three centuries ago. Until then, the Canon of the Mass
had never been placed into the hands of the ordinary faithful, much less
had anyone dared to translate it into the vernacular. Indeed, St. Basil could
have said in France then what he said in Caesarea in the fourth century.

If there had been written liturgical books in the first four centuries, how
is it, asks Fr. Le Brun, that the holy doctors did not appeal to them when
refuting heretics? After all, from the fifth century onwards, such texts are
regularly invoked in controversies to establish the Church's faith.

We shall reply first that, when the authors of this early period appeal to
tradition and custom concerning the holy mysteries, they always mean —
as our opponents admit — liturgical custom and tradition. Why then do
they not cite any specific text? First, we grant that liturgical books were
rare in the times when the discipline of secrecy prevailed. They were carefully kept hidden, and their contents, intended only to aid the memory
of priests and bishops, were scarcely known to the faithful. Accordingly,
they could not be revealed in public writings without inconvenience. Furthermore, one must recognize that if written liturgical books had existed
at this time, as we believe we have demonstrated, they belonged to each
particular Church rather than being in universal use.

How, then, could the Fathers have appealed to texts that did not represent
a substantial portion of the Church even in a single fixed expression? It was
thus more natural to appeal to tradition and custom, which these liturgical
books expressed in diverse forms. But at the time of the Church's Peace,
it was felt necessary to reinforce the argument drawn from tradition and
custom by subjecting liturgical prayers to the approval of councils, while
churches of the same province were obliged to adopt the same rites and
formulas. This is why, from then on, liturgical texts came to be cited much
more often in theological debates; they had become more widely known
and more broadly adopted among the particular Churches.

---

[14] St. Basil, *De Spiritu sancto*, ch. 27.

But then, our illustrious opponents will say, what of the *disciplina arcani*, the secrecy of the mysteries, if the sacred formulas were entrusted to writing?

The discipline of secrecy did indeed exist in the early Church. Evidence of it can still be found in the fifth century, in clear passages from St. John Chrysostom, St. Augustine, Theodoret and St. Cyril of Alexandria. It would, however, be a grave error to suppose that the *disciplina arcani* was always so absolute that it was never set aside. In the second century, this law did not prevent St. Justin Martyr, writing under the eyes of the Roman Pontiff, from expounding the mysteries of Baptism, the Eucharist, and the Christian Sacrifice in his first Apology, addressed to the emperors, with a clarity and breadth that surpass anything we find in the writings of that period intended for the faithful.

Even so, is the very existence of liturgical books an breach of the "discipline of secrecy"? Upon reflection, one must see it rather as a confirmation of that very discipline. These books existed, but they were kept secret. We could even grant, if need be, that they were not always brought to the altar, but rather, they served to support the priest's memory, to keep pure the deposit of tradition, and to prevent alterations which could have arisen without this aid. It was not necessary for there to be many copies; the common people did not read them, and indeed they were not written for them. How, then, could the Fathers have cited books that were not in circulation? From this perspective, it seems to us that everything can be reconciled without difficulty.

We are therefore persuaded that we have firmly established this proposition, and we regard the existence of liturgical books in the early Church, at least from the second century onwards, as an established scientific fact. It follows that the liturgical forms, so important for the mysteries they express and contain, were fixed at a time close to that of the apostles, and that the "supplications, orations, intercessions, and thanksgivings" prescribed by St. Paul were determined early on, and have come down to us altered only by small additions or slight modifications that have not substantially altered their meaning or form.

27

The Language of Liturgical Books

I F, BY TRADITION, LITURGICAL BOOKS have a style and form of composition that is proper to them, it is no less a fact that they are not written in every language. Should we attribute this to mere accident, or does it arise from purposeful design? Has the Church, by upholding the principle of a liturgical and non-vernacular language in her divine services, failed in her duty to the faithful? The present chapter aims to answer the first of these questions. As for the second, it was resolved by the Church herself at the Council of Trent, where she expressed herself as follows: "If anyone says that Mass should be celebrated only in the vulgar tongue, let him be anathema."[1]

When a diluted form of Calvinism — which produced so many evils in France under the name of Jansenism — had revived in this matter the same doctrines that the Council of Trent had excoriated, the Church, in the apostolic constitution *Unigenitus*, condemned Quesnel's saccharine proposal in these terms: "To deprive the simple people of the consolation of uniting their voices to that of the whole Church is a practice contrary to that of the apostles and to God's intention."[2]

We must now examine, in keeping with the scope of these *Institutions*, the origin of this law and the motive that prompted the exclusion of vernacular languages from the divine service.

THE THREE LANGUAGES OF THE INSCRIPTION OF THE CROSS
In the first place, it is completely false that the liturgy was celebrated in the vulgar language of every people among whom the Faith was proclaimed, even in the earliest days of Christianity. We dare to affirm that, until the fourth century, three particular languages, Syriac [*or Hebrew*], Greek and Latin, were the only ones used at the altar. This imparts to them a very special liturgical dignity, and wonderfully confirms the principle of using sacred rather than vernacular languages in the liturgy.

The firm and sublime teaching of Robert Bellarmine and certain other redoubtable theologians of the sixteenth century, including that of the Sorbonne in its memorable censure of Erasmus in 1526, found support in men both learned and resolute. The great Cardinal Giovanni Bona always

---

[1] Council of Trent, Session 22, can. 9: "Si quis dixerit lingua tantum vulgari missam celebrari debere, anathema sit."
[2] Pope Clement XI, Bull *Unigenitus* (8 September 1713), prop. 86.

upheld the Church's practice as a point of doctrine that must be taught affirmatively and not simply excused. But it must be acknowledged that, after a certain era, authors who treated the subject with perfect clarity became increasingly rare.

Nevertheless, it would have been easy to understand the Church's motives for using the sacred languages at the altar by recalling the ancient discipline of secrecy surrounding the mysteries. Certainly, the Church has modified her customs in this respect [*i.e., concealing the mysteries of the Faith from the unbaptized*], but she could not abandon the principle itself. The mysteries remain as profound as ever, and the heart of man, weighed down to the earth, remains as frail and as dangerous as before.

One could also have recalled the teaching of St. Basil who, in his book *On the Holy Spirit*, forcefully expresses the Church's thinking on the need to surround holy things with mystery: "Moses, in his wisdom," he writes,

> knew that things that are familiar and easily accessible are exposed to contempt, but that those which are rare and set apart from common contact naturally excite the greatest zeal and admiration. In imitation of him, the Apostles and the Fathers established, from the very beginning, various rites in the Church, and preserved the dignity of the mysteries by secrecy and silence; for what is uttered in the ears of the vulgar is in no wise a mystery any longer.[3]

It is thus that we begin with the bold certitude that there are certain sacred languages that have been set apart from others by divine election, to serve as intermediaries between heaven and earth.

The dignity of the three tongues that proclaimed the kingship of the Crucified One on Calvary did not only strike the mystical writers of the Middle Ages. Joseph de Maistre († 1821) recognized the consecration [*of these languages*][4] no less than did the devout Honorius of Autun († 1151),[5] both of whom simply repeated what St. Hilary of Poitiers had already said in the fourth century. "It is principally in these three languages [Hebrew, Greek and Latin] that the mystery of God's will is manifested; and it was Pilate's task to write prophetically, in these three languages, that the Lord Jesus Christ is the King of the Jews."[6]

God thus guided the hand of the Roman governor both in the choice of languages that appeared on the inscription, as in the terms in which it was conceived, and His divine Spirit, speaking to men in the Holy Scriptures, was also to consecrate three languages, the same ones that the

---

[3] St. Basil, *De Spiritu Sancto*, ch. 27, n. 66.
[4] Joseph de Maistre, *Soirées de Saint-Pétersbourg* (Paris, 1821), vol. 2, n. 7.
[5] Honorius Augustodunensis, *Gemma animæ*, bk. 1, ch. 92.
[6] St. Hilary of Poitiers, *Prologus in librum Psalmorum*, n. 15: "His maxime tribus linguis sacramentum voluntatis Dei . . . ex quo illud Pilati fuit, ut in his tribus linguis regem Iudæorum Dominum Iesum Christum esse præscriberet."

Jewish people, being gathered from the four winds of heaven for the feast of the Passover, could read on the title raised above the Redeemer's head.

THE THREE LANGUAGES OF SACRED SCRIPTURE

With Christ having come down to redeem us, and His Testament thrown open for our salvation by His death, according to the mind of the Apostle (cf. Heb. 9:15–17), the divine Spirit, inspirer of the Scriptures, gave the books of the New Covenant in the same three languages of the title of the Cross. St. Matthew wrote his Gospel in Syriac, the common Hebrew of his time. Papias, a disciple of the apostles, St. Irenaeus, St. Pantaenus, Origen, Eusebius, St. Athanasius, St. Epiphanius, St. Jerome, and St. Augustine all bear witness to this fact.

The Greek language was honored to serve as the language of the Gospels of St. Luke and St. John and the Acts and Epistles of the Apostles, except perhaps the Epistle of St. Paul to the Hebrews, which would have been written in their own tongue. Christianity, after having been preached in Jerusalem in the language of Israel, was then to extend first to the gentiles of the Greek language.

The *Liber Pontificalis* states directly that St. Mark, composing his Gospel in Rome under the eyes of St. Peter who confirmed it, wrote in the Latin language, which is corroborated by Eusebius and St. Jerome.[7] St. Gregory of Nazianzen likewise states expressly that St. Mark wrote his Gospel for the Latin people.[8]

[*Dom Guéranger goes on to demonstrate that the first complete translations, or "versions," of the Scriptures were composed, very early on, in each of these three languages.*]

The principle of sacred languages thus clearly holds firm with regard to the translations of Sacred Scripture. At the outset, such versions were confined to the three principal tongues, and were slow to increase in number. Only a few others — Coptic, Ethiopian, Armenian, and Slavonic — were eventually deemed worthy of being read in church. Other vernacular languages were reserved for the private use of the faithful, when indeed they were not the work of heretics.

THE THREE SACRED LANGUAGES IN THE LITURGY

Once this point is settled in relation to Sacred Scripture, it becomes evident that the liturgy must, for the same reasons, lay claim to the privilege of sacred languages.

First of all, the liturgy is composed in large part of passages from Sacred Scripture, destined to be read before the assembly of the faithful. If the Church deemed that the majesty of an unchangeable text was necessary to

---

7 *Liber Pontificalis*, ch. 1: Peter, 1:118.
8 St. Gregory of Nazianzen, *Poema* 12 and 21.

preserve reverence for the holy books entrusted to the faithful, was not this mysterious reserve even more appropriate for the fragments of Scripture read from the height of the ambo during the celebration of the mysteries?

Nevertheless, in time every nation in Europe came to possess its own version of the Bible. And yet the private reading of Sacred Scripture is one thing, the solemn, liturgical proclamation quite another. The latter must be grave and mysterious, like the divine oracles. It must not be subject to the vicissitudes of language, lest it falls into banality and familiarity.

Moreover, by reading Scripture in the sacred languages during the divine services, the Church has merely continued the traditions of the ancient Law. It is well known that the Hebrew language ceased to be a vernacular language in Judea shortly after the return from the Babylonian captivity. Nevertheless, this did not prevent the continued reading of the Law and the prayers in pure Hebrew in the Temple and synagogues, even though the people, who by now only used the Syro-Chaldean dialect, could no longer understand the tongue of their forefathers. After the liturgical reading of particular passages, Chaldaic paraphrases on these same passages were read. This custom of reading the Law and the various prayers in non-vernacular Hebrew was so innate to the traditions of the Temple of Jerusalem that modern Jews are still faithful to it, in whatever country they may be dispersed.

From all of this, we conclude that, since Scripture readings in non-vernacular languages are an essential and significant part of the liturgy, as the custom has always been among all Churches, the liturgy admits by the same token the use of sacred languages.

Secondly, the liturgy is a collection of formulas designed to accompany the celebration of the Holy Sacrifice and the administration of the Sacraments, all of which pertain to the proper and incommunicable ministry of priests. By its very nature, therefore, the liturgy is reserved for the clergy to a greater extent than Scripture itself. A layman may well possess greater exegetical knowledge than that of many priests; the simplicity of his faith may also dispose him to derive great fruit from the reading of the holy books which, as the Apostle teaches, were written for our instruction (cf. Rom. 15:4). But should we conclude from such cases that the common believer would equally benefit from a personal knowledge of the liturgical prayers?

His ear may hear, through the mouth of the priest, the accents of a foreign language, but his heart will have grasped it all. Is it in our urban churches, where every layman can can follow the Mass with a translation, or in the rustic parish churches of the countryside—so frequented still in provinces far from the capital—that one finds greater recollection, better observance of reverence for the house of God, and a deeper sense of the mysteries of the Faith? If the faithful can live in the faith and charity of Jesus Christ without needing the Scripture in their vernacular, they can all the more compensate by the same means for the immediate understanding of the liturgical language.

ONE FIXED LANGUAGE TO EXPRESS ETERNAL TRUTHS

Furthermore, since the liturgy is, as Bossuet so beautifully put it, "the principal instrument of tradition,"[9] it is crucial that its formulas be ancient and therefore inviolable. Now, it is the nature of living languages to vary and develop constantly. The language of liturgical books must remain outside of these fluctuations, for the preservation of the truths that these books contain depends on it.

But while it is important that the language of the liturgical books should be fixed and inviolable — and not merely national — it is also in its nature to be mysterious; it must not, therefore, be vulgar. There is a tendency that has spread through the entire world because it is grounded in nature, which causes men to veil holy things under the shadow of mysterious words. The prophets, guided by the inspiration of the Holy Spirit, shrouded the oracles that they uttered in riddles. The Incarnate Word, conversing with men, spoke to them in parables. The whole of Sacred Scripture, replete with literary figures of the boldest kind and filled from beginning to end with allusions plucked from the Eastern mind, will always be, in spite of translations, a mysterious book for the common man.

Rationalists who call themselves Christians must acknowledge that the no amount of knowledge of the holy books can ever replace the exercise of faith. In the dim light of the present life, men need to adore the mysteries, not reduce them to a carnal understanding.

Now, if this is true of the Holy Scriptures, why should it not be true, and with even greater reason, of the liturgy, in which the mysteries that were simply announced in the holy books are enacted? The Church has made a special application of this principle by laying down the inviolable and universal law that the most solemn prayers of the Sacrifice are to be recited at the altar in a low voice, no matter the language in which they are pronounced.

We must take note of this venerable law, which teaches us how greatly the Church desires to shroud her relations with God in mystery. If he is attentive, the Catholic reader will perceive one and the same principle at work in the law which prescribes the reading of the Canon in a low voice, and in that which requires the use of a non-vernacular language in the liturgy.

God has imbued sacred words with power. Does the form of the Sacraments need to be understood by those upon whom they operate? Does the effect of sacramentals depend on the comprehension of the faithful to whom the Church applies them?

---

[9] Bossuet, *Instruction sur les États d'Oraison*, in *Œuvres de Bossuet* (Versailles, 1812), vol. 5, p. 208.

We cannot resist quoting a magnificent passage from Origen, who, over fifteen centuries ago, explained the marvelous effects produced in souls through the mere pronunciation of the words of Sacred Scripture, even by those who do not understand them. God grant that this teaching, so lofty yet simple, not seem too novel to our readers!

> There are some things that seem obscure, but which, by the very fact that they penetrate our ears, nevertheless bring great profit to our souls. If the gentiles have believed that certain poems which they call enchantments, certain names, whispered by those who profess magic, which are not even understood by those who invoke them, put snakes to sleep or compel them out of their deepest caves; if it is said that such words have the power to drive out fevers and diseases from the human body, and that they can even sometimes throw souls into a kind of ecstasy, when the faith of Christ does not impede their effect; how much more powerful and efficacious must we believe the recitation of the words and names of Holy Scripture?
>
> Just as, among the unbelievers, the evil powers, as soon as they hear these names or formulas, hasten to lend their assistance to the work for which they feel they have been invoked, according to the words that have been uttered, obeying the man to whose service they have dedicated themselves; how much more do the heavenly Virtues and angels of God who are with us, as the Lord taught His Church even in the case of little children, rejoice when they hear the words of Scripture and the names they read coming out of our mouths, like pious enchantments.
>
> And indeed, even if we do not understand the words uttered by our mouths, these Virtues who assist us understand them, and invited as if by a song that delights their ears, hasten to our aid . . .
>
> It is an incontestable truth that there are a great number of Virtues in our midst, to whom the care of our souls and bodies has been entrusted. Since they are holy, they delight in hearing us read the Scriptures, but their solicitude for us redoubles when we utter words that guide our spirit to prayer while leaving our understanding in the dark. The holy Apostle said so, revealing a mystery worthy of admiration for man, when he taught that it can sometimes happen that the spirit within us prays, even while our understanding remains inactive (1 Cor. 14:14) . . .
>
> Thus, by pious contemplation of this kind, we draw to ourselves the company and assistance of the Divine Virtues, while at the same moment, in uttering these words and names, we repel the snares of the evil powers and the incursions of malignant demons.[10]

We have indulged in the pleasure of quoting this long passage, which explains better than any manner of argumentation the influence of holy

---

[10] Origen, *Homilies on Joshua*, Homily 20.

words on the multitude gathered in the presence of the mysteries. What Origen says here about Sacred Scripture applies, *mutatis mutandis,* to the liturgy.

INSTRUCTION FROM THE PULPIT

But although the Church knows that the words of the liturgy, even when pronounced in an unfamiliar language, pour sanctifying grace upon the faithful and unite them to the divine object of her mysteries, she does not for that reason want this people, whom she brings forth into the divine light, to be ignorant of the treasures of truth and life concealed in the sacred words.

While the priest is forbidden to use the vernacular in those dread moments when he is placed between heaven and earth as a powerful mediator uniting the one to the other, he is also commanded to instruct the faithful from the pulpit, not only in the general truths of religion, but especially those contained within the liturgical words. Here is the formal decree of the holy Council of Trent, which expresses the Church's intention on this subject:

> Although the Mass contains a great deal of instruction for the faith-ful, the Fathers did not think it expedient to celebrate it everywhere in the vernacular. For this reason, each Church will retain its ancient rites, approved by the holy Roman Church, Mother and Teacher of all Churches; but, lest Christ's sheep go hungry, and the little children cry out for bread when there is no one to break it for them, the holy Council orders pastors and all those with care of souls to explain often during the celebration of Mass, by themselves or through others, something of the formulas read at Mass; and among other things to expound some details on the mystery of this most holy sacrifice, especially on Sundays and feasts.[11]

The Church has therefore made solicitous provision for the instruction of her faithful, and it is not to keep them in ignorance that she has prescribed the use of sacred languages in the celebration of the mysteries. Protestantism has destroyed religion by abolishing sacrifice. It no longer has an altar, only a table; and whatever remains of Christianity there is found only in the pulpit.

The Catholic Church rightly glories in the pulpit of truth, for "faith comes through hearing" (Rom. 10:17). From this pulpit, she proclaims her immutable and victorious doctrine in the language of the people who listen to her. But her mission is not solely to instruct these people. If she reveals divine truths to them, it is in order to unite them to God through the mysteries of the altar. Having enlightened their faith, she puts them in communication with God through love.

Once she has aroused in them the desire for the infinite Good, in whose presence there is neither the learned nor the ignorant, she ascends like

---

[11] Council of Trent, Session 22, ch. 8.

Moses upon the mountain, and her voice no longer speaks to the ear, but to the heart. The accents of a mysterious tongue alone resonate in the holy assembly, transporting the mind beyond the limits of the present. Even those who understand this language are warned that something extraordinary is being accomplished. Soon, the words of this sacred language are enveloped in a silence in whose midst God alone may listen, yet the symbolic ceremonies always continue, and by their visible forms they never cease to elevate the holy people to a love of invisible things.

Such is the act of religion in the Catholic Church; in contact at the same moment with the needs of humanity and the infinite, ever sublime and simple, yet too simple to be understood by minds that believe they can reason about what belongs to sentiment.

OTHER LITURGICAL LANGUAGES

We have therefore no qualms about conceding that the early Church celebrated the sacred mysteries in the vernacular. This was as true of the liturgy as it was of the sacred Scriptures of the New Testament. Such was the privilege of the first age, and so it had to be. Time alone can turn a vulgar language into a sacred one: man does not invent languages *a priori*. If, in the early Church, the vernacular language was used at the altar, this privilege, during the first three centuries, did not extend to languages other than the three that had appeared on the title of the Savior's Cross: Hebrew (or Syriac), Greek and Latin.

These three languages alone reigned in the sanctuary until the Peace of the Church, just as they alone contained, during this period, the texts or versions of the Holy Scriptures. During these three centuries, many nations were called to the light of the Gospel, but since it must be acknowledged that they did not possess versions of the sacred text in their own languages, we maintain that neither did they celebrate the liturgy in the vernacular tongue.

But the time came when liturgical languages began to multiply. We should not assume, however, that every Christian people had its own liturgical tongue; here again, we encounter the presence of privilege. In the fourth century, Upper Egypt began to enjoy a translation of the holy books into Coptic. The custom of celebrating the liturgy in the same language in this region can be traced back to the same period. The use of Coptic gradually spread to the whole of Egypt, with the progress of Monophysitism, which erected a wall of separation between the Christians of Egypt and the Greeks who remained Catholic. The Muslim invasion and the barbarism that attended it completed the ruin of the Greek language in Egypt, and Coptic soon reigned alone in the liturgy.

Beyond the three languages of the title of the Cross, there are three other languages in the East that are currently admitted into the liturgy: Coptic, Ethiopian, and Armenian, to which one may add Slavonic. The whole question is whether the Coptic, Armenian, and Ethiopian in which all these Churches celebrate the liturgy are more vernacular languages than Latin in the West. They certainly were at the outset, but the fact is that they are no more vernacular today than Latin, and this has been the case for many centuries, such that the eastern Churches, despite the diversity of their liturgical languages, celebrate the divine service, no less than we do, in a language that is no longer understood by the people.

Thus, there were three sacred languages from the beginning. Three other main ones [*Coptic, Armenian, Ethiopian*] were then added to them, but as soon as these latter made contact with the mysteries of the altar, they too became immutable and imperishable. Peoples intermingle and redefine themselves, they see their political state overturned and emigrate to other climes, yet the liturgical language survives all things and does not give way before these revolutions. Consecrated to the secrets of eternity, it is no longer of time; the people venerate it as the link that binds them to heaven, as the sacred veil that covers the object of their adoration. It is the link between the past and the present, the sign of brotherhood that triumphs over all distances and unites the most disparate races.

In the midst of paganism, the ancient Romans understood this immutability of language in public prayer. Quintilian informs us that the verses sung by the Salian priests were so ancient that they were barely understood, yet the majesty of religion had not allowed them to be changed.[12] We have seen that the Jews, before Christianity, read the Law and prayers in Hebrew during their religious assemblies, even though the people no longer understood the language. Would it not be refusing to acknowledge the obvious, to overlook in all these instances the expression of a natural law in accordance with the spirit of religion?

A DISASTROUS PAPAL INDULGENCE

In the ninth century, however, a slight contradiction to everything that we have described thus far arose. A new liturgical language, Slavonic, appeared in the West, and Rome accepted and recognized it.

Shortly after the middle of the ninth century, the Slavs received the good news of the Gospel through the ministry of two holy Greek monks, Cyril and Methodius. These apostles had come from Constantinople, and after their initial sojourn in Bulgaria, where they planted the Faith, the saints continued on to Moravia, where they remained. Having left the Greek-speaking Churches, they headed for the West, where the Latin language alone reigned at the altar. Moravia, which they evangelized, seemed even to have already received some glimpses of the preaching of the missionaries sent by the Apostolic See. The two saints were to be the civilizers of the

---

[12] Quintilian, *Institutio Oratoria*, bk. 1, ch. 6: "Carmina Saliorum vix sacerdotibus suis intellecta, sed quæ mutari vetat Religio."

Slavic peoples, among whom their preaching had carved an immense furrow of evangelical light, and gave them an alphabet with which these peoples could henceforth write their language.

Sts. Cyril and Methodius believed that they should not only translate the holy books into this language, but also use it in the celebration of the divine service. Nevertheless, it is likely that they did not initially pursue this innovation, but only gave way to it later, in the hope of accelerating the conversion of the peoples to whose salvation they had dedicated themselves.

In fact, in 866, the two saints were summoned to Rome by St. Nicholas I, who had written to them with great benevolence. His successor Pope Adrian II consecrated St. Methodius as bishop, and we see no trace of the discontent that the use of Slavonic in the liturgy would arouse in Rome a few years later.

It was only under Pope John VIII, who succeeded Adrian II, that this fact attracted the attention of the Holy See. In 879, the Pontiff wrote:

> We have also heard that you sing Mass in the barbaric, that is, in the Slavic language, which is why we have already condemned this practice in our letters addressed to you by Paul, Bishop of Ancona, that you would no longer celebrate the solemnities of Holy Mass in that tongue, but henceforth either in Latin or in Greek, in accordance with the practice of the Church of God spread throughout the earth and among all nations. As for preaching, however, you may do so in the language of the people; for the Psalmist exhorts all nations to praise the Lord (Ps. 116:1), and the Apostle says: *Let every tongue confess that the Lord Jesus is in the glory of God the Father* (Philip. 2:11).[13]

With these words, the Apostolic See showed that the two sacred languages, Greek and Latin, were sufficiently established not to share with others the honor of serving at the altar.

Nevertheless, by one of those caprices to which Pope John VIII was prone and which have motivated posterity's severe judgments on his character, this Pontiff, who was soon to give the Church the sad spectacle of rehabilitating Photius,[14] soon relaxed his strictness on the Slavonic language in the liturgy. Let us examine the Pontiff's words.

> We order that the praises and works of Christ Our Lord be celebrated in this same language [Slavonic]; for Sacred Scripture does not teach us to praise the Lord in three languages only, but in every tongue, when it commands: *Praise the Lord, all ye nations, praise him, all ye peoples* (Ps. 116:1). So, too, did the

---

[13] Pope John VIII, Epistle to Methodius, in *Monumenta Germaniæ Historica: Epistolæ,* vol. 5, p. 161.

[14] Photius I, the Patriarch of Constantinople who broke with the Church of Rome in 858, was subsequently recognized by John VIII as the legitimate Patriarch of Constantinople, which further fomented the disastrous Photian Schism.

Apostles, being filled with the Holy Spirit, relate in all tongues the wonders of God (Acts 2:11). So it was that Paul, the heavenly trumpet, utters this admonition: *Let every tongue confess that the Lord Jesus is in the glory of God the Father* (Philip. 2:11)...[15]

The contradiction between this letter to Prince Svatopluk of Moravia and that to St. Methodius could not be more glaring; indeed, the same texts of Scripture are used in the opposite sense. The Pontiff must, therefore, have acted out of impulse or weakness in one case or the other.

These examples of human frailty are rare on the Chair of St. Peter, but history makes a record of them, and the sons of the Church have no interest in concealing them, because they know that He who assured the Roman Pontiffs of the infallibility of their faith in teaching did not spare them from all fault in the exercise of supreme government.

People today are so unfamiliar with ecclesiastical history that we would not be surprised to learn that we will meet with reproach for the severity of our judgment on Pope John VIII. We will therefore take cover behind the great authority of Baronius, who will doubtless escape charges of disordered passion against Popes who do not share his ideas:

> The fact that Pope John, rather than meting out tortures to that most iniquitous knave [*i.e., Photius*], made bold to pay him a tidy salary, bears a great mark of infamy against his own reputation and the pontifical chair... Being wholly sundered of all virility, frail of mind, bereft of priestly constancy and manful vigor, this was no Pope like Nicholas or Adrian, but he was called, by way of derision, a Popess.[16]

The first result of John VIII's concession was to stop the progress of the Latin language, which for nearly three centuries had been marching victoriously in its conquest of the North. This ordinance set the limits of European unity, which, but for the intervention of St. Gregory VII, would have ended just short of Bohemia.

Perhaps this indulgence helped the spread of the faith among the Slavs for a time, but observe the fruits that it would bear in the future. At the beginning of the eleventh century, the Church of Constantinople, then in communion with the Holy See, began the conquest of Ruthenia and Muscovy for the Christian faith. The apostles that she sent were no more conscientious about the liturgical language than St. Cyril and St. Methodius had been for the Western Slavs. The new missionaries therefore gave the Ruthenian converts the Greek liturgy in Slavonic, and an immense part of Europe was formed on the basis of a liturgical language that was neither that of Rome nor of Constantinople.

---

[15] Pope John VIII, Epistle to Svatopluk, in *Monumenta Germaniæ Historica: Epistolæ*, vol. 5, p. 190.

[16] Baronius, *Annales ecclesiastici*, ad annum 879, n. 5.

Such, then, was the consequence of Pope John VIII's concession, and the reader can now judge whether this disastrous indulgence can invalidate the principles we have expressed above on the importance of not multiplying liturgical languages. With respect to the question of law, it should be noted that the Pontiff granted the use of Slavonic in the Divine Liturgy as a dispensation from common law, and that he did so only after protesting against the work of St. Methodius.

The form of language into which the two holy monks had translated the Scriptures, and to which they soon entrusted the liturgy, grew old and fell out of common use. After a few centuries, therefore, the divine service ceased to be celebrated in the language of the people among the Slavs, because the liturgy had imparted its immutability to the language which had at first served as its interpreter.

The great and saintly archdeacon Hildebrand soon ascended the Chair of St. Peter under the name of Gregory VII, and the question of the liturgy in the Slavonic language merited his attention. The Duke of Bohemia, Vratislaus, had asked him to extend to his people, who were also of Slavic race, the dispensation that John VIII had accorded to Svatopluk for Moravia. Gregory steadfastly refused, and, without either accusing his predecessor or going back on a *fait accompli*, he proclaimed the Church's principles on liturgical languages. Replying to this prince in a letter dated 1080, Gregory VII writes:

> As for your desire that we give our consent to the celebration of the Divine Office in the Slavonic language in your country, you should know that we can in no way accede to this request. For those who have given serious thought to this matter, it is clear that it was not without reason that Almighty God was pleased to keep Sacred Scripture hidden in certain places, for fear that if it were laid bare before the eyes of all men it would become familiar and exposed to contempt, or that, if it were misconstrued by mediocre minds, it would lead them into error.
>
> Nor does it serve as an excuse to say that certain religious men [*i.e., Sts. Cyril and Methodius*] condescended to the desires of a simple-minded people or left them uncorrected; for the early Church herself had concealed many things which the holy Fathers later corrected, after subjecting them to delicate examination, once Christendom had been strengthened and the true religion propagated. For this reason, by the authority of Blessed Peter, we forbid you to carry out what your people imprudently ask of us, and, for the honor of Almighty God, we enjoin you to oppose this vain temerity with all your might.[17]

In these few lines, St. Gregory VII vigorously enunciated the Church's

---

[17] Gregory VII, Epistle to Vratislaus II, in *Codex diplomaticus et epistolaris regni Bohemiæ* (Prague, 1908), vol. I, p. 88.

sentiment, which has always been not to present the mysteries before the eyes of the vulgar without a veil. The Pope excused the concession made before him and proclaimed that this principle was one of such frequent application that the necessities which arose at the time of the Church's establishment cannot prudently be adopted as laws for subsequent centuries.

The Christian faith reigned in Bohemia, where it was established and maintained with the Latin liturgy. To introduce the use of the vernacular into this Church would have been to demote it to the conditions of childhood. By extending the frontiers of the Latin language as far as Bohemia, St. Gregory VII advancing them as far as Poland, which, by remaining Latin, was thus consecrated as the Catholic bulwark of Europe on the Asian side.

As for the provinces in which the Slavonic language was already established, there was no longer any reason to change the practice. The Apostolic See took upon itself the duty to protect this observance in the Churches where the language was legitimately used in divine service.

ERASMUS AND VOCAL PRAYER

The heresy of the sixteenth century, which sought to annihilate the Christian religion by destroying the notion of sacrifice and priesthood, declared war on the mysterious practices with which all the Churches had seen fit to shroud man's relationship with the divinity.

But the anti-liturgical movement of Luther and Calvin was not only foreshadowed by John Wycliffe and Jan Hus; as early as the twelfth century, the Waldensians and Albigensians defied the entire Church. These sectarians, who were the first to claim that the Bible should be interpreted by private judgment, were also the first to protest against the liturgical language and to celebrate the mysteries and Sacraments in the vernacular tongue. They made this practice one of the fundamental articles of their sect, and the first French version of the Holy Scriptures was their work. This was a radical shift, and it was not without reason that the French Calvinists of the seventeenth century proclaimed the Waldensians and Albigensians as their forefathers.

The anti-liturgical heresy was suppressed and even extinguished for a time by Catholic arms [*i.e., the Albigensian Crusade*], but it was to reawaken with terrible success three centuries later. When it erupted, triumphant over the ancient faith in many lands, several of its tendencies were imprudently admitted by shortsighted Catholics, leading to the establishment of a moderate rationalism in certain Catholic countries. This paved the way for that second outpouring of the Protestant spirit known as Jansenism.

Erasmus is perhaps the most complete representative of these perilous tendencies. Resolute in remaining a Catholic, he embraced but mitigated many of the ideas advanced by the Reformers, and he was more than once on the brink of disaster. The Sorbonne was shaken by the publication of his writings, which in a thousand places breathed the spirit of Luther without accepting his excesses, and in 1526, a famous censure from this Faculty summarized and proscribed the dangerous system this scholar had formulated, mainly in his *Paraphrases* of the New Testament.

Erasmus had not condemned the Church's practice regarding sacred languages — his prudent reserve always preserved him from the final excesses — but he expressed himself as follows: "To me it seems indecorous, or rather ridiculous, that ignorant men and mere girls may be seen mumbling their Psalms and prayers to God in the fashion of parrots, for they do not understand what they are saying." [18] The Faculty addressed the scholar of Rotterdam's unseemly assertion in these terms:

> This proposition, which diverts the simple, the uneducated, and foolish women from the vocal prayer according to the rites and customs of the Church, as if it were useless unless understood by them, is impious and erroneous, opening the way to the error of the Bohemians, who attempted to celebrate the ecclesiastical Office in the vulgar language...
>
> For indeed, the Church's intention in her prayers is not only to instruct us by the arrangement of words, but also to ensure that, by conforming ourselves to her purpose, as her members, we pronounce the praises of God, that we render the thanks due to Him, and that we implore the things that are needful for us. Therefore, on account of such intention in prayer, the affection is inflamed by the gift of God, the intellect is enlightened, man's frailty is exalted, and a fruit pleasing to God and glorious to the soul is produced.
>
> Such too is the intention engendered by those who recite vocal prayers without understanding the words. They are like a legate who does not grasp the words his lord has given him to bear, yet who, by transmitting them according to the order he has received, fulfills an office pleasing to his lord and to the one to whom he is sent.
>
> Furthermore, a great number of passages from the Prophets are sung in the Church, which, although they are not understood by many of the cantors, are nevertheless useful and meritorious to those who pronounce them; for indeed, by singing them, one renders a pleasing service to the divine Truth, who taught and revealed them.
>
> From which it certainly follows that the fruit of prayer does not reside solely in the comprehension of words and, moreover, that it is a pernicious error to imagine that vocal prayer has no other purpose than to procure understanding, whereas this kind of prayer is done principally to inflame man's affection, so that the soul, by elevating itself to God with piety and devotion in the aforementioned manner, is rejuvenated; that it is not frustrated, but rather obtains what its intention seeks; and likewise, that

---

[18] Erasmus, *Paraphrase on Matthew*, Preface.

the intellect merits illumination as well as other profitable and necessary graces. Now, all these effects are far more precious than the mere understanding of words, which is of little use until the affection for God is aroused. Even if the Psalms were translated into the vernacular, not because of that would the simple and ignorant reach a full understanding of them.[19]

The moral character of the opponents of the Church's practice on this point, from the Waldensians and Albigensians to Quesnel and Abbé Chatel,[20] itself proves the legitimacy, we could almost say the necessity, of sacred languages for the prayers of the liturgy. Only a religion without mystery, which is to say a human religion, could exclude the mysterious patterns of language.

THE CHINESE LANGUAGE IN THE ROMAN LITURGY

It had been thirty years since Fr. Matteo Ricci, of the Society of Jesus, had gloriously opened the apostolate of the vast empire of China. At this time, the zealous missionaries entrusted with continuing his work, hoping that the use of the Chinese language in divine service would consolidate the conquests of the Gospel, presented a petition to Pope Paul V requesting leave to adopt this means. By a decree dated 25 January 1615, the Pope granted their request. A Brief was even drawn up, but it remained in Rome and was never sent to China.[21] According to Fr. Daniello Bartoli, the Society's historian, the superiors of the order foresaw the disadvantages of this concession and did not see fit to implement it.

In 1667, a second petition composed by Fr. François de Rougemont once again put the matter before the Holy See. A congregation of cardinals, bishops, and distinguished theologians was charged with examining the missionaries' request. The decision seemed so difficult that the Apostolic See refrained from issuing a decree.

In 1678, the learned Fr. Ferdinand Verbiest drew up a third petition, to be presented to Pope Innocent XI, along the same lines as the first two, and attached to it was a copy of the Roman Missal translated and printed in Chinese. Fr. Philippe Couplet, Procurator of the Jesuit Mission in China, had come to Europe to push for the approval and use of the Chinese Missal. He spent several years in Rome, but was unable to obtain what he desired from the Holy See.

The final attempt made by the Jesuits in China occurred in 1697. A fourth petition was presented to Pope Innocent XII, but like the previous ones it obtained no result. Since then, the question has advanced no further;

---

[19] D'Argentré, *Collectio Judiciorum*, 2:61.
[20] Ferdinand-François Chatel (1795–1857) was a French priest who, embracing Gallicanism and liberal ideas, fell into schism. He founded an independent sect he dubbed the *Église catholique française* (French Catholic Church), which adopted a vernacular liturgy.
[21] Pope Benedict XIV, *De Missæ sacrificio*, bk. 2, ch. 2, n. 13.

indeed, it has even ceased to be discussed, and it has become obvious, for the missionaries as for everyone else, that the intention of the Apostolic See is not to grant the Churches of China the use of the vernacular in the liturgy.

The missionaries acknowledge that the faith can make progress among the Chinese people without the help of the requested means, which were especially aimed towards the mandarins and the literati, whose prejudices and delicate pride they wished to accommodate. Is there not reason to fear that this privileged caste, before which the Apostolic See would have to kowtow, having become the sole custodian of the whole Catholic religion [*in China*], may once again withdraw into an unbreakable isolation? And is it not a delusion to hope that in the future the learned class will show a more favorable disposition toward the Latin tongue?[22]

As for the claim that, if the Savior had been born in China, and if the Gospels had been written in Chinese, the peoples of Europe would have found it burdensome to learn that language, and that it would have been desirable for the apostles of our lands to dispense us from it, the reality is that God, in His mercy, did not proceed in this way. He first prepared all things in favor of the peoples that He deigned to call first, by gathering them all in the Roman Empire, the precursor of Christ's empire. Three languages — Hebrew, Greek and Latin — represented the vast majority of the peoples who made up this dominion. These three languages, having been consecrated on the title of the Savior's Cross, were sufficient for the first foundation of the Church. The language spoken by Christ Himself would prove the least fertile, and it received only a small portion of the Holy Scriptures of the New Testament.

In the history of the Church, hypotheses explain little: facts shed more light. Have we not seen that, in the first three centuries, many nations were admitted to the Faith, without the Scriptures nor the liturgy being translated for them?

PULPIT AND ALTAR

A clear distinction must be drawn between preaching and the celebration of the Holy Sacrifice. Indeed, if the apostles had gone out to preach the Gospel throughout the world in the Syro-Chaldean language, it is doubtful that they would have converted many people. Yet God had made provision

---

[22] In the conversion of the Chinese, the Jesuit mission especially directed its attention towards the educated elites: the mandarins and literati. By accommodating the Roman Liturgy to the language of the Chinese literati, the Jesuits hoped to secure their more rapid conversion. Writing at a time when China had recently been forced to reopen to the West after some two centuries of isolation under the Qing, renewing hopes for its conversion, Guéranger expresses the worry that a Chinese liturgy would allow even a converted upper class to once again revert to its policy of restricting contact with Europe, including the Holy See. Moreover, he expresses skepticism about the very policy of focusing on the conversion of the mandarins, given their instinctual rejection of anything non-Chinese, including the Latin tongue.

for this difficulty by giving the apostles the understanding of all languages, and the people the facility to understand the apostles in whatever tongue they expressed themselves.

It is necessary here to make a crucial distinction between pulpit and altar. From the pulpit, the vernacular is indispensable; at the altar, it can be discarded, even as it had been from the beginnings of Christianity, as innumerable historical examples have proved. Secondly, it is not correct to assume that the apostles used only the Syro-Chaldean language as an instrument of evangelical preaching; to do so would be to forget the miracle of Pentecost.

As for the liturgy, we have recognized and established that it existed in three languages, just as the Holy Scriptures, at the time of the apostles. We have noted the privilege of these three vernacular and sacred languages, which represent by their extension the limits of the Roman Empire. Since that time, the honor of being employed in the divine service has been accorded to a very small number of other tongues. All languages, however, have been admitted for the preaching of the Gospel. It is therefore essential not to confuse here the twofold use that the Church can make of languages.

HEBREW AND GREEK IN THE ROMAN LITURGY

We must not fail to mention the use of the three original sacred languages in the Roman liturgy, as on the title of the Cross. The Latin formulas undoubtedly constitute the basis of the prayers of the Church of Rome. However, Hebrew figures with honor into the same liturgy, first in the triumphal *Alleluia*, which the missionaries of the Roman Pontiff taught not only to the barbarians of Germania and Scandinavia, but even to the islanders dwelling beyond seas untraversed by Solomon's fleets. In the chant of the Trisagion, before entering into the Canon of the Sacrifice, Rome proclaims the thrice-holy God, Lord *of Hosts*, but she does not translate the sacred term, and the Latin ear will hear *Sabaoth* resound unto the gates of eternity. The third Hebrew word preserved in the Latin liturgy is *Hosanna*, which recalls Christ's triumph and cannot be translated without losing much of its force and grandeur. Finally, the fourth is the *Amen*, a conclusion and assent by which the Christian people unite themselves to all of the homage and supplication that the priest and Pontiff address to the divine majesty.

The language of the Septuagint, which is also the language of the New Testament, is likewise glorified in the Latin liturgy. Nine times at the altar, the Roman Church repeats *Kyrie* or *Christe eleison*. This Byzantine invocation also opens the Litanies and appears on certain days in the Hours of the Office. On Good Friday, among the chants accompanying the adoration of the Cross, Rome sounds the Trisagion in Greek, with the words written in Latin letters: *Agios, o Theos, Agios ischyros, Agios athanatos, eleison imas!*

When the Roman Pontiff solemnly celebrates the holy mysteries, following the Epistle chanted by the Latin subdeacon, the Greek subdeacon delivers it in the language of his Church. A Greek deacon also recites the Gospel in Greek, after the Latin deacon has chanted it in the language of Rome. In the past, this mingling of the two languages was more common in that Church that is both Mother and Teacher. We learn from an ancient author quoted by Dom Martène that the *Gloria in excelsis* was sung in Greek at the Midnight Mass of Christmas.[23] Likewise, the *Liber Pontificalis* relates that the twelve lessons of Holy Saturday and the six of Pentecost Saturday were chanted alternately in both languages.[24] The union of sacred languages was even more striking in 1409, during the coronation ceremony of Alexander V at the Council of Pisa. According to the Acts of the Council, the Epistle and Gospel were chanted in Hebrew, Greek, and Latin.[25]

We hasten now to bring this long chapter to a close and to draw a conclusion from the many facts assembled here. Thus, it has been demonstrated that the liturgical books — on which the science of the liturgy is founded, and whose original form dates back to the early centuries of Christianity — are entitled to our respect because of the mysterious and sacred character of the languages in which they are written. We have seen that this character is inherent to them, to the extent that the once living languages which had been accorded the honor of serving as the organ of the liturgy retain this prerogative even after they have ceased to be spoken. Finally, the unanimity of the various Churches in this practice, and the fondness of heretics for the vulgar tongue in divine services, have helped us understand how the holy Council of Trent was compelled to pronounce a dogmatic definition on this matter, which at first glance seemed to concern only discipline.

---

[23] Dom Edmund Martène, *De antiquis Ecclesiæ ritibus* (Antwerp, 1736), vol. 1, p. 279.
[24] *Liber Pontificalis*, ch. 106: Benedict III, 2:147.
[25] Luc d'Achery, *Spicilegium* (Paris, 1723), vol. 6, p. 334.

28

The Translation of Liturgical Books into the Vernacular

AVING ESTABLISHED THE PRINCIPLE AND conditions of liturgical languages, it may seem superfluous to examine the fittingness of translating liturgical books into the vernacular. Indeed, we have shown that such translations cannot not be used in the celebration of the sacred mysteries without violating the spirit and laws of the Church.

But is it permissible to place such translations into the hands of the ordinary faithful, so that they may unite themselves with a deeper under-standing to the mysteries celebrated before them, or to the Divine Offices chanted in church? Has the practice, which has prevailed in France for almost two centuries, of translating the prayers of the Mass and the Office, arisen without objections and in accordance with the spirit of the Church? Ought this practice to be abolished, or would it not be preferable to subject it to rules designed to mitigate its dangers?

A DANGEROUS FAMILIARITY

However entrenched the custom of translating the Mass and Office may be in France, we cannot refrain from stating that this custom, even if it were too late to abolish it, is totally contrary to the spirit of the Church. It would thus have been better had the competent authority not relaxed the stringent rules with which it initially sought to resist it.

This is the teaching of the Sorbonne, of the bishops of the Assembly of 1660, and of the Apostolic See. This teaching is founded first and foremost on the very principle by virtue of which the Church celebrates the liturgy in a non-vernacular language. One of the principal reasons for this universal law is the danger of exposing the sacred formulas to profane curiosity and the crude interpretations of the multitude, and ultimately of fostering a familiarity that would be hazardous to the respect for the mysteries.

It is true that, even with the establishment of liturgical translations, the sacred language is maintained in the Church. The Church's intention is nonetheless frustrated, and many of the same perils that would result from the celebration of the divine service in the vernacular persist unabated.

It is well known that the Jansenists were the authors and propagators of this revolution in the Churches of France, and that the ultimate aim of this heretical sect's maneuver was to lead the faithful, step by step, to desire the replacement of Latin with the vernacular in the liturgy. In the places where they managed to impose their will, the Jansenists were seen celebrating the sacred mysteries in French. Quesnel's eighty-sixth proposition bears ample witness to the Calvinist intentions of the party in all the works it undertook to re-establish "the rights of the faithful," allegedly violated by Rome's obstinacy in keeping the faithful isolated from public prayer.

It is common knowledge that the Divine Offices consist largely of passages and even simple verses from Sacred Scripture. Accordingly, if the Church judged it necessary to restrict indiscriminate access to the Scriptures, should not her reticence towards permitting translations of the liturgy be seen as a direct consequence of the prudent discipline she had so wisely enacted?

Among Protestants, the use of the Bible in the vernacular and the introduction of popular language into the divine service were nothing more than the application of the same principle. Could the Catholic Church have done otherwise than counteract this system? And was not the Jansenist sect, so adept at imitating Calvin in every respect, entirely consistent in promoting these two maxims: to proclaim as a universal and indispensable duty the reading of Sacred Scripture, and to introduce translations of the entire liturgy into the hands of the faithful?

Now, it is with great pleasure that we record here the words of the pious and courageous Bishop of Langres to his diocesan clergy on this subject:

> The best thing for the faithful to do while the priest sings the Mass would certainly be to adhere inwardly to his words, even without comprehending them; to pray what he is praying, even without knowing it. This is exactly what the early Christians did, first during all the centuries when the liturgy was transmitted only by oral tradition, and for a long time thereafter. That is why, after the priest's mysterious prayers in a low voice, the faithful simply responded *Amen*, "so be it," an act of faith sublime in its simplicity. It is as if they had said: We do not know what suits us best, but God does. We do not know what glorifies the Lord best, but the Church does, and it is the Church who has just spoken, for it is in her name and by her express ordinance that the priest has just spoken. It is the Church who has put on his lips the prayers that he has just uttered. We therefore adhere to them, whatever they may be, for we can ask for nothing better than what the Church asks, we can say nothing better than what the Church says. So be it, then, so be it! *Amen, Amen!*[1]

A STRONGLY MOTIVATED OPPOSITION

We now come to the second question: [*Whether it is permissible to place translations of liturgical books in the hands of the faithful.*] Having considered

---

[1] Bishop of Langres, *Instruction pastorale de Mgr l'évêque de Langres sur le chant de l'Eglise* (Paris, 1846), 11.

the principles of translating liturgical books, let us see whether, in practice, this innovation was not the object of the most strenuous objections in France itself at the time that this practice was implanted by a fervent and obdurate sect.

We cannot here provide all the details of the sessions of the Assembly for the condemnation of Missals in French, but we must insert a precious and solemn document, the encyclical letter that the prelates sent to all the bishops of France, urging them to forbid, on pain of excommunication, all translations of the Mass into the vernacular language. Here is the content of this important encyclical:

> We had reason to believe that this blessed alliance of sovereign, spiritual, and temporal authorities had forever put to rest those fatal novelties of our day which have caused so much turmoil and harm in the Church . . .
>
> These innovations . . . are versions of the Roman Missal in the vulgar language, against the practice of the Church and the doctrine of the councils and Fathers, under the pretext of the instruction and consolation of the faithful. The enemy of the faith and of our salvation has long used the deceptive appearances of piety and devotion to introduce his errors. This is how all heresies have subtly crept into the bosom of the Church, and our eyes and minds are never deceived except by the false colors of resemblance . . .
>
> This is why the Church, in order to perform the divine sacrifice worthily, has received by apostolic tradition the orders and formularies of the consecrations she makes in her Masses and liturgies, and these holy books, which contain her orders and sacred ceremonies, have always remained in the possession of the priests.
>
> It is true that the Fathers have, from time immemorial, desired and labored with great care to ensure that the faithful should be instructed in the truth and majesty of these divine mysteries; that they should be present at the celebration and that, as a part of the Church, they should join their intentions to the action of the priest, who is its one and only true agent of sacrifice, under the authority of Jesus Christ; but they have never presented to the laity these sacred formularies to serve them as books of devotion in assisting at the mysteries.
>
> From this, one cannot justly accuse these holy Fathers of having been negligent in providing the necessary means for the instruction of Christians in piety and in the use of these mysteries, under the pretext that they did not introduce versions of the Missal in vulgar languages, since they explained their importance and effect to them with such diligence and care.
>
> This is the means that the holy Council of Trent prescribed to maintain orthodox doctrine and to excite the devotion of the faithful, ordering that the bishops, and by their orders, parish

priests and preachers explain the mysteries of the Mass to the people on Sundays and feast days, judging that their advancement in doctrine and piety would be greater and more assured by these instructions than if this divine sacrifice were celebrated in the vulgar tongue, as the heretics have falsely tried to persuade was necessary to instruct the people.[2]

TWO HUNDRED THOUSAND COPIES OF THE ORDINARY OF THE MASS IN FRENCH

Later, it was felt that the revocation of the Edict of Nantes called for a solemn demonstration in favor of liturgical translations.[3] The original idea of using this means to convert Protestants came from Paul Pellisson.[4] It was he who, as early as 1676, in concert with the royal court and several bishops, first printed and distributed a five-volume Latin-French Missal throughout the kingdom. That same year, he also published an Ordinary of the Mass that was reprinted for the same purpose by the Bishop of Saintes in 1681.

This reprinting was done with extraordinary extravagance after the publication of the Edict of Revocation in 1685. François de Harlay, by order of His Majesty, ordered the printing of one hundred thousand copies of the Catholic "Hours" preceded by the Ordinary of the Mass in French. Shortly after, another hundred thousand copies of the Ordinary alone were published by Martin and Muguet, printers in Versailles. All this, it was said, would produce great effects towards accelerating the conversion of Protestants.

Such a measure, implemented without the consent of the Holy See, which would assuredly not have sanctioned it, emancipated all Catholics in France from the obligation imposed on them in 1660 to learn the language of the Church if they wished to read the Canon. Did it have any great effect on the conversion of the so-called "reformed"? It is difficult to draw such a conclusion today.

However accurate the translations of the liturgy may have been, by offering simple laymen the interpretation of the sacred formulas, they remained no less formally contrary to the spirit of the Church in respect to the principle of sacred language and respect for the mysteries. From the very time that these formulas were first conceived in a language that the people still spoke, it had been the inviolable custom of the Church to recite them secretly at the altar.

---

[2] Archbishop of Rouen, *Encyclical Letter to the Bishops of France* (7 January 1661).
[3] The Edict of Nantes, signed by King Henry IV in 1598, granted religious liberty to the Huguenots in France. The edict was revoked by Louis XIV in 1685, which prompted churchmen to consider the best means to draw French Protestants back into the Church.
[4] Paul Pellisson (1624–1693), born to Calvinist parents, became so noteworthy as a historian that he was employed by Louis XIV while still a Protestant. He converted in 1670 and was eventually ordained to the subdiaconate. As a Catholic, he worked to ensure the conversion of his former coreligionists.

In this way, the seventeenth century had been defeated in its resistance to translations of the liturgy. Consequently, the eighteenth century saw the complete overhaul of the liturgy itself in a great number of the Churches of France.

WHAT NOW?

We have no doubt that the pages we have just written will a surprise many of our readers, especially at a time when, in matters of religion, so many are prepared to accept established practice as legitimate right.

No one, after the arguments and evidence we have set out, can any longer maintain that the translations of the liturgy for the use of the faithful are in themselves in conformity with the spirit of the Church. Must we conclude from this that all missalettes must be immediately cast into the flames, and that the faithful of France must henceforth be forbidden an inveterate custom which most of them practice all the more innocently because they have never heard it condemned?

In our estimation, it is too late to undertake such a reform with any success. But it is no less evident that the laws and the spirit of the Church in this matter demand at least some restrictions on the unlimited use that the faithful make of these translations. One of the reasons why we believe that an absolute suppression of the translations in use would be inopportune is the length of time that has elapsed since the faithful of France began to enjoy this toleration. Severe measures, without any preparation to enable the faithful to understand the reasons for this conduct, would result in an unhappy disturbance.

It therefore remains to satisfy the spirit of the Church, which, until the end of the ages, will be to treat holy things with mystery, as well as to reconcile the demands of the current situation with the rulings of the councils and the Apostolic See. To our thinking, the way to achieve this result would be, first of all, to stress to the faithful the merit they would obtain in following the Church in her chants and ceremonies, since these chants are meant to unite the prayers of the people to those of the priests, and these ceremonies to instruct and edify those present.

Once that had been done, it would seem permissible to apply to the prayers of the liturgy the rule by which the Holy See saw fit to soften the general discipline prohibiting the use of Sacred Scripture in the vernacular. On 13 June 1757, the Sacred Congregation of the Index issued, by order of Benedict XIV, a decree stating that henceforth versions of the Bible in the vernacular could be permitted indiscriminately to the faithful, "if these same versions had been approved by the Holy See, or if they were published with annotations extracted from the Fathers of the Church or other learned and Catholic authors."[5]

---

[5] *Decretum Sacræ Congregationis Indicis* (13 June 1757).

As things stand in France, the spirit of this decree could be applied in practice, adjusted to circumstance. One could envision translations of the Introits, Collects, Epistles, Gospels, and so on, for the Missal; and of the Psalms, hymns, lessons, orations, and so on, for the Breviary, if they were accompanied by notes or glosses clarifying difficult passages, preventing misunderstandings, and explaining the meaning the Church attaches to such words or rites, all drawn from the teaching of the Fathers and orthodox doctors. Such translations would appear to be legitimized by the spirit of the 1757 decree and would be freed from some of the dangers which led the Church to declare the translations of the liturgy contrary to her spirit.[6]

But in order to satisfy the principle of sacred language, and to maintain the august secrecy which must surround the deepest of our mysteries, it seems evident to us that this freedom should never extend to the Ordinary of the Mass, even if the translation were accompanied by notes and explanations. It is principally this sacred prayer that the Council of Trent, Alexander VII, and the Assembly of 1660 identified as not to be exposed, without profanation or peril, to the eyes of the vulgar. It is by means of their translations of the prayers of the Offertory and Canon that the Jansenists attempted to alter the notion of the Christian Sacrifice and the part that the faithful play in it. Finally, the Ordinary of the Mass, composed almost entirely of the words of the Church, differs essentially from the other prayers or readings in the Missal and Breviary, most of which are taken from Sacred Scripture.

We have just seen that the Church deemed it necessary to soften her restrictions on the use of the Bible when the translations were accompanied by annotations designed to clarify the text and prevent misinterpretation. But Sacred Scripture does not cease be such when used in the liturgy, nor does the 1757 decree confer upon ecclesiastical compositions the status of Scripture.

It seems to us that, by proceeding in this way detailed above,[7] we would arrive at a reconciliation between ancient principles and the necessities of the present age, and that we would eliminate a contradiction that must no longer exist between the inviolable law, which prescribes the use of the sacred language at the altar, and a practice unlawfully introduced, which renders this prescription almost illusory.

An entire volume would be needed to show in full, even for the learned faithful, everything that the Ordinary of the Mass contains in terms of depth of expression, imagery, word choice, and dogmatic action often

---

[6] Such are the translations with commentary that constitute Dom Guéranger's *Liturgical Year*, a work which saw numerous editions in the latter half of the nineteenth century.

[7] Namely, with a translated Missal containing a thorough explanation of the Mass texts, excepting the Ordinary of the Mass, which should be known only in Latin.

concentrated in a single phrase, and forms drawn partly from the Latin of the first two Christian centuries, partly from the genius of Holy Scripture.[8]

We readily agree that such a thorough elucidation of the Ordinary of the Mass would be of great help in assisting the faithful to unite themselves with the priest and the whole Church in the action of the Holy Sacrifice. But can one truly expect the average layman to arrive at such an understanding of so profound a text, when it is not uncommon to hear even priests admit that the prayers of the Offertory and the Canon are not without obscurities even for them?

Such is the majesty of the liturgical books, that they must be protected from the familiarity of the common people by the sacred language in which they were written; by the mysterious silence of the altar in the most sublime moments; and by the extreme reserve that must govern the translation of the formulas these books contain.

---

[8] One such work already exists, and Dom Guéranger praised it in a preceding chapter; the book is Fr. Pierre Le Brun's *Explication de la Messe.*

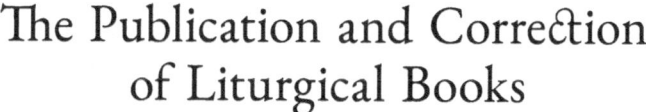

29

The Publication and Correction
of Liturgical Books

INCE THE BOOKS OF THE LITURGY ARE of such great importance in the Church and command a universal veneration from the faithful, not only as the principal instrument of tradition but also because of their great antiquity and the mysterious character of the languages in which they are written, it follows that the publication and correction of these books is of the utmost interest for Christian society as a whole.

We shall not here discuss the composition of these books, properly speaking, which is lost in the mists of time. The centuries may have introduced certain additions and modifications to the primitive liturgies, but their substance is contemporary with the origin of the Churches. It is for this very reason that the recent Breviaries of France — composed according to a novel plan so many centuries after the foundation of the Churches for which they are intended — lack one of the essential characteristics of any true liturgy.

One cannot, therefore, regard St. Gregory as the author of the Sacramentary, Antiphonary, and Responsorial which bear his name. His work on these books was nothing more than a simple correction. He reduced the Sacramentary of St. Gelasius and made a more discerning selection of the pieces chanted at Mass and at the Divine Office, but he was not the author of the liturgical corpus that we call Gregorian.

It is with even greater reason that one is bound to the same judgment about St. Gregory VII, Gregory IX, and St. Pius V in the works that they directed or undertook on the liturgical books, and what we say here must also be understood of those great figures who, for the last twelve centuries, have generally been regarded as the fathers of the various liturgies, whether of the East or the West. They revised, emended, and enriched the books of divine service; nevertheless, they are not, strictly speaking, their authors.

THE CRAZE FOR DIOCESAN LITURGIES

The ease of obtaining liturgical books for each diocese at low cost and in sufficient numbers by means of the printing press led many Churches to fall victim to the craze for adopting a particular Breviary and Missal that they had that had hitherto resisted.

The unity of Catholic prayers was by this means being torn asunder to the peril of the Churches, as St. Pius V would later forcefully remark. This is why the Council of Trent saw no other way to save the Latin liturgy than to entrust its correction to the Roman Pontiff. This was to declare that unity alone could remedy so grievous an abuse, and at the same time to choose the best means of obtaining pure, irreproachable texts.

By exempting those Churches which already had a particular Breviary and Missal [*of at least two-hundred years' use*] from the obligation to accept the new liturgical books, St. Pius V drew a line of demarcation intended to save from destruction those local usages which could command a certain respect. It was, in fact, since the mid-fourteenth century that the craze for creating diocesan books had intensified, and that the products of local creativity had begun to show more clearly the marks of coarseness and ignorance.

It was just that the Roman liturgy should regain the ground it had lost since that time, and the Apostolic See assuredly displayed moderation by asserting its claims no more forcefully than it did. This condescension was appreciated, and we observed that the very Churches which found themselves covered by this exception for the most part adopted the new books.[1]

Undoubtedly, the ease with which copies could be obtained was one reason for many of the Churches to make this choice. Nevertheless, the respect that was inspired by the correction of the Breviary and Missal, so carefully revised from the best manuscripts and by the most capable liturgists in Rome, made no slight contribution to accelerate this happy and peaceful revolution.

⁕❧⁕

Liturgical books are of an importance so far superior to all others that the authority of the "first pastors," exercised in accordance with established discipline, is the only way to give them the necessary gravity. The antiquity which is the chief glory of these books must always be respected, and the correction to which they are occasionally subjected in the course of the centuries is accomplished above all by purifying the texts through collation with the original sources.

---

[1] See above, chapter 15.

Liturgical Books
Before the Printing Press

HE CEREMONIES OF THE LITURGY SURPASS in beauty, grandeur, and loftiness, all the ceremonies of the State. Sacred chants move the soul beyond profane melodies; the arts, when devoted to the service of the divine, have produced more masterpieces than when they have been employed to decorate the pompous dwellings of the powerful. Liturgical books should therefore participate in this general law. With respect to their form, they should be the most extraordinary of all books, and indeed they once were.

The liturgical books on which our investigation will focus are first and foremost those used for the Sacrifice, among which we include not only the "plenary Missal," which has been in general use for some eight centuries, but also: the venerable collections known as Sacramentaries, containing the sacrosanct Canon, the orations, and Prefaces; Evangeliaries, intended for use at the altar; Epistolaries, which contain either the continuous text of the apostolic Epistles or fragments excerpted for liturgical use; Benedictionals, compiled from the Sacramentaries and forming separate books, and so on. Next come the books intended for the Divine Office, among which we include not only Breviaries, but also Psalters, Antiphonaries, Lectionaries, and so on.

In preceding centuries, Christian society was so vigilant in preserving the texts that were to serve at the altar and in the choir that Charlemagne, in the midst of the governance of his immense empire, saw fit not only to have Evangeliaries, Psalters, and Sacramentaries produced before his eyes, as it were, by the most adept calligraphers—either to be used for divine worship in his chapel, or to be offered by him as gifts to prelates or churches—but he also prescribed in his capitularies that this task should only be entrusted to men of a mature age who could offer suitable guarantees of their precision.[1]

Foremost among the scribes who devoted their labors to the production of altar books, even from the fourth century, we place St. Eusebius, Bishop of Vercelli, whom the most ancient tradition represents as having personally written the venerable Evangeliary preserved today in the treasury of his church.[2]

---

[1] Charlemagne, *Admonitio generalis*, ch. 72, in *Monumenta Germaniæ Historica: Capitularia* I, 60.
[2] Jean Mabillon, *Iter Italicum Litterarium* (Paris, 1687).

THE SCRIPTS OF THE MANUSCRIPTS

These pious copyists were too deeply aware of the sanctity of liturgical texts to use, in their transcriptions, profane letters dedicated to expressing purely human sentiments. The script of liturgical books was always the noblest and most dignified. In the production of ordinary manuscripts, one script would give way to another; however, the older styles endured longer in the production of divine service books, for they possessed a more ancient and venerable air, and they recalled the past in a manner most fitting to the mysterious texts they were meant to reproduce.

Capitals in liturgical manuscripts are usually of the kind called "rustic," especially when they run for one or more consecutive lines, yet in the Evangeliaries and Sacramentaries of the eighth and ninth centuries, one sometimes finds capitals combining the nobility and refinement of the finest classical Roman inscriptions.

The Uncial hand—a small capital script, rounded to be written more swiftly, which has such a grave and elegant appearance—as it was used for the whole contents of a single volume, did not endure beyond the eighth century in ordinary manuscripts, but it extended into the tenth century for liturgical books. This rule is applicable to manuscripts of both the Latin and Greek Church. Uncial only completely disappeared with the invasion of Gothic script, which nevertheless borrowed many of its features, particularly for capitals.

Bereft of the majesty imparted by the Uncial script, liturgical books descended to minuscule. This script was originally the Roman hand, which had declined under the Merovingians and lost much of its original grace and harmony. It was left to Charlemagne to restore the script and make it worthy of altar books.

Caroline minuscule required too delicate a hand to retain its prerogative for long in a time as little preoccupied with elegance as the tenth and eleventh centuries. The calligrapher's pen thence set out to find a mode of writing whose easy regularity, compact joining of letters, and somewhat monotonous harmony would bear a permanent relation to the fixity which the genius of Scholasticism imbued upon all intellectual pursuits. Accordingly, Gothic script gradually took shape, and it was fundamentally a degeneration of Roman minuscule, but having now become heavy, compact, full of angular strokes, and enhanced by capitals borrowed from Uncial, and even from Roman minuscule.

The unquestionable gravity of Gothic script ensured its custody of the books of the liturgy for many centuries to come, and we can affirm that the most remarkable manuscripts produced in this script from the thirteenth to the fifteenth centuries are those which the piety of our fathers consecrated to divine worship.

31

Liturgical Books Since the Invention of Printing

 HE INVENTION OF THE ART OF TYPOG-
raphy after the first half of the fifteenth century was bound
to exert an important influence over liturgical books. These
were the most numerous books of all, and this new manner
of production was of a nature that readily applied to them,
such that the Churches and clergy could not fail to have recourse to it.

The importance of manuscripts would diminish, although all the while
they continued to fight, until our own day, to maintain at least a shadow
of their former glory. One cannot help but feel a pang of regret for those
venerable Evangeliaries, those precious Sacramentaries, those age-old books
containing the choir's chants — all successively banished from the sanctuary
they once adorned, and destined to perish in such great numbers through
the carelessness of the very men who had employed them for so long in
the divine service.

Printing takes pride in opening its annals with the celebrated Mainz
Psalter of 1457. This is the liturgical book that inaugurates the history
of European printing, as if to consecrate this great art to God and His
Church. No sooner had the signal been given by the publication of the
Mainz Psalter than the desire for a printed Missal and Breviary became
universal in all the Churches of the West.

The particular characteristics of liturgical books are their gravity, elegance,
and correctness. The fifteenth century did not fall too far short of its task [*to
embody these characteristics*], and one is struck by the imposing appearance
of the Breviaries, Missals, and other books of divine service that this period
produced in such large numbers. The layout of the text, the generally skillful
variation of red and black ink, not to mention the illustrated miniatures,
place these editions among the most precious of incunables.[1]

Additionally, there are three special characteristics that have been specific
to liturgical printing from the outset. The first of these is the durability of
the material on which the texts were printed. During the centuries in which
only manuscripts were known, liturgical books were generally written on
parchment; printing preserved this precious advantage, at least to a certain

---

[1] Incunables are the editions that date to the beginning of the printing press. The word
derives from the Latin *incunabulum* which means "cradle" — not to be confused with
"palimpsests," from the Greek *palin* ("again") and *psestos* ("rubbed smooth"), which are
manuscripts written on parchment whose original writing was effaced to copy a new text.

extent. It would perhaps be impossible to name a single edition of a Missal or Breviary, let alone of other liturgical books, which did not have a more or less considerable number of copies on vellum throughout the fifteenth and up to the middle of the sixteenth centuries. As the sixteenth century progressed, vellum disappeared from even the most meticulously produced copies, but many Missals printed during this period still reserved its use for the Canon of the Mass.

The second attribute of liturgical books is the choice of typeface. The script used in the printing of liturgical books in this early period was, and for a long time after remained, Gothic, although Roman typeface appeared in Italy from the very beginning of typographical art. Nevertheless, the books of the liturgy adhered for a long time to the angular and somewhat barbaric script to which it had been subjected for almost four centuries. It would have been costly to change suddenly to a typeface whose use would deprive the new books of the familial resemblance with the manuscripts from which they originated. The transition took place gradually, with some Missals and Breviaries featuring a Roman title with the body of the text in Gothic. For others, the text was in Roman, but the Gothic still appeared on the title, as a final farewell to the Middle Ages.

The third characteristic is the use of vermilion for the titles of the divine service books, and generally for all the rules of the liturgy, which for this reason are called *rubrics* ("red"). Nothing contributes more to setting these books apart from all the others, and to assigning them a particular physiognomy, than this diversity of colors which immediately strikes the eye and announces a particular and mysterious purpose.

It remains for us to say something about the monuments of calligraphy applied to these same books after the invention of the typographical art. The regrets we expressed at finding so many masterpieces of art and patient labor disappear from the altar and the choir, to be replaced by the products (undoubtedly marvelous though they were) of a process that has as much to do with mechanics as with intelligence — these regrets were felt by all those who cherish traditions. In many places, manuscripts continued to possess the honors that they had previously enjoyed.

Indeed, one may even affirm that the use of manuscripts has never entirely ceased in the great churches, principally for choir books. They are found to this day in the cathedrals and monasteries of foreign countries, and in France, before the persecution that marked the end of the last century, nothing was more common than to see spread out on the lectern these enormous, splendid in-folio volumes on parchment, reminiscent of the days of old.

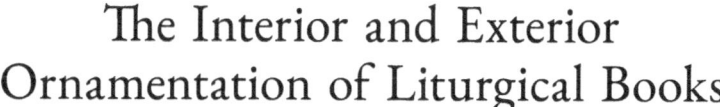

32

The Interior and Exterior Ornamentation of Liturgical Books

T IS FAITH THAT REVEALS THE IMPOR-
tance of liturgical books and manifests in them the instru-
ments of divine praise and the channels of heavenly graces.
Now, faith has been the principle of all the marvels of Christian artistry, and what it has done for churches, for altar
vessels, and for all the objects that serve in divine worship, it had to do
proportionally for the books of the liturgy.

DYED VELLUM

In the waning days of the Roman Empire, on the eve of the triumph of
Christianity, we already find examples of the use of purple dye on vellum
as a preparation for a book destined for the emperor's use.[1] Christian piety
soon seized upon this luxury for application to sacred books, and as early
as the fourth century we see it practiced by monks in the East, according
to the testimony of St. Ephrem and St. Jerome. Liturgical books were
naturally among the first texts to share this distinction, and they alone
enjoyed it for many centuries.

But purple was not the only color used to embellish the vellum of these
books. Later, violet and azure were also used, and one may judge of the
magnificence these rich colors conferred upon a volume by the splendor
still possessed today by liturgical manuscripts dyed in these precious colors,
faded though they are by the passage of centuries.

In the ninth century, the continued use of purple on liturgical manuscripts became less lavish. This reserve was inspired by economy, since
purple dye could only be obtained for an entire volume at a vast expense.

CHRYSOGRAPHS, OR GOLD-WRITTEN BOOKS

This preparation of vellum with purple, violet, and azure called for a
complementary ink that was never lacking. On such precious pages, it
was only possible to write in letters of gold or silver. Indeed, this practice
was constantly observed, although manuscripts on colored vellum written
entirely in silver letters are rare.

---

[1] The son of the Roman Emperor Maximinus Thrax was reputedly given "the books
of Homer, all purple, written in gold letters" (*Historia Augusta, Maximini Duo Iuli
Capitolini*, ch. 30).

The use of gold for lettering in liturgical books was not tied so closely to purple, azure, or violet manuscripts that it was not also used on plain vellum. Thus, many Evangeliaries, Psalters and Sacramentaries that have only a few colored pages are written in gold letters throughout.

Although the number of liturgical manuscripts written entirely in gold letters is necessarily limited, the use of gold is nonetheless frequent (albeit in a smaller proportion) on a considerable number of Evangeliaries, Sacramentaries, and other books of divine service dating from the eighth, ninth, and tenth centuries.

On this point, as on so many others, the Carolingian era reached the highest degree of magnificence and grandeur. The tenth century quickly descended from this elevation, and gold disappeared from liturgical books during the eleventh to thirteenth centuries, with a few rare exceptions.

The fourteenth century revived the use of gold as an ornament for letters and for the graceful and varied frames with which it enriched liturgical books. The fifteenth and sixteenth centuries imitated the practice, and this rich golden color has generally preserved, on manuscripts from this latter period, a clarity and splendor that the passage of time, and perhaps the inferiority of means, have taken away from most of the works left to us by the Carolingian chrysographers.

ILLUMINATIONS

The desire to give more luster and majesty to writing, especially at the beginning of a book, gave liturgical calligraphers the idea of adorning the initials of texts with particular care, and for this they had to employ the aid of illustration. From the seventh century onwards, the kind of ornamentation of liturgical manuscripts in the Latin Church was destined to undergo a rich development. The *Missale Francorum*, the *Missale Gothicum*, and the *Sacramentarium Gallicanum* in the Vatican Library — precious eighth-century monuments originally from the Abbey of Fleury — already feature letters timidly decorated with flowerets and birds at the beginning of certain Prefaces and orations.

Gold, the most vivid colors, and all the inventions of a light and dexterous hand were employed to make these initials so many marvelous works of art. Often, at the head of an Evangeliary, the first letter, which extends over two-thirds of the upper part of the page and then filigrees down to the bottom, presents twelve or more inches of decoration.

Towards the end of the twelfth century, the reign of the illuminators began in earnest. Their art, which had only just begun to be applied to all kinds of books, was devoted in a special way to those of the liturgy. Illuminators usually borrowed the elements of their rich page borders from the plant kingdom, imitating its foliage, flowers, and fruit with astonishing veracity. Often, too, they tried their hand at rendering insects and precious stones, and succeeded in doing so with rare felicity. The brushes of liturgical artists have preserved the costumes, attitudes, and sacred furnishings with a detail and abundance that cannot be too highly appreciated.

The revolution which nearly laid waste to the liturgy in France, and which began with the Breviary of Vienne in 1678, was fatal in its results to the ancient practice of adorning books of the divine service with pious illustrations. It was hardly to be expected that this aesthetic principle would survive amidst the wreckage of so many traditions.

The Breviary of Vienne appeared in 1678 with the rubrics in black, while more or less mediocre engravings were still present. François de Harlay's Breviary of Paris retained the use of red, but without engravings. The entire liturgy of Cluny, with the exception of an etching for the Canon and the Missal frontispiece, displayed the same dearth of engravings. Everything pointed to the imminent decay of the matter itself, which no longer had enough vigor to protect the form.

BINDINGS

Finally, it remains for us to recount the efforts made by Catholic piety in ancient times to adorn the exteriors of liturgical books. The immediate purpose of binding books is to protect them, but it can also be directed towards a higher end: that of bearing witness to the reverence that these books inspire. We may therefore report this as another triumph of liturgical books, for it can be said that they have achieved honors in book-binding that other books have never attained.

The principal ornaments used to embellish liturgical books fall into three categories: chiseled ivory, gold or silver plates, and precious stones.

The use of ivory tablets seems to us to derive from the ancient consular diptychs, which depicted in relief a figure clothed with the dignity of consul. From an early period, the Christian Church adopted not only the name but also the form of the consular diptychs for liturgical services. The lists of proper names to be recited at the altar were placed between two covers of solid material, hence the name *diptych* ("two tablets"). This type of binding would have been more or less opulent, since the tablets it protected were destined to appear on the altar itself. Later, a large number of liturgical books, particularly Evangeliaries, were outwardly adorned with richly carved ivory panels.

The number of ivory bindings dedicated to liturgical books seems to have been quite considerable, as can be seen from the large quantity that has been preserved in state deposits of antiquities and church treasuries, but even more so from the details provided on the subject in monastic chronicles.

From ivory bindings, we may turn to the bindings which owe their principal ornament to the panels of precious metal of which they are formed. The limited dimensions of ivory plates necessitated the use of a solid metal to affix these precious bas-reliefs to the covers of liturgical books, which were generally of a large format. This was an occasion for those charming arabesque borders wrought by goldsmiths which richly complement the decoration of so many beautiful bindings in which ivory forms the centerpiece.

But it was hardly equal to the piety of our forefathers to use gold and silver as mere accessories in the ornamentation of liturgical bindings. In more than one instance, it was their wish that the books of divine service be presented to the people only within a binding completely formed by panels of these precious metals.

Among many other precious metal bindings preserved in the Bibliothèque Nationale de France, we may cite the Evangeliary that was used in the royal chapel of St. Louis IX, the Sainte-Chapelle Gospels. This book is covered in gilt silver and decorated with impressive scenes representing the Resurrection of Jesus Christ on one side and on the other the Savior on the Cross, with the Blessed Virgin and St. John.

The third element of ornamentation used in the binding of liturgical books, surpassing all the others in magnificence and enduring over many centuries, is the practice of setting precious stones in the cover of these books. One of the princes of the liturgical science, the pious abbot Rupert of Deutz, celebrates the exalted propriety of this practice as follows:

> It is with good reason that the books of the Gospel are decorated with gold, silver, and precious stones; for in them gleams the gold of heavenly wisdom, in them shines the silver of an eloquence founded on the Faith, in them flash the precious stones of miracles, of those prodigies wrought by the hands of Christ, by those hands which, according to the words of the divine Canticle, *are turned and as of gold, full of hyacinths* (Song 7:6).[2]

---

[2] Rupert of Deutz, *De divinis officiis*, bk. 2, ch. 23.

CONCLUSION

S WE COME TO THE END OF THIS BOOK, intended as an introduction to the part of our *Institutions* devoted to the books of the liturgy—the very wellsprings of all liturgical science—let us cast a glance backward to measure the ground we have covered. From the origin of the Church, we have seen that the books of the liturgy were the object of a precise and authorized composition. That they enjoy the glory of being written in sacred and inviolable languages to which they are entrusted as to a precious deposit. That they can only be published or corrected by the highest authority in the Church. And finally, that the respect they have inspired in the centuries of faith has placed them, in terms of execution and richness, as far above ordinary books as their purpose is above the affairs of this world.

We have taken great pains to describe the marvels that the Catholic spirit was able to produce for the decoration of liturgical books. May the details we have painstakingly compiled inspire greater respect for these venerable books! Now, it must be recognized that the dignity of the liturgical books is such that there is nothing so precious that cannot, with propriety, be employed in their embellishment, and that parsimony [*in the production of liturgical books*] is an index of the weakening of the faith, for it attests that the books of the liturgy have lost their importance. We must conclude from the accounts we have put before the reader's eyes that the genius of the liturgy is eminently favorable to aesthetics, and that the arts cannot too highly honor the divine services to which they are indebted. At the same time, we must conclude that nothing is more capable of freezing and annihilating all inspiration than the decadence of the traditional spirit in the things of divine service.

In tracing the importance which the Catholic ages placed on bearing witness to their religion with the books of the liturgy, more than once we were painfully affected by the memory of so many cruel spoliations of which our churches have been victims, in the greater part of Europe, and which have brought about the violent destruction of so many monuments of the arts and of faith. But we have felt even greater remorse when we thought of the general atrophy which, for nearly three centuries, seems to have taken hold of minds and hearts, such that if we seek some consolation in the memories of a better time, we are reduced to going back in time to ages long past. Faith, without being extinguished, has become drowsy. A stubborn sleep has increasingly extended its unhappy influence. We are afraid of waking up, and we are ready to be scandalized at any word which would recall in some way the vitality of ages past. Unless we awake, however, the *more abundant life* of which the Savior speaks (Jn. 10:10) will not resume its course in our societies, which perish only because it is missing. Yet it is easy to see that the centuries that enjoyed this life drew it solely from faith, and that the liturgy was for them the great means by which this faith was nourished and manifested to the outside world.

INDEX